£39.99

W0246573

Digital Technologies of the Self

Digital Technologies of the Self

Edited by

Yasmine Abbas and Fred Dervin

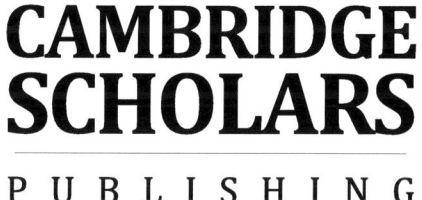

CAMBRIDGE
SCHOLARS

P U B L I S H I N G

Digital Technologies of the Self, Edited by Yasmine Abbas and Fred Dervin

This book first published 2009

Cambridge Scholars Publishing

12 Back Chapman Street, Newcastle upon Tyne, NE6 2XX, UK

British Library Cataloguing in Publication Data
A catalogue record for this book is available from the British Library

Copyright © 2009 by Yasmine Abbas and Fred Dervin and contributors

ISBN (10): 1-4438-1419-9, ISBN (13): 978-1-4438-1419-5

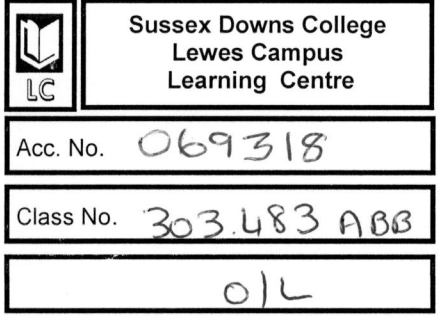

TABLE OF CONTENTS

INTRODUCTION

FRED DERVIN AND YASMINE ABBAS

I find, first of all, that I pass from state to state. I am warm or cold, I am merry or sad, I work or I do nothing, I look at what is around me or I think of something else. Sensations, feelings, volitions, ideas – such are the changes into which my existence is divided and which color it in turns. I change, then, without ceasing. But this is not saying enough. Change is far more radical than we are at first inclined to suppose.

For I speak of each of my states as if it formed a block and were a separate whole. I say indeed that I change, but the change seems to me to reside in the passage from one state to the next: of each state, taken separately, I am apt, to think that, it remains the same during all the time that it prevails. Nevertheless, a slight effort of attention would reveal to me that there is no feeling, no idea, no volition which is not undergoing change every moment: if a mental state ceased to vary, its duration would cease to flow. (Bergson 1911, 1-2).

Though we had common intellectual interests and were living in "neighbouring" countries (Denmark and Finland) when we put together this book project, we have never actually physically met. Nor, with one exception, have we met the authors of the chapters that compose this volume.

Our interaction during the editing process of the book and its French companion (Dervin & Abbas, 2009) took place via "plugged-in technobodies" (Turkle 1995, 177) and several technological devices, often on the move, rushing between various professional obligations in our respective countries or in far-off places and spaces. Whatever the nature of our disembodied encounters, we *know* each other in the sense that through the many and varied "tethering devices" (or our "identity accessories", Turkle 2006, 223) we have used for direct (Skype, Twitter, etc.) or indirect (website, blog) interaction, we have created an often-shifting picture of who we are — *representations* we want to come forward as "auctors" (authors/actors) of our lives (Bauman 2008, 52) who "create and shape things as much as… [we] might be a product of that creation and shaping".

This may not be surprising to the reader, as millions of people interact daily through such technologies, without relying on physical cues to interact or even having spoken to each other.

This book is about people like us and, in a way, most hypermodern individuals (Aubert 2004). Its title is inspired by the "technologies of the self" theorized by Michel Foucault in the early 1980s that seem to fit well with the investigation of the contemporary "living webs" (i.e., the internet and all the technologies attached to it). According to the philosopher, these technologies "permit individuals to effect by their own means or with the help of others a certain number of operations on their own bodies and souls, thoughts, conduct and way of being, so as to transform themselves in order to attain a certain state of happiness, purity, wisdom, perfection or immortality" (Foucault 1988, 18).

Dealing with their usages during, among other periods, the Hellenistic age, Foucault (ibid., 27) explains how writing about the self was an important aspect of taking care of oneself. Writing was used in "taking notes on oneself to be re-read, writing treatises and letters to friends to help them and keeping notebooks in order to reactivate for oneself the truths one needed" (ibid.). Without wishing to engage with exaggerated comparison, the link with the possibilities of interpersonal spaces created by web 2.0 and 3.0 technologies is clear, as more and more people (rich and poor, female and male, educated and non-educated...) take care of themselves with these technologies.

These technologies enable the individual's self/selves to emerge publicly and to be worked upon with its/their "disciples", be they companions in virtual worlds (Boellstorff 2008), readers (for example, of a blog), listeners (Podcasts), or viewers (YouTube, Dailymotion...). With high-speed internet access, omnipresent digital tapestries (Abbas 2008) and increasingly generous storage (portable computers, iPhones, USB keys, memory cards...), the opportunities for staging and transforming the self/selves have become nearly limitless — be they within or based on the technologies. What is important about these technologies is that they allow for multiple encounters and often "the promise of affection, conversation, a sense of new beginnings" (Turkle 2008, 125).

Questions of identities, which cannot be separated from taking care of oneself — the self being modelled by processes of identity creation — have never mattered more than with computers and the internet. Most researchers have now moved away from transcendentalist concepts of identity and dispelled the idea that identity is a given or an artefact. As such, in a book titled *The Plural Self*, Cooper and Rowan (1999, 1) assert that "the notion of a unified self begins to stand out like a relic from a bygone era". The sociologist Michel Maffesoli (1988) refers to the same phenomenon when he calls for the end of "the fantasy of unicity" in our postmodern worlds (note the plural) and allow full plurality to emerge.

The concept of identity is now omnipresent in research. The issue of the plurality of the self and multiple identities is not actually new, however. Lewis and Todd (2004, 43) remind us that the question "How can the self be one yet many?" has tormented philosophers and writers for centuries. The two psychologists also add that "It is a question that bridges worlds as different as Buddhist meditation, psychoanalysis and cognitive sciences" (ibid.). Researchers face the tricky fact that identity is both a scientific concept (a researcher analyzes the construction of identities in discourse) and a daily experience for every human being (I define who I am and I am defined by others whenever I interact).

This introduction is intended to propose reflections on identity, selfhood and new technologies. A review of the literature on identity is beyond our scope, especially as it seems that most scholars or researchers in the humanities and the social sciences have dealt directly or indirectly with the notion: Zygmunt Bauman, Pierre Bourdieu, Anthony Giddens, Claude Lévi-Strauss, Michel Maffesoli, Paul Ricoeur, Charles Taylor and more.[1]

Just over a century ago, the French philosopher Henri Bergson published one of his most famous works, *Creative Evolution* (1907). The book, whose main message was that *everything changes*, clearly set the tone for the idea that identity and the self evolve all the time: the concept is now labelled "social constructionism" (Berger and Luckmann 1966). For Bergson, states of being undergo change every moment and are not separate wholes. In this book, identity will be also considered as changing in a permanent construction process and thus plural and highly changeable.

However, we do not see identity as a "free from all" activity; hence the chapters in this book attempt a move from "soft constructionism" (we all have a limitless freedom to be who we want to be) and will not follow the procedure of starting out "'knowing' the identities whose very construction ought to be precisely the issue under investigation" (Kulick 1999, 6). We need to bear in mind that many elements external to the self represent a "coercive force" on identity construction and may thus orientate the self towards an undesirable/unstable identity (Brubaker & Cooper 2000, 1). This force is embodied by the physical, mental and

---

[1] The *Oxford Handbook of Internet Psychology* (Joinson et al., 2007) and *Self Identity and Everyday Life* (Ferguson, 2009) are good companions to the points made in what follows.

dialogical presence of others when we interact, be it directly or indirectly. Besides, the situation and context of interaction play a vital role in the construction of the self/selves and of the other (ibid, 14). We agree with Ewing (1990, 258) that what emerges from acts of interaction and the "forces" represented by these elements are "new selves from their available set of self-representations" — and representations only. These representations may mean, willy-nilly, having to "solidify" one aspect of the self (Bauman 2004; Hermans 2004), as will be explained *infra*.

In 1995 Sherry Turkle wrote a seminal book, *Life on the Screen: Identity in the Age of the Internet*, which will allow us to link the notion of identity with digital technologies of the self. For the MIT Professor, digital technologies represent "objects-to-think-with" for thinking about postmodern selves" (Turkle 1995, 185), i.e., they allow us to explore and invent multiple selves rather than discover *a* self (Bauman 2004, 15). Digital technologies of the self in the "expressivist turn" of the living webs (Allard 2007) seem to contribute to the daily experience of (invisible) multiple identifications by allowing them to "expand" and to be "validated" (Turkle 2008, 128) beyond the limits of the individual's space-time.

In our era of high uncertainty, one composed of multifaceted, complex, ambiguous and unpredictable moments (Hermans and Dimaggio 2007), the web represents a utopia where change is allowed to occur "without ceasing" (Bergson 1911) through unlimited possible contacts with billions of individuals who can help each other to construct and invent new selves and reinforce old ones. According to Hermans (2004, 305), digital technologies of the self can also "mediate between us and ourselves, in this way transforming the content and scope of our self-dialogues". For example, when a blogger writes about her/his daily life or thoughts, just like in Hellenistic times when writing to a friend or oneself, she/he transforms her/himself through dialogues with their own selves (especially if they reread their entries and the comments left by their "co-constructors").

New technologies of the self add more to this process of multiple self-discoveries than mere letter-writing to one interlocutor. Anonymity is one important difference. In her work on "multi-user domains" (MUD), Turkle (1993, 185) was one of the first to show how anonymity "provides ample room for individuals to express unexplored parts of themselves" more easily than in face-to-face interaction. "Super-selves" can be invented (Jauréguiberry 2004), allowing individuals to boost their projected identities: "The plain may represent themselves as glamorous; the introverted can try out being bold. People dream the dreamhouses in the virtual that they cannot afford in the real. They plant virtual gardens. They take online jobs of great responsibility…" (Turkle 2008, 125).

Just as physical travel "affords fantasy because it entails escaping the gaze and expectations of home communities" (Gillespie 2006, 63), digital technologies of the self can contribute to self-disclosure (revealing secrets, confessing…), transvestism (trying on new identities to test the self and the other), fantasising, etc. The fact that most of the others that we encounter online are anonymous, unknown or invented characters creates a "strangers on the train" effect (McKenna et al. 2002) that facilitates all these phenomena.

But this is not always the case. Anonymity can be relative. In Turkle's discussion of the "tethered self" triggered by new technologies (2006), she explains how the omnipresence of relational artefacts such as mobile phones is pulling down boundaries between social roles, allowing individuals present in the physical space of their use to witness mishmashing or disclosure of multiple identities: Turkle gives the example of the professional who answers the phone to her daughter in front of her colleagues — and thus revealing an identity that others may not be aware of (e.g., "I heard her talk to her daughter; her tone was very unpleasant"). The same can go for the internet: for example, IP addresses can often be identified[2] and force the mask to drop. Moreover, clues can always lead to the auctor's physical identity. In a February 2009 article published in the English newspaper the *Daily Mail*, a blogger indicated that she regretted writing some of her posts for this reason: "It's impossible to remain anonymous once you've disclosed your approximate location, your profession, the number, age and gender of your children and the nationality of your husband. I was 'discovered' by friends who found out that I had a blog and when I refused to give them its address, they simply put in a few relevant search words on Google and there I was".

Though (re-)inventions, confessions and multiple identifications are made easy online, certain practices of digital technologies of the self can also have a negative impact on one's identity construction. First of all, the internet in itself is full of identity "thieves", spammers, spies, attackers and rumourmongers who can spoil, confiscate, or transform somebody's identity. Secondly, the new technologies can serve as a platform for the building up and strengthening of "solid identities" (Bauman 2004). Hermans (2004, 315) makes clear that the internet has the potential to reduce identity and rid it off its (potential) complexity. An example from

---

[2] Check for instance, http://www.find-ip-address.org/

the Finnish context will illustrate this point. In January 2009 a nationalist anti-immigrant hate group created a site requesting the eviction of refugees from Finland in the social networking community Facebook. More than 15,000 web surfers joined the community and were led to enact a solid Finnish identity, as opposed to the solid negative identity imposed on refugees by the "community leaders".

The many and varied facets of new technologies of the self resemble a lot what is taking place in the "real" world. Actually, the dichotomy between the "real" and the "virtual" worlds seems increasingly to be losing its grip on reality. In his book on virtual worlds, the anthropologist Boellstorff (2008, 29) goes in that direction when he tells us that "forms of selfhood and sociality characterizing virtual worlds are profoundly human". Moreover, what takes place in the living web necessarily must "rework the virtuality that characterizes human being in the actual world" (ibid.), i.e., the inherent multiplicity and changeability of each individual. So whatever actions, discourses or emotions that one discovers on the web cannot be separated from the "real world" or discarded as having no influence whatever on the individual. In the complex identification processes in which we are all involved (with more or less freedom), our presence "out there" plays an increasingly important role. Going back to Bergson again: "There is no feeling, no idea, no volition which is not undergoing change every moment: if a mental state ceased to vary, its duration would cease to flow" (1911). Digital technologies also contribute to this.

The goal of this book is to explore the various aspects of how technologies contribute to the expression, (co-)construction and enactment of identitie(s) of mobile individuals involved in short-term (expatriates, businessmen, trainees, exchange students…), long-term (migrants, refugees, exiles…) and inter-/intra- and/or transnational mobilities. "Hypermobility", which intertwines the physical with the digital, causes the multiplication of encounters and narratives about others and the self. Migrants, refugees, intermittently mobile individuals, virtual residents use technologies ranging from the simple phone call to recorded and exhibited sound, images, videos and writing to testify of their being, and assert a sense of belonging to places and communities. For this reason, we have invited researchers from different disciplines to tackle from various angles the question of co-creation of identity and to analyze several platforms and behaviours in these digital technologies of the self. The compilation offers a comprehensive analysis of how people that are mobile, mentally, physically and/or digitally co-create their identity.

Responding to the call for proposal for the book cover, Daisy Ginsberg, a master graduate of the Design Interactions department of the Royal College of Art (UK) submitted a photograph from her project *Microbe Controllers: Biological Landscaping at Home*.[3] She writes that:

> Microbes are being genetically engineered to create biological computers, infiltrating the previously grey technology of silicon with a new green dimension. Microbe Controllers considers a domestic landscape where engineered microscopic organisms are cultivated to perform useful tasks in the home. Aware of this microscopic landscape around us, will our attitudes to what we accord "living" status change?

Her project inspired us to think that bio-engineered technologies relate to digital technologies of the self. This book, starting from the cover, is meant to inspire a multitude of reflections on identities and their co-construction.

The volume is divided in four sections. In the first section, "Surveillance and Identity", the authors investigate how power and knowledge operate between physical and digital worlds. In the second, "Digital Political Identity", we examine how identity is a tool for engagement in the realm of politics in virtual worlds. The third section, "We Surf Therefore I Am", explores how the focus on the self occurs from an introvert perspective (videogame immersion) and an extrovert one (blogs and podcasts) and always involves the other in its construction (for better or worse...). The last section, "Identity Gathering", examines how our collection of digital artefacts, places and friends participate in the construction of our identity.

1. Surveillance and Identity

In the first chapter, Katja de Vries explores how ambient intelligent (AmI) devices that anticipate the needs of users affect the ways in which one constructs his/her self. AmI objects that individuals use are endowed with memory and differentiate users in subtle manners. These objects are part of a larger network, and the data they collect are at the mercy of marketers and manufacturers. If the object transforms according to a person — i.e., individual — the self is subject to easy profiling, and this paradoxically participates to a certain unification of identity.

---

[3] http://www.daisyginsberg.com/projects/microbecontrollers.html

In the second chapter, Jed Brubaker examines the non-persistent subject through the survey of about 10,000 craigslist advertisements in the San Francisco, New York City and Washington, D.C, metropolitan areas. Brubaker writes that individuals leaving online notes (that are more likely to result in a "missed connection") "engage in practices of self-description, balancing disclosure and anonymity in these public posts". They construct an ephemeral identity. As Saul Alinsky writes, it might just be "a desperate search for personal identity — to let other people know that at least you are alive" (Alinsky 1971). However, Brubaker examines how, in the new spaces between the physical and digital, power and knowledge operate.

2. Digital Political Identity

In the first chapter of this section, Mutlu Binark and Günseli Bayraktutan Sütcü explore "Turkishness" through looking at online gamers. Basing their work on an analysis of *SilkRoad Online*[4], the authors focus on the virtual identities and community practices of Turkish players in relation to international political agenda, such as the rise of xenophobia and ethnic nationalism. They show how players internalize and are made to resort to an ethnic nationalist ideology through building up an invented *superself* in online guilds.

The second chapter reveals how politics is enhanced through the use of technologies and can help to creation identification. Both Barack Obama's blurred identity — neither black nor white — and his innovative use of social networking during the 2009 U.S. presidential campaign inspired Yasmine Abbas to elaborate on the interrelated concepts of mobility, identity and space. Participants in the mobilization during the 2009 campaign co-constructed their identity as well as that of the candidate. The author elaborates on how today's political mobilization is about "identity-sharing" or "peer-to-peer identity".

3. We Surf Therefore I Am

In the first chapter of this section, Olivier Mauco addresses the notion of the "second self" in investigating avatars (representations of the self in videogames and virtual worlds). According to Mauco, avatars are more

---

[4] *SilkRoad Online* is a well-known "massively multiplayer online role-playing game".

likely to be a crossover between the local social determinism and the technological constraints. So contrary to postmodern thinking, play introduces a focus on the individual.

In their chapter, Fred Dervin and Tanja Riikonen talk about "ego-casting" and demonstrate how the presence of others online contributes to the dramatization of the self and the other. Looking at three podcasts recorded by individuals who have "in-between identities" (or so-called "bi-national/bi-cultural"), the authors examine how a theory of the dialogical self (i.e., the insertion of many and varied voices in one's own discourse) can help to reveal the complexity of the identification process which is taking place online, and to which the potential presence of millions of unknown people can contribute in acts of reflexivity on the self/selves.

4. Identity Gathering

In the first chapter of the last section, Cati Vaucelle investigates a new breed of collectors: the collector of digital artefacts and information, brought about by neo-nomadism (Abbas 2008). The digital world can tie the object of the collection to an infinite number of features, the metadata; yet it enables the collector to strengthen her/his narcissism; the practice of online gift giving participates in defining the identity of the collector.

Finally, Michael O' Regan elaborates on the place/couch collection through social networking practices. This particular act of mobility, travelling from couch to couch and its preparation through Internet technologies, enables to stage the self and perform dwelling. The online presence (blog, social networking sites) corroborates a physical reality (the couch), increasing the complexity of concepts such as reciprocity, reputation and locality in the process.

Acknowledgment

The editors wish to thank Leighton Walter and Mari Nozac'h for their indispensable help during the editing process.

Bibliography

Abbas, Y. (2008) "Environnement néo-nomades, système écologique ?" In Dervin, F. and Ljalikova, A. (eds.). *Regards Sur Les Mondes Hypermobiles*. Paris : L'Harmattan. 19-36.

Allard, L. (2007) "Blogs, Podcast, Tags, Mashups, Locative Medias Le tournant expressiviste du web" in *MédiaMorphoses* 21: 57-62.

Aubert, N. (ed.) (2004) *L'individu hypermoderne*. Ramonville Saint-Agne: Collection Sociologie Clinique. Éditions Erès.

Bauman, Z. (2004) *Identity: Conversations with Benedetto Vecchi.* Cambridge: Polity.

—. (2008) *The Art of Life.* Cambridge: Polity.

Berger, P.L. and Luckmann, T. (1966) *The Social Construction of Reality: A Treatise its the Sociology of Knowledge.* Garden City, New York: Anchor Books.

Bergson, H. (1911) *Creative Evolution.* Translated by Arthur Mitchell. New York: Henry Holt and Company.

Boellstorff, T. (2008) *Coming of Age in Second Life: An Anthropologist Explores the Virtually human.* Princeton: Princeton University Press.

Brubaker, R. and Cooper, F. (2000) "Beyond 'identity'". *Theory & Society* 29. 1-47.

Cooper, M. and Rowan, J. (eds.) (1999) *The Plural Self: Multiplicity in Everyday Life.* London: Sage.

Dervin, F. and Abbas, Y. (eds.) (2009) *Technologies numériques du soi et (co-) constructions identitaires.* Paris: L'harmattan.

Ewing, K.P. (1990) "The Illusion of Wholeness: Culture, Self, and the Experience of Inconsistency". *Ethos* 3 (18). 251-278.

Foucault, M. [Martin, L.H., Gutman, H. and P.H. Hutton, (eds.)] (1988) *Technologies of the Self: A Seminar with Michel Foucault.* London: Tavistock.

Gillespie, A. (2006) *Becoming other: From social interaction to self-reflection.* Greenwich, CT: Information Age Publishing.

Hermans, H.J.M. (2004) "Introduction: the dialogical self in a global and digital age". *Identity* 4 (4). 297-320.

Hermans, H.J.M., and Dimaggio, G. (2007) "Self, identity, and globalisation in times of uncertainty: A dialogical analysis". *Review of General Psychology* 11 (1). 31-61.

Jauréguiberry, F. (2004) "Hypermodernité et manipulation de soi". In Aubert, N. (ed.). *L'individu hypermoderne.* Toulouse: Érès. 155-168.

Joinson, A., McKenna, K., Postmes, T. and Reips U.-D. (eds.) (2007) *Oxford Handbook of Internet Psychology* (Oxford Library of Psychology). Oxford: OUP.

Katz, J.E. and M. Aakhus (eds.) (2008) *Perpetual Contact: Mobile Communication, Private Talk, Public Performance.* Cambridge: Cambridge University Press.

Kulick, D. (1999) "Language & gender/sexuality". *Language & Culture Mailing List: Online Symposium.* http://www.language-culture.org/archives/subs/ kulick-don/index.html.

Lewis, M. D., and Todd, R. (2004) "Toward a neuropspychological model of internal dialogue: Implications for theory and clinical practice". In Hermans, H. J. M. and Dimaggio C. (eds.) *The dialogical self in psychotherapy.* New York: Brunner Routledge. 43-59.

Maffesoli, M. (1988) *Le temps des tribus.* Paris: Méridiens Klincksieck.

McKenna, K.Y.A., A.S. Green and M.E.J. Gleason. (2002) "Relationship formation on the internet: What's the big attraction?". *Journal of Social Issues.* 58 (1). 9-31.

Turkle, S. (1995) *Life on the Screen: identity in the age of the Internet.* New York: Simon and Schuster.

—. (2006) "Tethering". In Jones, C.A. (ed.). *Sensorium: Embodied Experience, Technology, and Contemporary Art.* Cambridge, MA: List Visual Art Center and MIT Press. 220-226.

—. (2008) "Always-on/Always-on-you: The Tethered Self". In Katz, J.E. (ed.). *Handbook of Mobile Communication Studies.* Cambridge, MA: MIT Press. 121-137.

SURVEILLANCE AND IDENTITY

CHAPTER ONE

IDENTITY IN A WORLD OF AMBIENT INTELLIGENCE

KATJA DE VRIES

1. Things That Think

Why limit the information society to a closed circuit of interconnected computers? With expanding wireless network connectivity and the miniaturization of computer chips we can envision a new informational revolution wherein *things* are endowed with intelligence. It was in 1988 at Xerox in California that the scientist Mark Weiser articulated a vision which he baptized "Ubiquitous Computing" (Weiser, Gold and Brown 1999) — a vision of things that function like silent and calm butlers in the background:

> microwave ovens that download new recipes [...] toys that are ever refreshed with new software and vocabularies, paint that cleans off dust and notifies you of intruders, walls that selectively dampen sounds [...]. (Weiser and Brown 1997, 78)

Crucial to Weiser's vision was that our relationship with such smart devices would be one of *dwelling* — something that fundamentally differs from the *interactions* we have with a contemporary personal computer:

> If you are only interacting with your spouse the relationship may be in trouble. We dwell with nature, and roommates and anything that we let enter us, and we it. Dwelling with computers means that they have their place, and we ours, and we co-exist comfortably. (Weiser 1996)

After Weiser launched his vision it began to proliferate at a fast pace, as the basic theme — "bringing the Internet and computing power into the world of physical objects" — turned out to be a fertile ground for endless variations. To trace all the instances of where and how the notion of ubiquitous computing (ubicomp) emerged and transformed is impossible, so I will restrict myself to some salient moments. Worth mentioning is, for instance, the founder of the MIT Media Lab, Nicholas Negroponte (1995). Elaborating on Weiser's vision, Negroponte contributed to its dissemination and laid the foundations of MIT's becoming one of the leaders in the field. In 1995 the Things That Think consortium was brought into being, later followed by project *Oxygen* at the MIT Artificial Intelligence Lab and by many more specialized research groups such as the *Tangible Media Group*. The movement spread to innumerable other universities. No self-respecting large company in communication, electronics, or information technology could stay behind: Motorola's *digital DNA*, Hewlett-Packard's *CoolTown*, Microsoft's *EasyLiving* and Philip's research at their *HomeLab* are just a few examples. Next to ubicomp, strongly related and overlapping notions like the "internet of things", "pervasive computing" and "ambient intelligence" popped up. All partake in a fair share of characteristics like pervasiveness, adaptivity, the capacity to anticipate, embeddedness, mobility ("everyware": Greenfield 2006), context awareness, personalization, and being turned "on" permanently. Meanwhile, a more general public had also acquainted itself with Weiser's vision. Ubicomp has found its way beyond the walls of the engineering groups and into other domains of academia, provoking legal (e.g., Wright et al. 2008), ethical (e.g., Albrecht and McIntyre 2005; Phillips and Wiegerling 2007) and geographical (e.g., Crang and Graham 2007; Thrift 2003) reflections. Moreover, today's interested layman will find not only plenty of popular scientific readings on the new developments (e.g., Greenfield 2006), but also has the possibility to acquaint him or herself with prototypes for smart fridges (keeping track of which products have been used up or are past their due dates) and smart laundry machines (automatically choosing the right program and amount of washing powder) in show houses such as the *Living Tomorrow* Pavilions in Brussels and Amsterdam, or in the accompanying glossy advertisement material (De Moor 2004).

For the philosophically inclined there are many paths one could explore in this protean field. One of the compelling issues on which I will focus in this chapter is how the permanent *identification* by smart environments might affect our experience of who we are, i.e., our *identity*. After all, the fact that ubicomp might be more than a hype and that in the decades to come a whole new category of things — which will recognize us, know who we are and anticipate us — could be brought into being, makes one wonder how the identification-based interaction (or "dwelling", as Mark Weiser (1996) would have described it) with these smart objects will compare with the interaction with more familiar beings such as friends, family, pets, governments, and organizations. Of particular interest are, of course, objects that are both *personalized* and have the capacity to *anticipate*. Because these two characteristics seem to be associated slightly more strongly and frequently with ambient intelligence (AmI)[1] than with the other similar concepts mentioned before, in this chapter I will stick to this particular notion, though more for the sake of simplicity and clarity than for dogmatic reasons. However, before turning to the question regarding how personalized anticipation could be realized in AmI devices (section 4), I will first (section 2) take a closer look at the processes that constitute our personal identity: what makes us who we are? Although this question could be addressed from many different philosophical positions, this chapter will take up the position of Foucault's later investigations into what he baptized "technologies of the self", as they can be applied in very elucidating ways in the context of AmI.

2. Identity

The notion of personal identity is full of ambiguities and misunderstandings. Either *identity* is understood as something very elusive and transcendental — becoming almost synonymous with "soul" — or it is understood in such a narrow sense that every connotation to selfhood is lost. Take for instance the modern buzzword "identity theft" (e.g., http://www.identitytheft.org.uk/) — even though the term may sound for the uninitiated as a magical bereavement of one's soul, in fact it only refers to the fact that a crime was committed by means of a fraudulently intercepted *identifier* (e.g., a credit card number). Thus, before addressing the question of how an AmI environment could affect personal identity, I will first have to unravel some of the conundrums that surround it. It will be argued that identity is fundamentally relational (section 2.1.), that it is a mechanism of iteration that — when practiced at the limits of ourselves — allows for self-transformation (section 2.2.), and that identity construction is a practice which can be induced by technological supports (section 2.3.).

2.1. Identity — a Relational Notion

One of the biggest fallacies about identity is the idea that one could

---

[1] An expression launched in 1998 by Philips; see for more details Aarts and Marzano 2003; Weber, Rabaey, and Aarts 2005; Wright et al. 2008.

have immediate access to who one is: "Even if I would have been born on a desert island and raised by wolves, I still would be an emancipated woman — because I feel that this is what I truly am!". Far from being a Cartesian *immediate* and transparent first-person intuition, identity is always an artifact constructed through words, tools and interactions with other beings. *Self*-understanding, according to Ricoeur[2], is never an "immediate intuition of the I" but always involves mediation by a "long detour through objectification, making reflection an interminable Odyssey" (Ricoeur 2008, 143, transl. *KdV*). Attributing communist ideas to a pre-Columbian American or a gay lifestyle to an ancient Roman is an anachronistic fallacy: even though from the present-day perspective we might identify a certain ancient Mayan as a communist *avant la lettre*, it is exactly in the necessity to specify this identification as *avant la lettre* that the anachronism becomes clear. In this way even the most private sense of identity is relational because it only exists insofar as it resonates with a world, i.e., insofar as it has the ability to function as a meaningfully differentiating shibboleth. Thus, when your credit card is stolen this might have disastrous effects for your financial situation but leave your identity as a credit card holder unaffected; however, if one would wake up one day in a world where nobody would have any idea what a credit card was ("An interesting piece of plastic — what is it for, sir?") this *would* affect one's identity. Identity is not a mine-ness in terms of property ("my credit card") but the difference that is produced in a relational facticity ("The war showed the cowards from the heroes"). Thus, from the macro-perspective the relational character of identity formation points toward its mediated nature and its co-constitution with a world. However, how then do we understand the phenomenological experience of identity as the preservation of self over and in time?

2.2. Identity at its Limits — a Moment-to-Moment Awareness of Oneself and Self-Transformation

One of the pivotal questions in the work of Foucault during the eight

---

[2] In his thinking on identity the French philosopher Paul Ricoeur greatly admired the "subjectivist' turn in Foucault's later works (Ricoeur 1998, 79): "It is to the extent that Foucault distanced himself from himself with his last two books that I felt closer to him". Even though explicit references to Foucault in Ricoeur's *Oneself as Another* are scarce (however e.g., Ricoeur, 1994, 2: "[…] *le souci de soi* (care of the self) — to borrow Michel Foucault's magnificent title") Foucault's ideas are present in the background.

years before his death in 1984 was how a relational understanding of the self could leave room for self-creation and self-transformation instead of implying that we are merely passively constituted by forces from the outside (Foucault 1985, 1986; Martin, Gutman and Hutton 1988). In fact, at first glance the word *identity* seems to be the absolute opposite of transformation because one's identity can only arise from a specific openness toward time and space wherein one experiences oneself as *identical* with oneself ("I am the same as I was yesterday") and with others ("We are the same: I am a woman like you"). As is nicely illustrated by its Medieval etymological ancestors, i.e., *idem* ("the same") and *identidem* ("time and again") (Groebner, Kyburz, and Peck 2007, 26-27; Ricoeur 1994, 2 and 115 ff.), identity involves the ability of subsuming oneself under a certain aspect (e.g., "myself," "my character" or "female") as being the same. However, what is crucial here is that an identity is not a passively accumulated sedimentation of pre-given sameness (the memorization of repeated identifications by others as "such-and-such") in a particular body, but that it is a *relation* which needs to be *enacted* over and over again. Identity is not a hidden entity that simply has to be memorized and deciphered in a hermeneutic practice: "If I will just keep digging in my soul, one day my true identity will come out". Even though interacting with people suffering from severe dementia makes one realize how memory is a necessary constituent of personal identity, memory alone is not enough. A person with a detailed recollection of what happened forty years ago who is not aware of himself living in the present has lost an ability that is constitutive for identity construction, i.e., the ability of activating one's memory in the *now*. Identity is constituted by memory — not memory understood as an epistemological gaze but as a mechanism of iteration that — when practiced at the limits of ourselves — allows for self-transformation. Or as Deleuze puts it, reformulating Foucault:

> Memory is the real name of the relation to oneself, or the affect on self by self. [...] The inside condenses the past (a long period of time) in ways that are not at all continuous but instead confront it with a future that comes from outside, exchange it and re-create it. To think means to be embedded in the present-time stratum that serves as a limit: what can I see and what can I say today? But this involves thinking of the past as it is condensed in the inside, in relation to oneself (there is a Greek in me, or a Christian, and so on). We will then think the past against the present, [...] that is, by making the past active and present to the outside so that something new will finally come about, [...]. (Deleuze 2000, 107 and 119; referring to Foucault 1985, 9)

The difficulty in Foucault's work of the 1980s on self-transformation is that it is easy to misread him as slipping into an exalted account of individualism and free agency (see Paras 2006). Yet Foucault does *not* endorse a naïve voluntarism when he writes about self-transformation. Instead of radically rejecting the given facticity of relations that constitutes who we are (e.g., "I am fed up with my macho lifestyle — let's erase my memory and move to a desert island"), Foucault proposes a reappropriation at the *limits* of ourselves (e.g., "This macho lifestyle of mine — I have to trace exactly how it works, to which aims it moves me, what it makes me do, how it makes me do that and what it operates upon"). Such "work done on the limits of ourselves" (Foucault 1984c, 46) can be understood as a tinkering *within* one's facticity: "a pragmatics of transformation that demands nothing less than a moment-to-moment awareness of the virtual nature of ourselves" (Varela 1999, 75, expanding on Foucault). However, it should be clear that many "technologies of the self" do not promote such a pragmatics of transformation but instead induce a pre-given kind of constitution of the self. Foucault disdainfully dismisses, for instance, the Californian "cult of the self" in the 1980s wherein one aims to decipher psychoanalytically one's "true self" (Foucault 1984a, 362) as something completely opposite to the transformatory pragmatics of life he envisions:

> The art of living is the art of killing psychology, of creating with oneself and with others unnamed individualities, beings, relations, qualities. If one can't manage to do that in one's life, that life is not worth living. (Foucault 2001a, 1075; transl. by Paras, 2006, 129)

2.3. The Materiality of "Technologies of the Self"

When Foucault uses the word *technology* in relation to the "self" (e.g., "the self is nothing else than the historical correlation of the technology built in our history", Foucault 1993, 222) the notion of technology should not be understood in the sense mechanical hardware, but in the sense of a "technique": "techniques of the self" and "technologies of the self" are used by Foucault as synonyms (Foucault 1993, 203). Foucault repeatedly underlines that in his famous notion of "technologies of the self," technology should not be understood as "hard technology, the technology of wood, of fire, of electricity" but as a kind of "practical rationality governed by a conscious goal" (Foucault 1984b, 255-256) or, to put it in other words, as a certain type of

> ...practical reason [...] which permits individuals to effect by their own

means or with the help of others a certain number of operations on their own bodies and souls, thoughts, conduct, and way of being, so as to transform themselves in order to attain a certain state of happiness, purity, wisdom, perfection, or immortality. (Foucault 1988, 18)

Yet even though this practical reason is not a "hard technology" in itself, it cannot be separated from the materiality — "its material instance" (Foucault 1977, 97) — that gives rise to it. Foucault stresses that the self-transformation an individual performs upon himself should be understood in terms of constituting oneself as a work of art or artifact:

> From the idea that the self is not given to us, I think that there is only one practical consequence: we have to create ourselves as a work of art. (Foucault 1984a, 351)

And:

> This transformation of one's self by one's own knowledge is, I think, something rather close to the aesthetic experience. Why should a painter work if he is not transformed by his own painting? (Foucault 2001b, 1355)

In the same way as the work of an artist is co-constituted by his material (e.g., not only would *Guernica* have looked quite differently if Picasso had used glass-engraving tools instead of paint and brushes, but without any material there would be no *Guernica* at all), technologies of the self, too, are co-constituted by their material instance. Take, for example, the way the experience of oneself, described by Foucault, "intensified and widened" (Foucault 1988, 28) in the first and second century A.D. The emergence of this novel way of experiencing oneself in the Hellenistic period — constituted by a technology of self-vigilance Foucault identifies as "care of the self" (*epimeleia heautou*) — can be understood in relation to the spreading use of a certain kind of notebooks for administrative and personal purposes. These material memory supports, which allowed for mental exercise and inspection of oneself, were called *hypomnémeta*[3] (Foucault 2001c; 1984a, 363-365):

> This new technology was as disrupting as the introduction of the computer in private life today. It seems to me the question of writing and the self must be posed in terms of the technical and material framework in which it

---

[3] For an elaboration on the material base (*hypomnémeta*) of different "technologies of the self" and the effect of contemporary audio-visual mass media ("*analogue hypomnémata*", Stiegler 2008, 314), see: *idem*, 257 ff.

arose. (Foucault 1984a, 363)

Even though Foucault emphasizes that techniques of the self do not necessarily require a lot of "material apparatus" (e.g., the little "voice" in your head telling you that you should be a good wife and stop flirting with others is not a "material' technology) and will often be "invisible" (Foucault 1984a, 369), it is clear that new sorts of *hypomnémeta* could facilitate the emergence of new ways of relating to oneself. A contemporary example of how new media allow for new forms of self-monitoring is for instance "Moodjam"[4] (http://moodjam.org/), an online tool to visualize one's moods as a palette of colorstripes tagged with a word to express the mood. After having accumulated enough records one could start discovering trends in one's own "inner palette" and those of others, thus in fact possibly creating a new way of relating to oneself: "I feel so blue-yellow striped today — but it is quite normal it seems in this period of the year". Or as the artist Jill Magid puts it:

> Self-surveillance is a way of seeing myself, via technology, in a way I could not otherwise. In self-surveillance I use a system or a technology as my mirror. The type of reflection I face is specific to the tool I am using. Who I appear to be in that reflection is unfamiliar. The process of coming to recognize myself as I appear there is what I call my work. (Magid and Lovink 2004)

3. *Please, Give Me Some Building Blocks to Tinker With!* Constructing One's Own Identity in between the Silent Operations of an *AmI* World

The troubles with privacy in an *AmI* world is that *AmI* technologies make the boundary between the public sphere and the private sphere — where one should arguably enjoy the right "to be let alone" (Warren and Brandeis 1890, 195) — less distinct. The public spaces in a world of *AmI* will no longer be places where one can dissolve in an anonymous crowd: both in and outside one's house one will be permanently recognized, identified and anticipated. The onset of this dissolution of the private sphere can already be experienced on the Internet.

---

[4] Moodjam is part of the larger Technologies about the Self (http://self.cs. cmu.edu/) project at the *Human-Computer Interaction Institute* at *Carnegie Mellon University* which explores several new technological forms of self-monitoring.

[T]oday the data bank of Amazon.com has simultaneous access to my most subtle preferences as well as to my Visa card. As soon as I purchase on the web, I erase the difference between the social, the economic and the psychological, just because of the range of traces I leave behind. (Latour 2007)

One of the ways to address the upcoming indifferentiation between the personal and public domain is to go beyond "the static conception of privacy as a right to seclusion or secrecy" and to redefine the right to privacy as "the freedom from unreasonable constraints on the construction of one's own identity" (Agre and Rotenberg 2001, 7). However, as was shown in the previous section, constructing one's own identity is not something we can decide upon as sovereign and autonomous individuals. While rejecting the naïve position of voluntaristic sovereignty in the creation of one's identity, a certain amount of creative transformatory power toward oneself might nevertheless be attained by a subtle tinkering within the facticity of one's life — at least, *if* one manages to create a moment-to-moment awareness toward one's facticity. Yet such awareness — what's more: any awareness at all! — might exactly be what is flagrantly lacking within certain forms of AmI technologies. AmI technologies are, for several reasons, intrinsically invisible technologies (cf. Hjelm 2005).

From the earliest beginnings, *ubicomp* founding father Mark Weiser stressed that the new smart technologies will have to function silently in the periphery of our attention, to enable us to focus on more interesting matters (Weiser and Brown 1996). Apart from these humanistic and ideological considerations, there might also be more practical reasons why designers would like to push the functioning of smart devices as far out of sight as possible. For example, users of a vehicle-navigation system that personalizes directions for individual drivers according to their driving style (inferred from data collected by discreet sensors and cameras) might like the directions they got, but would become upset about the infringement on their autonomy (see different results, however, in: Barkhuus and Dey 2003) when they were told about the personalization that had taken place:

This suggests [...] that contextual computing needs to be discreet: such systems are, in effect, judging people and trying to influence their behaviour. Systems that manipulate people [...] may have to keep quiet about it to work. (Economist 2007, 22)

Moreover, a designer might justify the fact that he or she "keeps quiet" about the identification and categorization which take place, precisely because it is "only" an intermediate step. Once again the rudimentary forms of this logic can be found on the Internet — when *Amazon* registers which books were browsed by a particular customer, the goal is not one of surveillance in itself, but merely a step in a process of "acting upon", i.e., discovering statistically significant patterns, making inferences and luring customers into buying more books by offering them statistically "personalized" selections of books. Such information technologies — which can function both on the Internet as well as in an "Internet of Things" — should therefore not be seen as a simple extension of the monitoring gaze of "Big Brother". What happens in "personalization" based on statistically inferred profiles is a moving away from a discourse of *seeing* toward a discourse of *acting*, i.e., from a discourse of "gaze", "surveillance" and "peeping into a personal sphere" (which can be both top-down or bottom-up; Haggerty and Ericson 2000) toward "operating upon actions", "manipulation by anticipation" and "freedom of identity construction". This new form of privacy intrusion is not an intrusive gaze looking for personal secrets but a vision enhanced with statistical algorithms, looking for "anonymous" patterns, which could function as the basis for a manipulative way of anticipation.

4. Identifications in a World of *AmI*

Not every smart device is a personalized device — especially not in the rudimentary forms of AmI devices now being brought to the market. For instance the "Ambient Umbrella"[5] anticipates the weather (the handle indicates when rain or snow is expected by glowing up in a particular light pattern) but does not adapt itself to any particular user. However, what happens when devices anticipate us in different ways according to how we are identified and profiled by them? What if the umbrella glows only for some particular people — people who are profiled as having a very low rain tolerance — when light drizzle is expected? To answer that question, two types of profiles need to be distinguished: unique user profiles and group profiles based on statistical inferences.

---

[5] See http://www.ambientdevices.com/products/umbrella.html

4.1. Unique User Profiles: "Magic Mirror on the Wall, Will You Produce a Difference Between Us All?"

At the moment, most prototypes of AmI devices seem to focus in particular on unique user profiles (cf. "direct individual" or "personal" profiles: Hildebrandt 2008). Such profiles do not correlate the preferred settings of different users, but "simply" activate the unique set of favourite settings upon identification of a particular user. This identification could take place in several ways. One could identify oneself by a fingerprint scan, pressing a key or entering a code, but the ideal for many AmI designers is for the identification to be more "discreet" (e.g., Ramalingam and Ambaye 2005). Such unobtrusive identification could, for instance, be a shower which can "sense who a user is from a user's body characteristics" and subsequently activate the preferred water temperature:

> An example of a learning heuristic is time sensitive adjustment to temperature of the water: after X minutes lower the temperature to Y where X and Y are input explicitly by the user or by the shower remembering how the user adjusted the temperature during the most recent shower. (Van Doren 2004, 2)

As soon as a smart device is endowed with a "memory" or a learning heuristic and is able to distinguish between different individuals, these individuals will suddenly become differentiated with respect to their daily practices. Whereas a pre-AmI family might never realize that each of the family members has slightly different preferences with respect to the temperature of their shower, the level of "toastedness" of their toast, the brightness and contrast of the television screen, the sound level of the audio installation, etc. (Van Doren 2004, 2), now everyone turns out to have a very specific profile in these day-to-day matters. Moreover, every reiterated interaction with the smart device will allow for an even more precise differentiation of one's individual taste — the toast a subtle fraction less toasted, the shower a little bit hotter, etc. Thus, what these devices do is not just mirroring us but in fact *producing* new differences and identities. Somewhat surprisingly, there are interesting similarities between Foucault's depiction of the Hellenistic "care of the self" and these AmI practices. In both cases new *hypomnémeta* allow for a memorization of "shallow" daily practices, "only deeds, not thoughts" (Foucault 1988, 30), that open novel domains for self-analysis and "a whole field of experience [...] which was earlier absent" (Foucault 1988, 28).

However, one of the big differences between the Hellenistic and the AmI technologies is the possibility of dissemination of the memorized daily practices. The behaviour stored in a *hypomnéma* of a Roman would in principle, unless sent to a friend as a letter, stay there. The behaviour stored in the smart toaster of a man of the AmI world, on the other hand, is a volatile entity that can theoretically spread itself instantaneously to other smart devices, to manufacturers, marketeers, etc. Given the fact that the AmI practices that are constitutive of new identities are the flipside of a very specific *technology of power*[6], i.e., constituting consumer-subjects with very specific preferences, desires and appetites, this volatility of personal profiles is a reason for concern. Moreover, even if data protection legislation is properly enacted and the profiles merely circulate *within* your house, it can still be a source for concern when the shower starts anticipating your preferred temperature based on the kind of coffee you just had. Of course, the temperature might happen to be precisely the one that you like, but when you lose track of the lines along which you are manipulated into a certain identity, tinkering with the constitutive facticity of your identity becomes difficult.

4.2. Group Profiles. *Here Is Your Coffee… It Is the Coffee that Other* "Young-Females-with-Happy-Facial-Expressions" *Like*!

At present the use of identifications into categories, similar to the Amazon logic of using group profiles[7] to make more specialized offers (*"Customers with Similar Searches Purchased…"*), is not yet widely spread within AmI prototypes. Yet there seems to be no particular reason why group-profiling practices (Custers 2004; Elmer 2004; Hildebrandt 2008; Schauer 2003) that play an increasingly important role in targeted advertising on the Internet, for example, would find no application within an AmI world. One of the advantages of group profiling is that one does *not* have to store an individual profile of one particular person. Thus a smart coffee machine based on group profiling could for instance proactively offer a different kind of coffee to women than to men because on average women like a different blend of coffee. Although this sounds like a contradiction in terms, one could call this *anonymous*

---

[6] "[T]echnologies of power […] determine the conduct of individuals and submit them to certain ends of domination, an objectivizing of the subject" (Foucault 1988, 18).
[7] *Profiling* is categorization based on the patterns discovered in data mining. *Data mining* is the algorithmic process of discovering interesting patterns ("knowledge") in large databases. Often this will be done with as little prior hypothesising as possible, so that unexpected patterns can emerge.

personalization. After all, statistical "stereotyping" of this kind could create a highly personalized experience: "I don't know how my coffee machine does it, but it makes exactly the coffee I like". Good targeting is an art in itself. Thus, a smart coffee machine with a smart camera that can distinguish between men and women does not access any personal or uniquely identifying information. However, one might of course accuse the machine of unwarranted statistical discrimination (cf. Gandy 2002).

Whereas the traces that users leave behind on the Internet are more or less up for grabs for data mining and statistical analysis, discreet automated extraction of analysable data from the real world is less evident. One of the ways to collect data in the "outside" world is by using smart cameras, i.e., cameras which are enhanced with software to analyse what they record. While machine vision (for a general introduction on "machine vision" and the more or less synonymous notions of "video analytics" and "smart CCTV" see: Davies 2005; Shapiro and Stockman 2001) is still far from being perfectly reliable, there is nevertheless some quite advanced software available. Such enhanced cameras can identify in real-time particular objects, recognize facial expressions or classify people according to gender, age, ethnicity, etc. (e.g., Wilhelm, Böhme and Gross 2005; Wu, Smith and Hancock 2008). One of the ways to "teach" a smart camera to distinguish a certain category is by showing it a large number of pictures from that category (e.g., "women") and letting it create an algorithm which forms the best common denominator for that category.

To a large extent such use of machine vision, which tries to imitate human vision, is a costly, resource intensive and difficult process. Consequently, technologies such as radio frequency identification (RFID), thermal or motion sensors are being used (Dai, Zheng, and Li 2007; Inman 2008; Ivanov et al. 2007). For example, the installation of a high-density of cheap and small motion detectors in a building turned out to be an interesting alternative to cameras:

> As digital video cameras get cheaper and smaller, CCTV systems are becoming more common. But as well as raising privacy concerns [...] the footage is difficult to search through or interpret quickly. [...]. The detectors collect much less information than the cameras. "It's not going to catch you picking your nose. You can only tell that some person went by [...] maybe this is better than living under thousands of cameras". But the motion-detector system still collects a lot of information. To find unusual or interesting patterns in the data, the researchers developed software to display movements of people around the building on a map in real time. People show up as a bright spot trailing a tail of lights that slowly fade away. (Inman 2008)

Thus, an additional benefit of using sensors which only generate "hot blobs" is that they are less privacy intrusive in the classical understanding of privacy (e.g., Caine, Fisk, and Rogers 2006; Ivanov et al. 2007).

> I've not seen this approach before in journals or at conferences [...] But I have seen it in fiction, for example the Marauder's map in Harry Potter. (Inman 2008)

While the use of devices to directly extract processable data from the physical world (smart cameras, sensor systems, etc.) in the field of *AmI* is still more focused on establishing unobtrusive unique user identifications, in retail management these technologies are already used for identification into categories ("This person is an Asian elderly female"). By taking a closer look at profiling practices in retail environments one could get a taste of how such practices could function in an *AmI* environment.

5. Smart Retail Surveillance

The main objective of CCTV cameras in shops used to be the discovery of *individuals*: e.g., a shoplifter or an employee engaging in some prohibited activity. However, the infrared sensors, dual lens cameras, digital-audio recorders and video-mining technology that together form new "smart retail surveillance systems"[8] are not used to discern you and me *in particular*, but concentrate on identifying "hot blobs" or moving "pixel clusters" immediately *as* belonging to a certain *category*: e.g., a "shopping unit", "shoplifter", "female customer" or "affluent early adopter" (Economist 2007b, 25).

---

[8] See http://www.brickstream.com/demo/behavioriq.php or http://www.videomining.com/technologies/main.html

Figure 1. An overview of an exemplary embodiment of "Automatic detection and aggregation of demographics and behavior of people". VideoMining Corporation has filed an application for a U.S. patent (Application No. 12,002,398) for this invention: Sharma et al. 2007, 2.

Patent Application Publication   May 8, 2008   Sheet 2 of 13   US 2008/0109397 A1

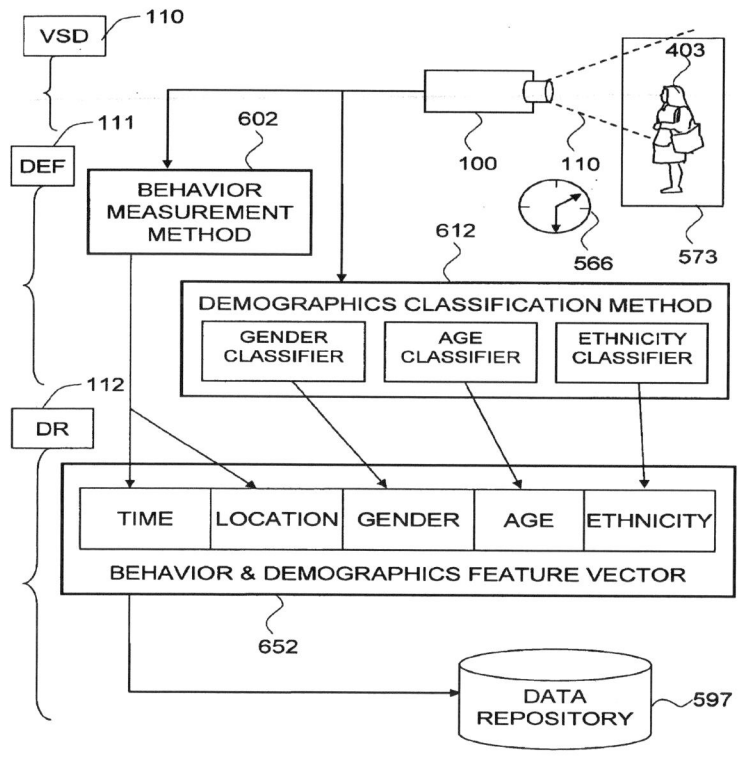

These productive and pragmatic categorizations are embedded in a process of retail pragmatics — for example, one could use them to enable shops to match the amount of "shopping units" with an appropriate number of available check-outs, to make customized offers to particular customers or to identify the hotspots in a shop for a particular category of customers. It is quite easy to imagine how these practices could be extended into fully fledged AmI technologies by linking them to, for instance, a "smart" supermarket basket or the mobile phones of customers.

6. How Can One Relate Oneself to Black-boxed Volatile Algorithms? Artistic Answers

Identity does not arise in a vacuum. Even though one could describe identity as the way we relate to ourselves, this loop is always mediated through the facticity of how we relate to our surroundings. Identity thus arises within the material instances of those relations: how I experience myself is a form of self-surveillance that can be mediated through a friend, a notebook, the *Moodjam*-application, or an AmI shower. In the differentiating questions emerging from a relation, one is forced to take a stance into a particular identity: a good or a bad friend, a lover of medium-hot or lukewarm showers, being in a blue-yellow or a pink-red mood, etc. Realizing that relations do not *mirror* a true or pre-given self but in fact are the *producers* of differentiations and identities can be a stepping-stone toward self-transformation. By retracing the tiny mechanisms producing our identities, "a moment-to-moment awareness of the virtual nature of ourselves" (Varela 1999, 75) can arise that will allow us to work "on the limits of ourselves" (Foucault 1984c, 46). However, in an AmI environment such awareness might be difficult to achieve. First, this can be the case because the identifications and the creation of personalized profiles that take place in AmI will often be a set of black-boxed intermediary steps in a process of being second-guessed by a smart device. As long as the personalized profiles are only based on our own behaviour and are not communicated with other devices, there is nothing special about this black-boxing. From the way one is anticipated, one can infer the mechanisms that produced the identity ("I am a *moccachino extra-strong* person — that is an identity that emerged in my re-iterated interactions with my smart coffee machine"). However, discreet identification methods might obscure the awareness of these mechanisms. Moreover, as soon as these black-boxed profiles begin to *circulate* between devices and environments (e.g., my smart coffee machine at home suddenly offers me a *moccachino extra-strong* based on the fact that I drink them at my work), it will become even more difficult to keep in touch with the way in which one's identity is produced (cf. Phillips 2005). Next to this deterritorialization of the identity-construction process, things become even more unclear when statistical stereotypes ("group profiles") are taken as a base for personalized anticipation (e.g., my smart coffee machine suddenly offers me a *double espresso* based on the fact that people who like hot showers like this kind of coffee too). A partly overlapping issue is the "inarticulateness" of some of the mechanisms underlying machine profiling: how to identify with an algorithm? (cf. Gandy 2002, 15).

Jason Salavon's *The Class of 1988* and Benjamin Males's *Target Project* are two works of art that could help to answer that question. The visual stereotypes of *The Class of 1988* (1998) create an intriguing atmosphere of serene aesthetics (see for further analysis: Viégas & Wattenberg, 2007). In *Target Project* the juxtaposition of smart CCTV pictures with alienating mathematical percentages and mosaics of skin colour representing particular neighbourhoods in London[9] leave the viewer with a feeling of discomfort. In both works "statistical stereotypes" appear to be much more than a mere intermediate step in a process of anticipatory personalization based on a machine-profile.

Conclusion

As the boundaries of the private and the public domain become less distinct within the information society, there is a need to reformulate the right to privacy. One way would be to understand privacy in terms of freedom of the creation of one's identity (Agre and Rotenberg 2001). Yet, how could one understand such freedom of identity construction in a way which does not rely on the naïve presupposition of a sovereign and autonomous subject able to act independently from the facticity of its world? The Foucauldian notion of "techniques of the self" opens up a way to envision how the materially and relationally constituted self could perform certain operations upon oneself "to attain a certain state of happiness, purity, wisdom, perfection, or immortality" (Foucault 1988, 18). The crucial condition for such techniques of the self is a certain degree of awareness of the functioning of these relational materialities and the possibilities lurking within them. Only when one is aware of the facticity in which a difference is produced ("the exam showed the good student from the bad") the possibilities or virtual nature of oneself ("if I understand how the exam works, I see how I could try to turn from a bad student into a good student") can be acted upon. Thus, an exam can differentiate the good student from the bad, a marriage can produce insights into what kind of spouse one is and an AmI shower can produce commercially exploitable differences between different preferences. One of the aspects distinguishing these loci of production of differences is their transparency about the way in which the differences are produced. Whereas an official exam will probably be rather transparent of what

---

[9] See for the mosaics: http://www.benjaminmales.com; for more technical details on the project: Kirk, 2008.

constitutes a good or a bad answer, in a marriage and an AmI shower this can be much more ambiguous. Moreover, when AmI technologies make use of volatile statistical clusters as the basis of their categorization, making an inference about the mechanisms underlying a certain personalised approach might be even more difficult than making an inference of the reasons underlying the way one is approached by one's spouse. When the temperature of your AmI shower adapts to you in such a silent way that you are hardly aware of the personalization, reappropriating this locus of difference within a "technique of the self" will become difficult. Thus, in thinking about identity and AmI, the crucial question is how to prevent the "statistical stereotype" and other mechanisms that underlie personalised anticipation to slip *beyond* the periphery of our attention — into complete invisibility. Artworks like Salavon's *The Class of 1988* (1998) and Males's *Target Project* (2008) form a good starting point to envision ways of bringing those mechanisms back to our "moment-to-moment awareness". After all, in our "dwelling" (Weiser 1996) with our spouses, friends and pets there is a long tradition of cultural knowledge available that helps us to act upon the possibilities lurking within the mechanisms of such relations; whereas in our dwelling with new AmI technologies we might benefit from a little prosthetic help from artworks like those of Salavon and Males.

Bibliography

Aarts, E. and Marzano, S. (eds.) (2003) *The New Everyday: Views on Ambient Intelligence*. Rotterdam: 010 Publishers.

Agre, P. E. and Rotenberg, M. (eds.) (2001) *Technology and Privacy: The New Landscape*. Cambridge, MA: MIT.

Albrecht, K., and McIntyre, L. (2005) *Spychips: How Major Corporations and Government Plan to Track Your Every Move with RFID*. Nashville: Nelson Current.

Barkhuus, L. and Dey, A. (2003) "Is Context-Aware Computing Taking Control away from the User? Three Levels of Interactivity Examined". In A. K. Dey, A. Schmidt, and J. F. McCarthy (eds.). *UbiComp 2003: Ubiquitous Computing (Proceedings of the 5th International Conference, Seattle)*. Berlin: Springer. 149-56.

Caine, K. E., Fisk, A. D. and Rogers, W. A. (2006) "Benefits and Privacy Concerns of a Home Equipped with a Visual Sensing System: A perspective from older Adults". Paper presented at the *Human Factors and Ergonomics Society* 50th Annual Meeting, San Francisco.

Crang, M. and Graham, S. (2007) Sentient Cities. *Information,*

Communication & Society 10 (6). 789-817.

Custers, B. H. M. 2004. *The Power of Knowledge: Ethical, Legal, and Technological Aspects of Data Mining and Group Profiling in Epidemiology.* Nijmegen: Wolf Legal Publishers.

Dai, C., Zheng, Y. and Li, X. (2007) "Pedestrian Detection and Tracking in Infrared Imagery Using Shape and Appearance". *Computer Vision and Image Understanding* 106 (2). 288-99.

Davies, E. R. (2005) *Machine Vision: Theory, Algorithms, Practicalities.* Amsterdam: Elsevier/Morgan Kaufmann.

De Moor, D. (ed.) (2004) *Living Tomorrow: Well-being — Today and Tomorrow.* Tielt: Lannoo.

Deleuze, G. (2000) *Foucault.* Minneapolis: University of Minnesota Press.

Economist (2007a) "The Trouble with Computers". September 8, 21-22.

—. (2007b) "Watching as You Shop: Retail Surveillance". December 8, 24-25.

Elmer, G. (2004) *Profiling Machines: Mapping the Personal Information Economy.* Cambridge, Mass.: MIT Press.

Foucault, M. (1977) "Two Lectures". In Gordon, C. (ed.). *Power/Knowledge: Selected Interviews and Other Writings, 1972-1977.* New York: Pantheon. 78-108.

—. (2001a) "Conversation avec Werner Schroeter". In *Dits et Écrits II, 1976-1988.* Paris: Gallimard. 1070-79.

—. (2001b) "Un interview de Michel Foucault par Stephen Riggins". In *Dits et Écrits II, 1976-1988.* Paris: Gallimard. 1344-57.

—. (2001c) "L'écriture de soi". In *Dits et Écrits II, 1976-1988.* Paris: Gallimard. 1234-49.

—. (1984a) "On the Genealogy of Ethics: An Overview of Work in Progress". Interview with H. Dreyfus and P. Rabinow. Berkeley, April 1983. In Rabinow, P. (ed.) *The Foucault Reader.* New York: Pantheon. 340-72.

—. (1984b) "Space, Knowledge, and Power". In Rabinow, P. (ed.) *The Foucault Reader.* New York: Pantheon. 239-56.

—. (1984c) "What Is Enlightenment?" In Rabinow, P. (ed.) *The Foucault Reader.* New York: Pantheon. 32-50.

—. (1985) *The Use of Pleasure*, vol. 2 of *The History of Sexuality.* New York: Random House.

—. (1986) *The Care of the Self,* vol. 3 of *The History of Sexuality.* New York: Random House.

—. (1988) "Technologies of the Self". In *Technologies of the Self. A Seminar with Michel Foucault,* eds. L. H. Martin, H. Gutman, and P. H. Hutton, 16-49. London: Tavistock.

—. (1993) "About the Beginning of the Hermeneutics of the Self: Two Lectures at Dartmouth". *Political Theory* 21 (2). 198-227.

Gandy, O. H. (2002) "Data Mining and Surveillance in the Post-9.11 Environment". Paper presented at the Annual meeting of IAMCR.

Greenfield, A. (2006) *Everyware: The Dawning Age of Ubiquitous Computing*. Berkeley: New Riders.

Groebner, V., Kyburz, M. and Peck, J. (2007) *Who Are You? Identification, Deception, and Surveillance in Early Modern Europe*. New York: Zone Books.

Haggerty, K. D. and Ericson, R. V. (2000) "The Surveillant Assemblage". *British Journal of Sociology* 51 (4). 605-22.

Hildebrandt, M. (2008) "Defining Profiling: A New Type of Knowledge?" In Hildebrandt, M. and Gutwirth, S. (eds.) *Profiling and the Identity of the European Citizen*. N.p.: Springer. 39-50.

Hjelm, S. I. (2005) "Visualizing the Vague: Invisible Computers in Contemporary Design". *Design Issues* 21 (2). 71-78.

Inman, M. 2008. "'Big Brother' Buildings Offer Less Invasive Security". *New Scientist*, April 9.

Ivanov, Y. A., Wren, C. R., Sorokin, A. and Kaur, I. (2007) "Visualizing the History of Living Spaces". *IEEE Transactions on Visualization and Computer Graphics* 13 (6). 1153-60.

Kirk, J. (2008) "CCTV Camera Identifies People by Race". *PC World*, July 14.

Latour, B. (2007) "Beware, Your Imagination Leaves Digital Traces". *The Times Higher Literary Supplement*, April 6.

Magid, J. and Lovink, G. (2004) "Surveillance, Performance, Self-Surveillance: Interview with Jill Magid". http://www.evidencelocker.net/img/artistTalk.pdf

Martin, L. H., Gutman, H. and Hutton, P. H. (eds.) (1988) *Technologies of the Self. A Seminar with Michel Foucault*. London: Tavistock Publications.

Negroponte, N. (1995) *Being Digital*. London: Hodder and Stoughton.

Paras, E. (2006) *Foucault 2.0: Beyond Power and Knowledge*. New York: Other Press.

Phillips, D. J. (2005) "From Privacy to Visibility: Context, Identity, and Power in Ubiquitous Computing Environments". *Social Text* 23 (2). 95-108.

Phillips, D. J., and Wiegerling, K. (eds.) (2007) *Ethical Challenges of Ubiquitious Computing*, vol. 8 of the *International Review of Information Ethics*.

Ramalingam, S., and Ambaye, D. (2005) "Stereo-based 3D Face

Recognition System for AmI". In Remagnino, P., Foresti, G. L. and Ellis, T. (eds.) *Ambient Intelligence. A Novel Paradigm*. Boston: Springer. 177-97.

Ricoeur, P. (1994) *Oneself as Another*. Chicago: The University of Chicago Press.

—. (1998) *Critique & Conviction : Conversations with François Azouvi and Marc de Launey*. New York: Columbia University Press.

—. (2008) "L'interprétation de soi. Allocution prononcée à Heidelberg en janvier 1990". In Zarka, Y. C. (ed.) *Paul Ricoeur. Interprétation et reconnaissance*. Paris: Presses Universitaires de France. 139-47

Sharma, R., Moon, H. and Jung N. (2007) "Automatic Detection and Aggregation of Demographics and Behavior of People". US Patent 12,002,398, filed Dec. 17, 2007, and published 8 May, 2008. Available at: www.google.com/patents

Schauer, F. F. (2003) *Profiles, Probabilities and Stereotypes*. Cambridge, Mass.: Belknap.

Shapiro, L. G. and Stockman, G.C. (2001) *Computer Vision*. Upper Saddle River, N.J.: Prentice-Hall.

Stiegler, B. (2008) *Prendre soin de la jeunesse et des générations*. Paris: Flammarion.

Thrift, N. (2003) "Closer to the Machine? Intelligent Environments, New Forms of Possession and the Rise of the Supertoy". *Cultural Geographies* 10. 389-407.

Van Doren, E. G. P. (2004) "Adaptivity of Ambient Intelligence to Fulfill Consumer Needs". US Patent 10,575,574, filed Oct 12, 2004, and published June 21, 2007. Available at: www.google.com/patents

Varela, F. J. (1999) *Ethical Know-How: Action, Wisdom and Cognition*. Stanford: Stanford University Press.

Viégas, F. B. and Wattenberg, M. (2007) "Artistic Data Visualization: Beyond Visual Analytics". In Schuler, D. (ed.) *Online Communities and Social Computing*. Berlin: Springer. 182-91

Warren, S. D. and Brandeis, L. D. (1890) "The Right to Privacy". *Harvard Law Review* 4 (5). 193-220.

Weber, W., Rabaey, J. M. and Aarts, E. (eds.) (2005) *Ambient Intelligence*. Berlin: Springer.

Weiser, M. (1996) "Open House". *ITP Review 2.0*, March. Available at: http://sandbox.xerox.com/hypertext/weiser/wholehouse.doc

Weiser, M. and Brown, J. S. (1997) "The Coming Age of Calm Technology". In Denning, P. J. and Metcalfe, R. M. (eds.) *Beyond Calculation: The Next Fifty Years*. New York: Copernicus-Springer. 75-85. Also available at:

http://www.ubiq.com/hypertext/weiser/acmfuture2endnote.htm

Weiser, M., Gold, R. and Brown. J. S. (1999) "The Origins of Ubiquitous Computing Research at PARC in the Late 1980s". *IBM Systems Journal* 38 (4). 693-96.

Wilhelm, T., Böhme, H.-J. and Gross, H.-M. (2005). "Face Recognition and Detection: Classification of Face Images for Gender, Age, Facial Expression, and Identity". *Lecture Notes in Computer Science* 3696. 569-74.

Wright, D., Gutwirth, S., Friedewald, M., Vildjiounaite, E. and Punie, Y. (eds.) (2008) *Safeguards in a World of Ambient Intelligence*. N.p.: Springer.

Wu, J., Smith, W. A. P. and Hancock, E. R. (2008) "Face Recognition: Facial Gender Classification Using Shape from Shading and Weighted Principal Geodesic Analysis". *Lecture Notes in Computer Science* 5112. 925-34.

CHAPTER TWO

I JUDGED YOU AT STARBUCKS:
IDENTIFICATION AND REGULATION
OF THE NON-PERSISTENT SUBJECT
ON CRAIGSLIST MISSED CONNECTIONS

JED BRUBAKER

In order for a man or a woman to be constituted as a subject, he or she must first be divided from the totality of the world, or the totality of the social body. For 'me' to emerge, a distinction must be made between the 'me' and the 'not-me.' The boundaries of the self are those lines that divide the self from all that which is not the self, which is beyond the self. (Gutman, 1988: 107)

SF bay area craigslist > missed connections
cute starbucks boy - w4m (downtown / civic / van ness) 19yr
Date: 2008-05-23 22:21:01 PST
You're tall and skinny and work at starbucks....
Just letting you know that I have a crush on you. :)[1]

Introduction

Many of the current discussions about identity on the internet address disclosure and privacy through the analysis of digital presence and self-presentation (Ellison et al. 2006; Lampe et al. 2007). This contrasts with earlier practices of anonymity seen in MOOs and MUDs that emphasized the empowering notion of the construction of self in deindividuated spaces (Dibbell 1998; Markham 1998). While the recent proliferation of social

---

[1] Posts to craigslist frequently include misspelled words, incomplete sentences, and typos. In order to present these posts in their original state, Missed Connections included in this chapter have not been altered.

networking sites has allowed users to develop persistent identities with profiles that can transcend a single interaction, there are many digital spaces in which user identities are not persistent and require the construction of a single-use identity for each interaction.

This chapter examines effects of this non-persistence in posts submitted to craigslist Missed Connections, an online equivalent to "I saw you" personal ads. Authors on Missed Connections submit anonymous posts that detail interpersonal interactions from the physical world with the hopes that their target will recognize the post and respond. Unaided by user profiles or accounts, authors describe themselves, their targets, and detail their encounters. Readers, meanwhile, interpret these descriptions of physical spaces, individuals, and interactions. Readers are cued only by the content of the original author's post. Despite the popularity of the site, however, there is no guarantee that the author's intended target will read the post, recognize the interaction, or respond. Anonymized by the craigslist system, and obscured by the volume and variety of content, Missed Connections authors engage in practices of self-description, balancing disclosure and anonymity in these public posts.

Users of sites like craigslist problematize our traditional understanding of identity and subjectivity. They construct social spaces but without an enduring presence. Physical bodies are not available by which to identify the participants, nor are pictures, usernames, or profiles. When they do occur, interactions are always delayed and, given that they may occur privately over email, are frequently invisible to the public readership. Interactions that are visible consist of non-persistent identities composed inside of posts that have no guarantee of reaching their desired target.

The anonymous user behavior on craigslist results in a lack of self-persistence that gives rise to new practices of self-definition. If "the individual which power has constituted is at the same time its vehicle" (Foucault 1980, 98), then we must explore the ways in which power, mediated by the anonymity of digital spaces, is expressed via new forms of subjectivity and through new sites of disciplinary regulation. Given these new forms of self-expression, unbound by bodies, physical space, previous self-descriptions, and the resulting persistence of self, we must consider the ways in which identity is communicated through what I am calling the "non-persistent subject".

In this chapter, I will share conclusions from over one year of research on the craigslist Missed Connections space. I read more than 10,000 advertisements[2] posted to the San Francisco Bay, New York City, and Washington, D.C. metropolitan areas with a particular focus on self-descriptions, anonymity, and deindividuated communication. While Missed Connections has been used for a number of purposes, this analysis is predominantly limited to prototypical posts written by authors that seek to reconnect with a specific target and the public responses to these posts. I am particularly interested in the ways individuals negotiate anonymity and identification across real and digital worlds. In addition to the work of Foucault, these readings are informed by Kristeva's theory of intertextuality (1980), and research on anonymity and self-presentation from the field of computer mediated communication (Lea and Spears 1992; Walther 1992; Walther 1996). Together, these theories provide a framework by which to understand the behavior of authors and readers and the potential implications of these brief interactions between otherwise anonymous individuals.

Foucault's anti-humanist approach to subjectivity is particularly pertinent when considering the non-persistent subject. His insights on power/knowledge, disciplinary categories and regulation, and our relationship with each through technologies of the self, provide an informing lens when considering dynamic self-presentation via text. Foucault (1977) claimed that practices of disciplinary regulation arose in the years following the middle-ages as the unified Church-regulation of a now mobile and educated population broke down. As result, new disciplines derived from prisons, hospitals, and schools emerged to create manageable categories for the population (Foucault 1977). As the population once again is fracturing in the face of virtualizing and mobile technologies, power has retreated, only to find new ways in which to articulate itself in dynamic environments and with new forms of subjectivity.

Online, we can selectively present ourselves (Walther 1992), but the identities we compose are selectively interpreted as well. In environments where bodies and identities are mutable, subjectivity can be understood as the interpreted presentation of individuality. Lacking a persistent physical or digital presence, the subjectivity produced by a Missed Connections author, and later interpreted by his readers, is distinct from the bodily and profile-centric subjectivities with which we are more familiar. This non-persistent subject is constructed as a single-use profile and need not

---

[2] Every submission to these cities between June 2007 and July 2008 was reviewed. These posts were automatically collected and catalogued by a custom software application written for this project.

account for issues of continuity or persistence. Authors can publicly craft their single-use subjects with ostensibly less fear of direct recourse, and as we will see, a greater level of candor.

While the anonymous format and short lifespan of posts on Missed Connections makes them ephemeral, authors do rely on persistent physical spaces, contexts, and ideas. Non-persistent subjects are composed of shared categorical, contextual, and cultural understandings. This allows authors to build their text-based profiles by drawing from shared cultural knowledge, relying on the reader's ability to interpret the profile and construct the appropriate subject. Participating in shared languages of self-description, however, also provides a vehicle by which authors and readers of Missed Connections are regulated. An effect of power, the non-persistent subject is established in relationship to the disciplinary categories to which he is assigned and by which he is identified. Thus by engaging in practices of self-description, craigslist authors craft text-based subjects that are always constrained by the language with which they are represented. Through the act of selective self-representation, authors must engage power/knowledge as they evaluate their presentation relative to the various disciplined categories by which the self is ultimately defined.

In considering the non-persistent subject, the goal of this project is three-fold. First, in order to understand the ways in which non-persistent subjects are constructed, I will examine practices of identification and presentation. Second, I will account for the ways in which non-persistent subjects are embedded in larger contexts through which readers understand the posts. Building on the self-identifying practices used in posts, I will examine the ways in which authors and the craigslist system embed posts into spatial and cultural contexts. Finally, I will consider the regulation of non-persistent subjects via public third-party responses. Missed Connections readers sometimes choose to publicly respond to posts by contributing a post of their own. These regulatory posts, however, are submitted anonymously, addressed to an individual who may never see the post.

The craigslist space is unique in many ways, but the ways in which users blend anonymous and non-anonymous aspects of themselves across variably persistent spaces is not. We need to consider the ways in which the deployment of persistent and non-persistent subjects across digital and physical spaces provides new spaces in which power/knowledge is reworked or redeployed. In the next section, I will present an overview of the technical functionality and typical use of the Missed Connections section. This will help to highlight the ways in which users work with and against the craigslist system.

1. Representing a Connection: Posting Encounters on Missed Connections

capitol south to l'enfant - m4m (orange line)
Date: 2008-04-22, 7:19AM EDT, Washington D.C.

Monday at about 10:30 am, I got on the metro at capitol south, you were with two other guys, you and I were in shorts and you had what appeared to be some hot pecs, you caught my glance and said hello. We all got off at L'Enfant. If you see this, coffee at Starbucks on the Hill?

craigslist is a community-focused Internet website that resembles the form and function of newspaper-based classified advertisements. The site was launched by Craig Newmark in 1995 and features advertisements (or "posts") that can be submitted free of charge.[3] The craigslist system is geographically divided into sub-sites (sometimes called "channels"), typically representing metropolitan areas such as "Washington D.C." and "SF bay area". Each channel features advertising areas including jobs, housing, for sale, and starting in 2000, a personals section that includes an area for "Missed Connections". craigslist's success has frequently been credited to its ease of use. Authors can quickly add content without a user account, and readers can anonymously search the large number of posts.[4] craigslist has increased in popularity over the years and is now the 45th most visited website on the internet, and the 12th most visited site inside the United States.[5]

Posts to Missed Connections are fairly formulaic. The typical Missed Connection describes a sighting or exchange that occurred in the real world, but did not result in the inter-personal connection desired by the author. An author will submit a post to craigslist that details the events of the encounter with a title and message, and then hope that his intended target will read the post, recognize the description, and respond. To this end, authors utilize myriad descriptive categories to identify the participants involved and the physical space in which the interaction occurred. Posts often include physical descriptions ("in shorts", "hot pecs"), logistical details ("you were with two other guys", "We all got off

---

[3] craigslist does charge for job and housing posts in select metropolitan areas. craigslist first began charging for listings in August 2004.
[4] On average, the New York City channel of craigslist Missed Connections received over 307 posts per day during the period of April 2008 to July 2008.
[5] Alexa.com ranking as of April 29, 2008.

at L'Enfant") and any interaction ("you caught my glance and said hello"). Many, like the post above, involve simple sightings and perceived romantic or sexual interest. Others might include contact on the dance floor; kind words shared in the lunch line, or repeated sightings at common locations like the gym. Virtually any interaction that does not result in the exchange of phone numbers, email addresses, or a name with which one can be found on Facebook might result in a Missed Connection.

Unlike other socially and romantically geared websites, Missed Connections is unique in its account-less format.[6] Sites such as Match.com, Facebook, and eHarmony allow users to register for an account and create profiles that include pictures, physical descriptions, personal interests and preferences. Missed Connections on the other hand, embedded in a site and format famous for selling bikes and futons, avoids profiles and persistent descriptions. Even the use of pictures is discouraged in the Missed Connections section. Where most social sites attempt to represent their users via personal attributes tethered to a user account, a Missed Connections author must construct a single-use identity with a title and single text box labeled "Description". Each post, and the details it conveys, is self-contained, allowing the author to customize their level of disclosure and anonymity.

While the subjects constructed for use in Missed Connections are contained within the post, some of the geographical and cultural contexts by which these interactions are interpreted are not. In addition to the details provided by Missed Connections authors, craigslist asks authors to select a geographical channel (e.g., Washington D.C., New York City, etc.), allows custom locations (e.g., "Connecticut Ave", "Castro", "In my dreams!"), and labels Missed Connections based on the author's gender and sexual preference (i.e., m4w, w4m, m4m, w4w). Along with the "Description", these details allow readers to categorize the participants and contexts the post describes based on their understandings of these categories. As authors and readers present and interpret identities in the anonymous craigslist environment, they construct non-persistent subjects that are understood relative to the persistent categories by which they are defined.

---

[6] craigslist allows user accounts for easy management of posts, but they are optional and do not include profiles. According to craigslist's help section: "You can manage posts efficiently with a craigslist user account. The process of creating posts, editing and deleting them, and re-posting ads that have expired is much easier. If you post frequently, or if you need to post paid ads, it makes sense to set up a user account".

2. The Foucauldian Connection

Foucault viewed the subject as the byproduct of social relationships. He drew on Nietzsche's theory of the subject as emerging from the interplay of language and power, defining the subject, not as a vehicle of power, but rather as the result of it:

> The individual is not to be conceived as a sort of elementary nucleus... In fact, it is already one of the prime effects of power that certain bodies, certain gestures, certain discourses, certain desires, come to be identified and constituted as individuals. (Foucault 1980, 98)

Foucault accounted for the subject's relationship to power with what he called "technologies of the self" (1988). Foucault's description of these technologies shows an expansion of his theories of confession and internalized disciplinary regulation to collectively explain the practices by which the subject continually inserts power/knowledge into his consciousness through practices or technologies of self-checking and self-knowledge.

For Foucault, our individuality is not subject to power. Instead, our understanding of ourselves as individuals exists because of power: "The individual... is not the vis-à-vis of power; it is, I believe, one of its prime effects... it is the element of its articulation. The individual which power has constituted is at the same time its vehicle" (1980, 98). In his lecture at the University of Vermont, Foucault (1983) explored this concept by turning to the Roman philosopher Seneca's practice of self-writing. This practice of journaling (which Foucault called "*hupomnemata*") established a technology of self-truth called "*exagoureusis*" in which the individual verbalized his thoughts in a continual manner. The continuous detailing and production of self-knowledge, often delivered in the presence of a master, allowed a more thorough self-categorization. Foucault argued that this active and public note-taking created a subject that had already submitted to the input of his master and their collective culture. In doing so, the entire known subject was simultaneously created and regulated by power.

Practices of self-writing and self-categorization are relevant to Missed Connections for several reasons. First, authors on Missed Connections capture thoughts, desires, and experiences that would not have otherwise been shared. Walther (1996) has argued that the rate of communication in computer-mediated environments provides users the opportunity to carefully craft their self-presentation. This may explain why craigslist users choose to present themselves online, rather than risk an interaction in the real world. Additionally, slower self-presentation may suggest a more significant consideration of the language used in these posts. Secondly, because posts are text-based, Missed Connections requires that users produce a self-knowledge in categorical terms. The importance of these categories may be more important online. Lea and Spears (1992), for one, have shown that individuals rely on social categories when formulating impressions of others in anonymous digital environments.

Finally, there is a difference between the message intended by a Missed Connections author and the way that message is interpreted by readers. In her theory of intertextuality, Kristeva (1980) claims that texts are unable to transfer meaning directly, but instead are mediated through a set of personal "codes" that influence our production and interpretation of meaning. In the case of a Missed Connection, these theories allow us to see how authors intertextually "read" a real world interaction, and selectively encode their understanding of that exchange in categorized terms online. Those reading the posts intertextually interpret the content based on their own understandings, while giving preference to the social categories the posts contain.

With today's technology, the ability to selectively represent oneself in mediated environments allows individuals to utilize various disciplinary categories while producing any number of non-persistent selves. Myriad digital environments provide authors with multiple audiences against which temporary and even contradictory subjectivities can develop. While the individual might have a need to integrate these duplicitous selves, the ability to selectively present an anonymous or non-persistent self to a specific set of "masters" provides the opportunity to experiment with various relationships with power. In the next section, I outline common patterns of representation utilized in Missed Connections in order to consider the relationships with power that emerge from user practices and the craigslist system.

3. Authoring the Non-Persistent Subject

Green Line towards Branch Ave (around 6:40p) - m4m (Green Line)
Date: 2008-08-25, 8:13PM EDT, Washington D.C.

You (BM) had on a red and white Old Navy T-shirt and jeans. I (BM) had on a black suit and greenish shirt and tie. We made eye contact several time before you got off at Naylor Road and waited for the train on the other side.
Maybe next time you can ride to Suitland with me.

Presenting ourselves is always an act of selective representation. Virtual environments, however, further constrain our representations through reductive technologies like profiles and instant messages. While I have suggested that the anonymity and structure of craigslist can empower users to explore new forms of self-presentation, authors are constrained by their intended audience's ability to intertextually interpret the posts. Authors present themselves in ways that ostensibly help them achieve their objective while emboldened by the anonymity of these spaces and the omissions that they allow.

Posts to Missed Connections exhibit a tension between anonymity and identification. On the one hand, authors use craigslist to anonymously recreate their interactions without fear of social ridicule or rejection. On the other, authors construct messages that detail themselves, their targets, and their interactions with the very objective of being identified, albeit by a specified audience. Posts are always selective and always have an objective. These are subjects looking to be recognized.

Reading through these posts, it is easy to view them as a type of confession. Missed Connections are saturated with individuals baring their souls. Foucault is well known for his analysis of confession (1990), and indeed Missed Connections appear to match the type of disciplinary technology. Confession is a practice intended "to bring the arcane conscientiae to light", cleansing the soul with its "purifying value" (Foucault 2005, 500). Foucault, however, also explored confession as a technology of self-knowledge "in which the speaking subject is also the subject of the statement" (1990, 61). Authors may post their Missed Connections in order to allow their "arcane conscientiae" come to the surface, but the practices of identification required to both author and read posts allow power to inject itself into the consciousness of craigslist users through the disciplinary categories they use.

These technologies of self-identification project a subject while leaving the author with the anxious hope of discovery. There is an anxiety in having correctly disciplined oneself into legible categories that the author's target will recognize and with which produce the intended response. Identification, however, is also a practice of distinguishing oneself from the masses. Following in the tradition of Rousseau's Confessions, these authors' self-descriptions establish individuality by separating the "self and society" (1988, 107).

When negotiating the balance between identification and anonymity, authors identify interactions and participants using a variety of techniques. Some authors create profiles of the participants by including short lists of familiar descriptive categories that frequently include physical attributes and material objects such as clothing. Others choose to describe participants in more evaluative terms by using qualitative descriptions. Finally, some authors choose to identify the participants by detailing an interaction. Each of these techniques allows the author to categorize the participants and interactions into short descriptions that communicate a number of subjective qualities.

When a 23-year-old in Washington D.C. posts "me: white, 5'9, grey t-shirt", he is identifying himself in physically descriptive terms. Without any additional information, however, this author must rely on the impression he made in the physical world to trigger the would-be reader's memory. The choice of these categories, however, is noteworthy. The use of performatively naturalized categories obscures the ways in which practices of identification organize non-persistent subjects into codified populations. For example, a 46-year-old's post into the "m4w" section of the San Francisco area about a "tall, blonde haired" target requires that he encode his target relative to these two categories.

This is not to suggest that categories are not without their utility. Categories certainly help the intended target find the appropriate post, but in their use, also place the author and reader into a position of regulation. Without user accounts, authors use visually descriptive terms to identify themselves and their targets in terms of regulated categories. Foucault reminds us of the constructed aspect of these categories when he writes that "for a long time ordinary individuality — the everyday individuality of everybody — remained below the threshold of description" (1977, 191).

The categories used in an author description may have varying meaning for different readers. The inclusion of a "grey t-shirt", for example, is fairly innocuous. While a t-shirt is certainly a legible category, its effectiveness at distinguishing the author from the crowd may render it unimportant. Other categories may carry greater levels of signification. One 25-year-old man in New York City, for example, describes his target as wearing "skin tight black leather jeans" featuring a "perfect ass" which the author describes as "f-cking hot". Through his descriptions, this author produces a subject that can be assigned to a variety of categories including "gay", "young" and "sexual". This is not to say that varied interpretations are not common. A reader might also interpret this subject as having an affiliation with S&M, gay leather culture, or even part of New York's Goth scene. And of course, this representation is written by the author in terms markedly different than those the target may ascribe to himself. Regardless of the accuracy of the author's descriptions, both author and reader must consider their relationship to the categorical terms by which he is defined.

Authors also use qualitative descriptions. "I am a very out going person", says one 20-year-old woman from the San Francisco area. In her extensive post she describes herself by listing activities she finds enjoyable: "I like to go out and go dancing, go to movies and I also like to just stay home and have a nice quit night, just cuddled next to the one I care for". Descriptions such as these move beyond descriptive lists to include selective and nuanced interpretations that qualify otherwise profile like descriptions.

Most posts include some interaction, but some skip descriptive and qualitative descriptions and rely on the interaction alone. "what i told you at the end of the night was the truth, i had to get home or else i would be in trouble!", posts a 21-year-old man about an interaction outside a Washington D.C. dance club. He skips codified self-descriptive practices, and instead attempts to reinforce the subject already presented during the originating interaction. These interaction-only posts lend themselves to narrative, and while the most descriptively rich, also limit the author's profile to the smallest deciphering audience. In a New York City post entitled "Hows your resume going", a 48-year-old man simply writes: "Saw you today we spoke briefly just wondering how it went---". Without including categories this author has avoided the production of the self Foucault described, but has possibly restricted the ways in which readers might find his post. This post may not appear when would-be readers search through content using physical descriptors in the craiglist search engine.

Typical authors blend a number of these techniques, sometimes with a douse of creative flair. A Wall Street businessman who describes himself as "damn good at anticipating the price of oil" writes to a "Non-herpetic hipster". He attempts to evoke a response by revealing an intimate conversation in which they "were talking about the practicalities of life and love, and divulged the shared fact of our Herpes-free bodies to one another, and how rare that made us in this crazy town".

Finally, some posts request that the would-be respondent provide the description instead. This authenticating request made by a 21-year-old is prototypical: "just tell me what my shirt looked like so that i know it's you!". While not included in every post, the regularity with which this kind of request appears may suggest that despite complex descriptions, readers often incorrectly identify themselves in posts. Authors may include these requests as a type of interpretation enforcement, allowing them to negotiate the terms under which they are willing to interact with their anonymous readers.

An author's description of his target results in a non-persistent subject for the target as well. Using the same descriptive techniques, authors produce a non-persistent subject against which readers can compare themselves. When reading through the posts, readers must engage in the same identity categorization as the author, creating a set of personal categories that he will compare with the non-persistent subject produced by the author. When reading one 35-year-old man's description of a target who was wearing "a gray skirt and black or dark gray top and red heels", readers must mentally scan their wardrobe for the matching articles of clothing, as well as outfit choices over the last several days that might fit the description.

Not only does this result in subjects that are categorized by each other, it would also suggest that authors craft the descriptions of their targets anticipating their response upon reading the post. One clear example involves authors apologizing for the post they submit. "Sorry, this is pretty random", writes 45-year-old man trying to reconnect with a woman after a traffic stopping connection in the Mission District of San Francisco. He proceeds to provide a demographic description of himself and a qualitative description of his target, but then apologizes for the descriptions themselves, mocking his writing ("[I] may not be all that creative") and the exposed nature of a craigslist ("if this is worded a little awkwardly, I'm having to edit for BIG BROTHER CRAIG.."). Not only does this author anticipate his reader's evaluation of him as "awkward" and less than "creative", he offers an interpretation of the Missed Connection system itself. This is one example of how authors detail participants, interactions, and even the craigslist system in ways that anticipate the judgments of their targets. Whether the author includes a description of his target or not, the subjects produced emerge, as Emile Benveniste's essay "Subjectivity in Language" suggests, in each other's presence: "*I* posits another person... to whom I say *you* and who says *you* to me" (1971, 729).

While authors carefully craft their descriptions, subjects deployed via the Missed Connection have no persistent existence beyond the post. When an author's craigslist "masters" read the author's post, regulation is limited to that which is included in the Missed Connection. As Nietzsche's *On the Genealogy of Morals* (1966) reminds us, subjectivity emerges out of the complex interplay between language and power, a fact that Foucault seizes to further his theory of disciplinary regulation. These digital bodies are pre-encoded and pre-regulated in their virtualized state. The subject summoned via text is always already categorized into regimes of power.

Then why turn to the restrained environment of craigslist in the first place? First, power/knowledge is not universally at the expense of the subject. Categorizations such as "hot pecs", "outgoing", and "perfect ass" can be channeled to an author's advantage. Secondly, the use of text allows authors to mediate the disciplinary practices of the real world by selectively choosing the categories by which they are identified. Ultimately, anonymous authorship on craigslist Missed Connections appears as a practice of controlled representation in which categorical fluidity is forfeited in exchange for a selectively regulated subject, constrained in his textual construction.

4. Contextualizing the Non-Persistent Subject

ATTN: Emily from Texas, Sightseeing - m4w
Date: 2008-08-18, 5:06PM EDT, New York City

We crossed paths several times while in New York City. Once at The Met, then the following day near NYU at Washington Square. And finally at a bar in Williamsburg at which point I came up to you and we spoke briefly-you introduced yourself as Emily sightseeing from Texas. I told you I was Chad sightseeing from LA.

While Missed Connections authors may selectively construct their subjects by including attributes and descriptions, subjects are also understood in relationship to their contexts. Here I am using contexts to refer to understandings outside of the non-persistent subject that communicate information with which readers may interpret posts. Knowingly or otherwise, authors often include contexts from the physical world when describing their interactions. craigslist's requirement of a geographical area and the option of specifying age, gender, and sexual orientation provide a large number of contexts with which readers can understand these non-persistent subjects. Many of these divisions create social spaces within the Missed Connections space (particularly sexual orientation), but each also represents a persistent context that transcends the individual post.

As readers interpret these persistent contexts, posts to Missed Connections bridge "real" and "digital" space. When "Chad" posts a New York Missed Connection about "Emily", readers may choose to interpret these non-persistent subjects based on their knowledge of men from Los Angeles, women from Texas, tourists in New York City, or any of the various places their paths crossed while visiting the Big Apple. As Castranova writes in his book *Synthetic Worlds*, "There is certainly a relationship between the synthetic world and the real one... People are crossing all the time... carrying their behavior assumptions and attitudes with them" (2006, 147). Authors ostensibly are seeking to bridge these spaces. The author's narrativized Missed Connection is the digital instantiation of a non-digital experience, but whose primary objective is to return to the real world.

Authors often bridge these spaces by including specific locations in their posts that are embedded with cultural meaning. One 23-year-old woman in the San Francisco area, for example, describes an encounter at "the drag king show at the White Horse on Wednesday night". This description places her and her target in a specific cultural context, as well allowing readers to infer characteristics about the author (namely, someone who would attend a drag king show).

Some contexts are unavoidable. The craigslist site requires that authors post Missed Connections into a geographical space, permitting readers to always make some base level of contextual interpretation. Other optional information such as gender and sexual preference, age, and specific location, each provide readers with information which he can use to understand the non-persistent subjects authored in the post.

Anonymity might suggest a separation from the restrictions of physical space, but unlike the fantastical MOOs and MUDs of the 1990s, Missed Connections seek to re-present the real world. Nowhere is this more apparent than in apologies for not establishing the desired connection in physical space and resorting to a Missed Connection. "I really think that this is a long shot, but it's worth a try", writes one 27-year-old man in Santa Clara about a Jamba Juice employee with "beautiful eyes and a great smile!". A woman in the Castro writing "to carly at the café" sums up the frustration of many authors nicely: "why didn't i get your number????".

Non-persistent subjects created by anonymous users may inhabit craigslist, but it is neither an autonomous digital space nor fully representative of the real world. Instead, craigslist acts as digital proxy for the real world. While craigslist authors selectively present personal attributes, a reader's interpretation of the various contexts communicated by the craigslist system cannot be avoided. Through the placement of non-persistent subjects into more persistent contexts, authors are able to anonymously work on themselves with new categorical terms while reworking contextual and cultural understandings as well.

5. Regulating the Non-Persistent Subject and his Contexts

re: Blooms in Fair Lakes
2008-05-23 11:10:35 EDT, Washington D.C.

Dude. You are a freak. Seek help. People like you scare the shit out of chicks. You actually followed somebody to their house??? What is wrong with you?

Amidst the various responses to Missed Connections, some readers choose to become authors themselves and write what I am calling a "public response". Because the craigslist system does not functionally allow users to publicly respond to posts, readers-turned-authors have taken a cue from email subject lines and internet forums and adopted a convention of their own: pre-pending the previous author's subject with "RE:" (e.g., "re: Blooms in Fair Lakes", seen above).

Respondents may also choose to address other public respondents in addition to the original author. Typically these posts will all share the original subject line, but multiple "RE:"s may or may not be added. This, however, is not always the case and readers must discern the conversation across a number of posts that puncture the stream of more conventional Missed Connections. When readers can decipher these conversations across responses, the Missed Connections section bends in the direction of an internet forum, allowing a discussion of posts and categories and the subjects they contain.

Public respondents post for a variety of reasons. Some, like this post made to the Washington D.C. site, ask for clarification: "Care to supply more details or are we all to just assume this is for any man or woman who has been ignored...?". Others may offer encouragement. "I know a posting from a stranger doesn't do much (perhaps nothing at all)", reads a response to the relationship struggles of one man, "but you'll be okay".

While public responses can undoubtedly serve a number of purposes for authors and readers alike, in this section I am turning my attention to the public response as a form of regulation. craigslist has been lauded for its community moderated flagging system, a system that allows the effective management of content by allowing readers to flag inappropriate posts for removal from the site. However, readers sometimes choose to regulate the site by authoring a public response instead, ostensibly when they consider the removal of the post unnecessary or insufficient. By replying publicly, the respondent seems to object not so much to the original post's presence on the Missed Connections site, but rather to its specific content. Given that the non-persistent subject is limited to the Missed Connections post, regulation resembles the "coercions that act upon the body, a calculated manipulation of its elements, its gestures, its behavior... [producing] subjected and practiced bodies, 'docile' bodies" (Foucault 1977, 11).

Some posts, like the one at the beginning of this section, take issue with specific actions (i.e., following a stranger to their house). Public responses also frequently address the way in which an author thinks. In response to one man's post about an altercation with a woman, a San Franciscan writes "that's your story Mr., but what about her perspective?". Another post responds to a Washington D.C. Missed Connection that originated in a sex club and resulted in a sexually transmitted disease. "Crabs huh?" the public response reads, "That should be the least of your concerns if you're getting banged at a bathhouse".

These posts seem to emulate real world conversations, yet they share a fervor often reserved for anonymous spaces that deindividuate their participants. I would suggest that the public response indicates a desire on behalf of the reader-turned-author to not only address to the original post in a way that does not include censorship, but rather through their authorship, highlight that which is objectionable.

While public responses are addressed at or around a specific post, their regulatory function cuts across categories and contexts. In fall of 2007, a young man posted an ad with an evocative title to his local m4m section. "I've missed the connection with DC", the title read simply. In a post that may have been more appropriate for craigslist's "Rants and Raves" section[7], he included the typical demographic and qualitative descriptions, but instead of identifying some person on the street as his target, he targeted his readers instead.

"Sometime last year", he wrote, "I thought it would be a rocking' fun-zone idea to move somewhere new... Washington, DC... I'll bet I find some great folks there--maybe a boyfriend, too. Flash forward to the present... I simply find myself disinterested... in most of the people here".

The man continued by offering himself as an "enigma" while talking to his "neo-panoptic" craigslist audience about the frustrations he had with the gay community in DC. But cutting through the thicker words and reappropriated Foucauldian theory, the theme of the post was clear: He was lonely.

---

[7] craigslist's "Rants and Raves" section provides a non-topic specific space for users to post content. As the title suggests, most of the posts in the section include a public complaint or praise for the topic.

The reactions of his "neo-panoptic" readers were intense. Rather then censor the post by flagging it for removal (and thereby dissolve the instantiated subject, the post, and its readership), public respondents attempted to target him directly. "Perhaps you should look at yourself and your attitude as the reason you're such an unhappy person", wrote one respondent, blaming the author for his situation. This response by a 26-year-old seemed to agree: "DC is the swamp of the self-important. Based on your Missed Connection, I think you'll do alright".

Other respondents could relate to this author's frustrations. "I'm just a bit disappointed with DC. And it's not for my lack of trying..", said a 23-year-old. Another post, added only a few minutes later, seemed to echo the sentiment: "I really expected [DC would provide] the opportunities to find someone that I clicked with... However, I have been extremely disappointed in what I've found". The conversation quickly degraded to, as one 25-year-old wrote, "lambasting the local gay community", leaving another to ask, "Is this a discussion about DC?".

Undoubtedly it was. Regulation of the non-persistent subject frequently touches upon his composing categories and contexts. "For you people thinking that DC will be the 'be-all-that-ends-all'...PUH LEEZ!" wrote one respondent, followed by "DC is a s---hole - an expensive ghetto full of uptight east coast types". Still another binds the context of Washington D.C. with the context of the gay community by writing "The gay men in this city need to get over their insecurities... It's the insecurities that keep them out of meaningful relationships".

And of course there was advice: Go to the bars, don't go to the bars, join a club, give it time, try online services, "keep your eyes open – he's out there", and sadly, "how about you all just, you know, shut the hell up?" or even "move". It is remarkable that amidst the variety of reactions technically available to these readers, rather than emailing the author directly (forfeiting their anonymity and potentially persisting the subject) or flagging the post for removal (potentially eliminating the subject), these readers chose to author a public response, reinforcing the very non-persistent subject and contexts with which they were taking issue.

From the perspective of a public respondent, a response seeks to rework the definitional categories, deploying an alternative or modified power/knowledge through an act of disciplinary regulation. Collectively, these regulatory practices, emboldened by anonymity, transform craigslist into a new site for disciplinary regulation. Through its anonymous text based interface, craigslist allows users to engage in a category-based relationship with power/knowledge. Employing languages of self-identification, users read interpersonal interactions while iteratively defining a restrictive discipline for Missed Connections, as well as the non-anonymous categories, interactions, and contexts from which these Missed Connections emerge. Bearing this in mind, we need to consider the motivations for regulation of this digital space.

In Joan Scott's essay entitled *Experience,* she reminds us that "Experience is a subject's history" and that "Language is the site of history's enactment" (1992, 33). The posts are based on authors' experiences of these categories and contexts, each of which is collaboratively constructed. "Since discourse is by definition shared", she continues, speaking to the way in which we use language to share our personal histories, "experience is collective as well as individual*".*

But if these experiences constitute the categories and contexts themselves, then any regulation must be considered across duplicitous environments. We can see the ways in which posts like those above can both confirm and contradict the collective experiences of a group such as the gay community, a community whose categorical cohesion is dependent on being made essential. Scott would seem to agree. "Identity is tied to notions of experience", she writes, "[but] both identity and experience are categories usually taken for granted…" (1992, 33).

If we acknowledge a connection between the content of Missed Connections and the contexts they represent we should question the ways in which the disciplinary regulation within the deceptively unstructured social space of craigslist feeds back into the real world to shape the essentialized concepts we have of men, women, grey t-shirt wearing club kids, the gay community, or even Washington D.C. If craigslist has created a space in which content is no longer exclusively censored, and the most extreme posts are now extremely regulated, then the words of Foucault seem quite apt when he describes a move "from the censorship of statements to the disciplinarization of enunciations… to a form of control that is now exercised on a disciplinary basis" (2003, 184). When we discipline the categories with which we represent our real world experiences, we discipline the subjects and contexts from which these experiences arise.

Conclusion

The anonymous practices of identification seen in Missed Connections show one way in which the non-persistent subject provides authors the ability to construct participants, interactions, and contexts in codified terms. Authors employ a variety of identifying practices that compose subjects out of disciplinary regulated categories, mapping the non-persistent subject into the "anonymous everyman" (Martin 1988, 51). Missed Connections publicly expose otherwise private interactions, relying on pre-determined categories with which to describe participants and contexts. In this way, craigslist provides a distinct proxy for the real world, allowing users to work on the "self" with languages of self-identification that facilitate regulation. On the one hand, authors can use the anonymous space to rework their subjective relationship with disciplinarized categories. On the other, posts such as those made by public respondents work to disciplinarize the very terms with which the non-persistent subject and his contexts are described. craigslist is a compelling example of how variably persistent subjects and contexts intersect with mediating technologies to allow the increasingly dynamic subject to remain within the purview of power.

craigslist Missed Connections creates a space that is technically more flexible than social websites that restrain users with persistent profiles that are structurally predetermined. This might suggest that craigslist should lead to the proliferation of diverse identities and experiences. The posts submitted, however, do not realize this potential. While the craigslist system appears to provide the technical freedom to represent any type of subject, the categorization of Missed Connections situates posts in relation to the real world they seek to represent. Despite the agency that Missed Connections provides authors in their descriptions, public responses by readers integrate posts into pre-existing and persistent understandings from less anonymous real world contexts.

How then do we understand forms of regulation such as those seen in the public response? As we vividly saw in the Washington D.C. example, the non-persistent subject cannot be managed with conventional forms of regulation; there is no guarantee that original authors ever witness the disciplining of their non-persistent subjects. Instead, the public response provides a vehicle through which it can address us all. The original post lays out the disciplinary categories inside and against which readers and respondents operate. As we read public responses, power/knowledge is deployed, and the categories against which we are always self-checking are further internalized.

In an age where persistent digital identities produce homogenized definitions of the very categories by which we understand ourselves, craigslist provides a space to rework these categories, and in doing so, rework ourselves. "I believe the great fantasy is the idea of a social body constituted by the universality of wills", Foucault wrote in his essay *Body/Power* (1980, 55). "The phenomenon of the social body is the effect not of a consensus but of the materiality of power operating on the very bodies of individuals". To this end, we articulate our identities with the hope of connections that will ultimately reify our own culture of the self.

It is not surprising then that each Missed Connection envisions its own future. These posts are embedded with an interpersonal potential, should the authors connect with their targets. Authors craft non-persistent subjects that, despite their limited lifespan, can represent the desire for something that endures. In their descriptions, authors detail their relevant self-understanding, producing a self-knowledge in pre-regulated terms. In their anonymity, these posts allow authors a dynamic production of the self without concern for continuity.

The regulation of the non-persistent subject seeks then, not to regulate the author, but the legitimacy of the future to which his post aspires. Contexts are embedded with these potentials as well. When public respondents seek to regulate shared experiential contexts such as "the gay community", not only do they disciplinarize the collective experience of that context, they also work to ensure the promises it contains. Be it Starbucks, non-herpetic hipsters, or Washington D.C., each of these categories hold a promise for its authors. As authors engage with categorized terms and contexts, they are not only entering into a relationship with the possible futures these regulated terms allow, they are reworking their own non-persistent selves across a variety of contexts and the promises their authorship might hold.

Acknowledgment

I would like to extend thanks the generous support of those who made this chapter possible. In particular, thanks goes to Mirjana Dedaic, Garrison LeMasters, and Matthew Tinkcom for their advice and guidance with the direction of this project, and to Patricia Fancher, Ramzi Fawaz, Kathryn Cornelius, and Steven Frost for their feedback along the way.

Bibliography

Benveniste, E. (1986) *Problems in General Linguistics*. In H. Adams & L. Searle (eds.). Critical Theory Since 1965. Gainesville: University of Florida Press.
Butler, J. (1999) *Gender Trouble: Feminism and the Subversion of Identity*. New York: Routledge.
Castronova, E. (2006) *Synthetic Worlds: The Business and Culture of Online Games*. Chicago: University Of Chicago Press.
Dibbell, J. (1998) *My Tiny Life: Crime and Passion in a Virtual World*.

New York: Holt Paperbacks.

Ellison, N., Heino, R. and Gibbs, J. (2006) "Managing Impressions Online: Self-Presentation Processes in the Online Dating Environment". *Journal of Computer-Mediated Communication* 11 (2). 415-441.

Foucault, M. (1977) *Discipline and Punish: The Birth of the Prison.* New York: Vintage.

—. (1980) *Power/Knowledge: Selected Interviews and Other Writings, 1972-1977.* New York: Pantheon.

—. (1983). *Michel Foucault: the Culture of Self.* Berkeley Language Center. Retrieved from: http://www.lib.berkeley.edu/MRC/audiofiles.html#foucault.

—. (1988) "Truth, Power, Self: An Interview with Michel Foucault" — October 25th, 1982. In Foucault, M. (ed.). *Technologies of the Self: A Seminar With Michel Foucault.* Amherst: University of Massachusetts Press.

—. (1990) *The History of Sexuality: An Introduction.* New York: Vintage.

—. (2003) *"Society Must Be Defended": Lectures at the College de France, 1975-76.* New York: Picador.

—. (2005). *The Hermeneutics of the Subject: Lectures at the College de France 1981-82.* New York: Palgrave Macmillan.

Gutman, H. (1988) "Rousseau's Confessions: A Technology of the Self". In Foucault, M. (ed.). *Technologies of the Self: A Seminar With Michel Foucault.* Amherst: University of Massachusetts Press.

Kristeva, J. (1980) *Desire in Language: A Semiotic Approach to Literature and Art.* New York: Columbia University Press.

Lampe, C. A. C., Ellison, N., and Steinfield, C. (2007) "A familiar face (book): profile elements as signals in an online social network". *Proceedings of the SIGCHI conference on Human factors in computing systems.* New York, NY: ACM Press. 435-444.

Lea, M., and Spears R. (1992) "Paralanguage and social perception in computer-mediated communication". *Journal of Organizational Computing* 2. 321-341.

Markham, A. N. (1998). *Life Online: Researching Real Experience in Virtual Space.* Lanham, MD: AltaMira Press.

Martin, L. H. (1988) "Technologies of the Self and Self-Knowledge in the Syrian Thomas Tradition". In Foucault, M. (ed.). *Technologies of the Self: A Seminar With Michel Foucault* Amherst: University of Massachusetts Press. 50-63.

Nietzsche, F. W. (1966) "On The Genealogy of Morals". In Kaufman, W. (ed.). *Basic Writing of Nietzsche* New York: Random House. 451-492.

Scott, J. W. (1992) "Experience". In Butler, J. and Scott, J. W. (eds.). *Feminists Theorize the Political*. New York: Routledge. 22-40.

Walther, J. B. (1992) "Interpersonal Effects in Computer-Mediated Interaction". *Communication Research* 57. 52-90.

—. (1996) "Computer-mediated communication: Impersonal, interpersonal, and hyperpersonal interaction". *Communication Research* 23. 3-43.

DIGITAL POLITICAL IDENTITY

CHAPTER THREE

PRACTICING IDENTITY IN THE DIGITAL GAME WORLD: THE TURKISH TRIBES' COMMUNITY PRACTICES IN "SILKROAD ONLINE"

MUTLU BINARK AND GÜNSELI BAYRAKTUTAN SÜTCÜ

Introduction

Playing digital games, especially massive multiplayer online role-playing games (hereafter abbreviated to MMORPG), is one of the most popular leisure activities among Turkish youth. After the September 12 1980 military coup in Turkey, the depoliticization process greatly affected public life. Government authorities considered digital games to be a legitimate leisure activity, and the spread of internet cafés supported the expansion of game-play in public places. Since then, video and PC games, text-based online games (such as MUDs), and mobile phone games have become popular. The marketing strategies of some game companies (e.g., K2 Network, Joymax) have also recently contributed to the attractiveness of online role-playing games. After noting the high number of players from Turkey, South Korean game companies have developed business connections in the country.

A new socializing pattern emerged among Turkish youth, called *immobile socialization* (Bakardjieva 2003), explains how they locate their real life through social networking and invest in building new social capital within cyberspace. Following Pierre Bourdieu's important notion, *habitus*, we believe that the online game player relocates her/his subjectivity positions and represents her/his identity-structuring determinations that previously had been produced in her/his real life, including experiences acquired in the family circle, network of friends, and in school and at work. Bourdieu explains the concept of habitus as a system of general generative schemes that enables a social scientist to analyze the behavior of agents in everyday situations. An agent's habitus is self-reflexive in that each time habitus is transmitted into practice or encounters itself as embodied within an agent's acts, tastes, preferences, or sayings (Bourdieu 1990; Calhoun 1993, 61-88; Brubaker 1993, 212-234), it becomes both an internalization and an incorporation of a granted culture, and becomes a social distinction among the agents. In MMORPG we could observe that players transfer their real life habitus to the game world[1], and use already produced habitus to construct a virtual identity.

For this paper we chose to analyze the newly emerged Turkish online game player culture through an examination of *Silkroad Online* (hereafter SRO), created by Joymax. Turkish online game players' re-embodied habitus in SRO becomes visible through the formation of Turkish guilds — in other words, tribes. Ethnically marked organizations designate the consensus on role playing in SRO and guide the coordination of the players' activities. Turkish youth reconstruct their real-life habitus in online environment by creating an avatar and participating in ethnically rooted guild organization. Hence, players in SRO reinforce Turkish identity through guild rituals and express pride in being Turkish with every game play. The habitus of Turkish players in cyberspace once more derives from the real-life determinants.

1. *Silkroad Online* World and the Turkish Players' Habitus

SRO is a free game and has almost 12 million players around the globe who bring their own social and cultural capital to this virtual world; 1.2 million of these are Turkish.[2] SRO is based on ancient Chinese and Korean mythologies (see http://www.joymax.co.kr and http://www.silkroadonline.net). A major motivation for Turkish youth to play SRO is that the game is free to download and play. Neither the game's story nor its mythological references are inherently attractive to Turkish players, a belief that is supported by our interviews with guild leaders. SRO has some common narrative features with other MMORPGs,

---

[1] Edward Castronova, names the place (interface) where people inhabit as a synthetic world and emphasizes that this synthetic world has outside implications caused by inside events (2005, 4; 7).
[2] Murat Yavuz Kaplan, an expert of the Turkish game Nette Hayat, provided this data in the interview carried out on April 4th 2008.

including the exploration of distant places and the aim to develop some solidarity among the players while fighting against monsters or undertaking difficult quests. Seeing the game's popularity among Turkish youth, in 2007 Joymax began distributing SRO in all internet cafés in Turkey by establishing a new payment system (such as premium cards) via the internet cafés' SRO accounts and membership IDs.[3]

Game magazines and internet forums promoted the reputation of SRO by distributing free installation CDs and advertising the game. Like many other examples of the genre, SRO is composed of 48 characters, 24 female and 24 male. Each player can choose a character and create an avatar from a given set of characters. The player can choose different clothes and accessories and hairstyles to customize the appearance of her/his avatar. The player then has to follow instructions from non-player characters and gain skill and experience points to survive in this virtual environment. The level upgrading system is the main feature of the game; therefore each player has to invest seriously in her/his virtual career. To survive in SRO, the players need to develop solidarity and form guilds.[4]

To better understand how Turkish players socialize in SRO, we will examine the identity practices of several different guild members and their leaders. We have three major assumptions: First, we assume that the increasing number of Turkish tribes being established in the digital game world is related to the international political discussions such as the global rise of xenophobia and ethnic nationalism. Thus Turkish players invest in establishing virtual tribes and even forming unions to protect themselves and fight against hostile foreigners in SRO. These ethnically rooted guilds provide players with a secure playing environment as well as protect them from cheating and illegal attacks from hackers.

Second, we assume that the formation of virtual identity is also key to understanding how players sense being part of the game. Virtual identity is represented through an avatar's body; its role-playing strategy. Players transfer their real-life habitus (i.e., cultural and social capital) to the virtual space through creating these virtual identities. In particular, players seek to

---

[3] In Turkey, a player pays at least 50 US dollars per month for a premium, a special pin code enabling rapid connection to SRO amongst other privileges. In order to manage this system, Joymax uses three ways: PayPal; local firms such as Game Sultan, GameTurk and Game Master; and internet café managers. Establishing a new payment system is important: although SRO is a free-to-play game, within the game world a player has to buy and trade some items using their credit cards.

[4] Guilds are called "tribes" among Turkish players.

establish similar social networks within SRO and prefer to interact with the players who have same cultural capital. For example, the player mostly interacts with members of his/her own guild, spending time with them and reconstructing a local culture and social life within this specific virtual world. Thus, the virtual identity is reinforced through this social networking, the social and cultural preferences.

Third, we assume that the guilds' members and leaders consider their organization as an "internship" first for the virtual life, then real life, if possible. Here, we mean that the internship is first established among players in the virtual life; once the suitable conditions are realized, this friendship can be transferred to real life. For that reason, we assert that Turkish guild leaders' online games turn out to be meticulous virtual careers. The leaders of Turkish tribes set economic and administrative rules and practice disciplinary techniques on the player members of the tribes.

2. Research Methods and Samples

Qualitative research techniques could make the cultural forms and contexts in which digital technologies are used more visible (Hine 2005, 1-13). The multi-method or combined method approach is much supported in social science research:

> Many qualitative researchers use a multi-method approach in their investigations in order to examine different levels of the same situation or focus on different aspects of the same phenomenon (Mann and Stewart 2002, 95).

In this qualitative study, a combination of five different research techniques is used: First, we conducted participant observation in both SRO and its related internet forums from summer 2006 to early autumn 2007. Second, we created an avatar in order to experience various role-playing strategies and took a "lurker" position, whereby a researcher could observe the interactions among the players without revealing her/his research identity and aims (Sanders 2005, 71; Orgad 2005, 54). The lurking position helps us to learn about the online culture (Chen et al. 2004, 165) and role-playing strategies among the Turkish players.[5] Within

---

[5] In this ethnographic research, we used a lurker position only to observe the environment, and did not conduct any interviews with other players. We also did

this virtual world we observed the Aege server where the Turkish guilds were first formed and on which most Turkish players prefer to play, giving it a high percentage of Turkish players. It is very common to establish guild-like organizations in MMORPGs because within them the players could assist each other and gain from the in-game economy. We observed at least 26 Turkish guilds[6] on the Aege server. From August 2006 to September 2007 we chose three particular Turkish guilds from this server to monitor: SkY, TurkishFire and Osmanlılar (The Ottomans). These guilds have been singled out by Turkish players in SRO-related forum sites because of their strictly documented and recorded administrative rules, as well as their reputation within the game world.

SkY, when it was established, had 41 members under the leadership of "Blue King_TR", a 29-year-old university graduate and sales representative. Recently, this guild has been reorganized, and now has 7 female and 43 male player members – this restructuring will be discussed in detail later. The guild's motto is "The secret friend of Turkish tribes is SkY". Osmanlılar is a guild established by an Internet café owner, and all the member players share the same offline social network and take it online. The guild leader was "Yavuz Sultan Selim", whose name is that of a 16th-century Ottoman Emperor. TurkishFire is one of the earliest Turkish guilds, established on the Aege server, and had opened the first internet forum on SRO news and events (http://www.turkishfire.forumup.com). Formerly led by "duster", the guild is now under the guidance of "crusade". The members of TurkishFire had been organized under "TC", an acronym for "Turkish Republic". Following reorganization, the guild's new leader has chosen a name for his avatar based on a religious mission conducted from 11th to 13th centuries. The coming of this guild's new name, "TC", has some connotations to the nation-state's unity, its secularity and its modern political administration, compared to Osmanlılar.

The third research technique we used was to create an avatar as a "suitable" member of the well-known Turkish guild, SkY, after receiving permission from the guild for the status of participant observer. For SkY,

---

not make any screenshots from game-play of this avatar. So, our avatar did not disturb the game environment and caused any ethical problems.

[6] These guilds are named TurkishFire, Dehşet, _Dreamover_, KingTurks, HeroTurks, Panterler, Turkiyem, Osmanlılar, SeverOfLife, Turk_Lokumu, The_Lords, OTTOMANS_TR, Tr_Grand_Tr, """Hero Turks"", AYYILDIZ, OZEL HAREKAT, RaDiKal, TuRK LoKuMu, Paradise, Ege, TC, Essiz, Disaster, Nizam-i Cedid, Elite Turks, KSK CARSI and SkY.

it is important to be a "suitable member", meaning the character has to be well built by arms and in possession of important skills such as healing and destroying powers. We recorded all the activities of this avatar. Fourth, we conducted an online open-ended questionnaire on the TurkishFire forum. We chose this forum, the first on SRO, because of its popularity among the guild leaders we interviewed. Finally, we conducted in-depth semi-structured interviews (Kivits 2005) with two tribe leaders.

While conducting our research, we were careful not to disturb these online communities and respected their rights in order to protect their privacy, confidentiality, and real-life identities. We also obtained their permission to use the findings of both questionnaires and interviews (Barnes 2004, 219). Having established a degree of honest online relationship[7] with the research participants, we moved to a face-to-face relationship with the tribe leaders.[8] Two agreed to meet us in August 2007. We conducted two recorded interviews with the guild leader of SkY, Blue King, lasting a total of 12 hours. He gave us permission to use all recorded materials about him and the tribe. With Osmanlılar's guild leader, "Yavuz Sultan Selim", we had a two-hour interview in his own Internet café. In contrast to Blue King, he asked us to protect his privacy and real-life identity. All quoted extracts from the interviews are used with the permission of these guild leaders. Their original grammar and spelling have been preserved.

3. Results and Discussion

Guilds in MMORPGs provide online game players with advantages, such as learning how to obtain valuable items (Taylor 2006). These organizations provide strategies on surviving in the game world while undertaking quests. Furthermore, for members of the same ethnic origin, the tribe offers online solidarity. Ethnically based online tribes reduce the need for member players to integrate and adjust themselves to the new and different conditions. On the contrary, they utilize already known codes and familiar cultural practices in their guild organizations. Moreover, the use

---

[7] The online relationship with the guild leaders lasted at least 3 months in order to obtain their confidence and the permission to conduct an ethnographic research with their guilds.

[8] According to Shani Orgad, combining online and offline interactions with informants, enhances the ways in which researchers are positioned in relation to their informants, and the ways they come to know them. As a consequence arguably, the analysis that is being produced is enriched (Orgad 2005, 62).

of common, native language (Turkish) strengthens the guild's social networking. The tribe members then carry over their online community into real life. We claim that this internship has both online and offline dimensions. For example, the leader of SkY, the character created as Blue King_TR, or in his new avatar, Blue King[9], employs various communication techniques to rule SkY and control its members. He uses MSN, participates in SRO-related forums, and from time to time meets with SkY members in his hometown. This continuous connectivity and the transformation of online relations to offline ones build the ties of "imagined community" among SkY members. Another example from the Aege server is that the members of Osmanlılar, who are residents of a small town near by İzmir[10], play SRO together in the internet café managed by the guild leader. Thus existing offline relations are reproduced in the formation of a specific guild — Osmanlılar. The guild leader of Osmanlılar, "Yavuz Sultan Selim" explains the membership policy of this tribe:

> In the game, most of the players don't know each other. They are from different cities. While establishing the Ottomans (Osmanlılar) tribe, our main aim was to know each other. If you act together, it will be good for the game. It is also more reliable... To play with someone whom you already know from the real life is better. I mean it is good for your security. For instance, you could be protected from hacking, acts such as stealing a character (Interview, August 31, 2007).

4. Research Findings

We discuss our research findings in the three following sections: the administrative and the economic rules of the guilds, the leadership, and the identity practices of Turkish tribes in the virtual world.

---

[9] "Blue King_TR" has been banned from SRO's administration from November 2006 to May 2007, because of a PayPal transmission error. The player character entered the game with a new avatar, named as "Blue King" since May 2007. Since his return to SRO, the restructuring process of SkY has began and still continues.

[10] İzmir is the third biggest city in Turkey in terms of population and is located on the Aegean Sea side.

4.1. The Guild as Modern Capitalist Enterprise:
The Administrative and Economic Rules

We found that guilds in online games operate similarly to modern capitalist enterprises. They have a hierarchical organizational structure, a leader, written and pre-determined rules to follow, and customs that are developed during the game. A player must accept the official rules, which are announced on the official website of the game, and also accept the authority of the guild leader. There are two ways of being a guild leader: either a player forms the guild and is the leader, or the member players nominate candidates and elect one from these candidates as a guild leader within the game environment. Official rules also determine the conditions of membership and leadership.

The ostensible reason for the existence of the Turkish guilds is to form a community to work, fight and survive together. T.L. Taylor emphasizes that interdependence is at the very heart of the game (2006, 32) and shows the possible means of social networking within the game, such as establishing pairs, pickup groups, friend groups, guild and ally groups and hybrid groups (2006, 37). Taylor also observes that there are two types of guilds; one is a family-like guild, sometimes called a social group, in which personal connections and playful engagement with the game are emphasized, and the other is a raiding guild, sometimes called an "uber guild", in which the players come together with a well-articulated commitment to complete a mission or a quest (*ibid.*, 43). Based on Taylor's classification, we could say that the Turkish tribes are all social groups. The guild leader of Osmanlılar, "Yavuz Sultan Selim", explains the necessity of being a member of the virtual community this way:

> One cannot live alone in real life. So, it is the same within the game world. How could I put in words? We need a patron or we need to join a community. Otherwise, you will be the loser within the game, or you are lost. No one knows you. One must belong to somewhere. The aim of the online game is related with this belonging and togetherness. Togetherness, to act together, to do tribe wars etc. are the things what we enjoy from online games. In the Silkroad Online there were no wars only tribe fights. But they opened European servers, so soon there will be castle wars. This makes the game more attractive... You can not do castle wars yourself alone. You need to be a member of the tribe, in other words the community. (Interview, August 31, 2007).

Castronova also emphasizes the necessity of establishing online communities by defining them as "forced cooperation" (2005, 115), stemming from the scarcity of the game resources (e.g., items, game money), so a solo player must either cooperate or come into conflict with the other players.

To survive in SRO, these virtual communities should have rules and regulations. The SRO website has official rules, and many of the guilds set alternative and more involved regulations for their members. These sometimes determine who is "an ideal player", emphasize the internship, and list the shared values and beliefs of the member players. According to Johan Huizinga, no play or game can exist without rules. They determine what "holds" in the temporary world circumscribed by play. Rules of a game are absolutely binding and allow no doubt (1970, 30).

Based on Huizinga's explanation, an ideal player member is one who strictly obeys the rules, and thus carries the game to further stages. The definition of the ideal player may differ according to different guild leaders. Being an active SRO member is the most important requirement for the leader of TurkishFire. Being an active member enables GuildLvlUp, meaning that members seriously invest in developing their virtual career, thus contributing to the guild's financial success. Members are expected not only to contribute financially but also to work hard for solidarity: When lower-level members ask for assistance from advanced players, the request has to be honored. For example, before selling any item in the market, an ideal member is expected to show their items on the guild's forum site, so that any lower level player can see it before it is offered to the server-wide population. This kind of protection mechanism supports solidarity among guild members. The economic and administrative TurkishFire guild rules are shown below (See Figure 1).

To be a member of Osmanlılar, it is necessary to live in the same town, and to use the same internet café while playing SRO. The guild leader of Osmanlılar explains the membership rules as follows:

> We didn't have many established rules. We ask our players "don't swear, and be respectful to the other players". We didn't want more than these. If you want to be assisted, let's act together, we said. That is all. (Interview, August 31, 2007).

Figure 1. TurkishFire Guild Rules[11]

1.	There is no restriction to being a member of our guild. We only expect our members to be active players. Also, each member will be expected to approve these rules without any exception.
2.	Our guild consists of active members. Friends who do not enter the game for a long time will be punished.
3.	No money is ever collected within the guild. Everybody could give/donate for GuildLvl Up.
4.	In collective activities done for the guild (i.e., trade), we will be very happy to see each other together at the day appointed. Both for the GuildLvlUp money, and for your own financial strength and of course for the unity of the guild you are expected to make the appointment.
5.	In order to diffuse in-guild solidarity at the lower levels, members should firstly publish their item demands in the guild's own forum site. Also, during the game all of your questions whether they are about the items or not, will be replied to.

As in Osmanlılar, trusting guild members is the most important requirement. For example, in SkY we observed that a sophisticated and distinct example among Turkish guilds on the Aege server is known to other Turkish SRO players by its well-defined hierarchical structure and the administrative techniques used by its leader. The recruitment policy of this guild also provides a set of rules to guide members' behavior (See Figure 2).

---

[11] http://turkishfire.forumup.com/viewtopic.php?t=791&mfourm=turkishfire. Accessed June 28, 2007. The original text is in Turkish and has been translated to English by the authors.

Figure 2. SkY Recruitement Policy[12]

Having an undergraduate degree or to have specific cultural capital is essential. Offensive and hate speech is strictly forbidden. Reflecting the ideals and values of the player's personality to the avatar is required. Being an active team player is expected. The most important criterion is to be an ethical and clean player. To create a strong character in the server is necessary. After they are selected, a new member must also accept the former rules and regulations, and is responsible for following them. There is no trial period; if the member acts or misbehaves against the guild interest, they will be thrown out of the guild without explanation.

The leader of SkY, Blue King, emphasizes the SkY soul and its basic characteristics as a community:

> I shall explain why a human being wants to play a game. Because he wants to display his power; to create a very good character... When we established the SkY, I asked the members if there was a good character within the game; they said 'yes'. Was there a good tribe within the game? The answer was 'yes'... what else, were there good caravan traders? Was there a good internship within the game? 'No'. So, that time I said that we were going to be a good team that will be our difference, and our strength will be originated from this point... Why is the SkY different and so special? Why does a player participate in the tribe, because of these reasons: one is to sell and receive an item; the other is chat. In our tribe, none of the players became a member because of item trade. I bought all the items myself. I gave them to the all the members generously... All I wanted from the members was to act ethically. In other words, I had some principles: I will offer all needed materials to the players, so don't be so greedy, be a member of the community, that's all. If a member plays for the sake of his interest instead of the tribe's, without any hesitation I cast out him from the tribe... (Interview, August 30, 2007).

From this statement, it is obvious that the members should act ethically, collaborate with the others in every instance, and communicate to establish the solidarity within both online or offline environments.

---

[12] http://silkroadturk.com/index.php/topic,47.0.html. Accessed June 28, 2007. The original text is in Turkish and has been translated to English by the authors.

As seen from the statements of Blue King, each community needs to emphasize its differences with the others. Also, according to Huizinga, the play "promotes the formation of social groupings which tend to surround themselves with secrecy and to stress their difference from the common world by disguise or other means" (1970, 32). One of the SkY members believes that:

> We have a confidential guild. Our members at least share the same cultural capital, and have education. The guild, indeed, is similar to a firm. A firm lives on the basis of capital and the loyalty of its labor force, same as our guild does. There is no guild like us in this game (Aa).

This statement also supports our contention that the online organizations within the game are similar to the modern capitalist enterprises, and the shared cultural capital is the main element of these organizations. Besides being a product of the culture industry and having economic value for some national economies (e.g., Korea) (Jin and Chee 2008, 38-58), SRO itself produces a financial market. The activities in the SRO essentially revolve around the trade issue. Players and guilds both fight for gold and other valuable items (e.g., silk), and either sell them in the market or transfer them to the guilds' treasury. Sometimes guilds experience the "misuses of the treasury", which lead to conflict among the member players. The leader of SkY, for example, once warned his players about using the treasury without making any contribution. According to Blue King, the member must work hard to develop SkY's treasury, and that's why he strictly regulates the uses of gold, silk and other valuable items. Blue King explains the importance of the economy within the game:

> Within the game you could only make money by opening stalls. You need to be a master at online economy. Only a naive player wants to make money from the caravan trading... We have our second-alt tribe, called "Troy" where we practice marketing. We give lectures on the basic requirements of economy. We have trade chars, and exercise sales, change the items at the stalls... We are 50 persons, and pay 50 US dollars to Korea. So our tribe members all together pay 2500 US dollars a month to Joymax, which is a serious amount of money (Interview, September 1, 2007).

Moreover, it should be emphasized that while this game is free to play, at the upper levels a player cannot survive without buying "premium" cards. The player also needs to buy some virtual silk that costs money in real life. These kinds of exchanges develop a game-related offline economy, and players have to spend their game-related budget (Castronova 2005,

170-204). The economy within the game is getting more attention by Turkish players because of the money made by some selling game-related items and even avatars at virtual markets. Players who want to establish strong avatars have to join the guild organizations. In a similar manner of the nation state's membership, membership in the tribe provides deep solidarity among the members, so each one feels equal, agrees on the disciplinary techniques for the sake of the tribe's existence, and practices the work ethic in cyberspace. Being a member of a tribe offers a feeling of inclusion for the players, and differentiates them from those who are excluded, creating two types of existence: "us" and "the others".

4.2. Leadership: Authority, Social Networking, and Virtual Career

In SRO guild leaders function like CEOs of multinational companies. They have the responsibility of regulating the financial resources and the administrative functions necessary to secure the "brotherhood" within the guilds. The leader has to play and be in the game much more than any ordinary player. Consequently, the guild leader reaches a high level skill: while the ordinary players spend no more than two hours per a day in SRO, the leader has to spend at least four hours within the game. This is almost equal to a part-time job in the offline world. The guild members expect the leader to have all the solutions; in any difficult situation, he/she is the first person to be asked for advice. The leader of Osmanlılar confirms this issue: "The leader of the tribe has more knowledge and items than the members. He gives to the members if they want it. It could be money, too" (Interview, August 31, 2007).

The leader has to apply her/his real-life qualifications — in other words, social and cultural capital — while managing the community.[13] The leader is able to monitor each player by using either the guild channel or a private chat channel. In some guilds it does not matter whether the leader practices his/her duties and responsibilities effectively. In SkY, however, the leadership has a strong strategic role. Blue King, following his return to the game, declared a new structuring policy and sought new

---

[13] We should also mention that there are very few female players and almost none of them are guild leaders among the Turkish tribes, playing on the Aege server. The assistant of the SkY leader is female; "Blue Queen" is a high level character in SRO. One of the female players is under the age of 18, and she is accepted because of the reference from her older brother. We could say that, based on our observation, online game playing is a male-dominated field.

members who could play harmoniously. He announced this new hierarchical order and its requirements on the forum site of TurkishFire, as well on the SRO Turk official web page.[14] According to the new order, there are three classes among the member players of SkY: the S class who, as players, are not expected to be active all the time as they are older members who, while still connected, no longer play actively. They have a position of honorary member and a privileged status: the leader calls them the "Palace" (in Turkish "hanedan"), referring to palace ("saray") life.

This strategy resembles "history making": creating a collective memory for the imagined community. Ks are commanders and are expected to play actively whenever and wherever they are. There will be five commanders (K1 to K5) and seven A soldiers (A1 to A7) under the control of each of these commanders. Ys are assistant members and can be considered the infrastructure of the guild; for example, a Y soldier is responsible for serving the guild in such duties as helping defense forces during caravan trade. In case of incompetence by K-class soldiers, they will go back to the Y class to be retrained. The leader, having defined these three classes, declares, "The future is ours. The best guild in Aege is SkY". What is more fascinating about this structuring is that Blue King also re-constructs the guild's name through this new recruitment policy: SkY. As Blue King stated:

> I organized the SkY composed of three parts, S, K and Y, which resemble the capital letters of the SkY. S means the Palace ("Saray"), where the players don't play the game so much. For example Cc, comes home at night, and plays for an hour. K consists of players who are in level 79 and 80. They are active, and online. Under their authority, there are 5 soldiers, so there are 35 soldiers. Y is composed of the assistant players, who don't master in the game. Just right now, we are working on recruiting female players in order to socialize the tribe. (Interview, August 30, 2007).

Guild leaders use certain strategies for ensuring members' commitment and the success of their guilds. The leader communicates with the member players both in the game and outside the game in other online places, like MSN or internet forums, as well as by phone. The leader holds meetings within the game, collects all the members and talks about certain necessary issues, like the administration of the guild's treasury or possible attacks from the other guilds and hackers. Furthermore, guild leaders sometimes organize "events" to entertain the member players in which the

---

[14] http://silkroadturk.com/index.php/topic,47.0.html. Accessed June 28, 2007.

players try to reach the target as quickly as possible and gain some gold. Thus, the online community ties are strengthened. SkY members sometimes meet in MSN and gather on one of the hills of the Aege map; the members of Osmanlılar always gather and play in the same internet café; the members of TurkishFire are active in online forums and discuss SRO-related issues, particularly on the guild's forum. The hill on which SkY members meet to discuss internal and external affairs bears the same name as the tribe.

In sum, creating some administrative and economic rules, and setting up some ethical principles addresses the "obsessive search for community" in the virtual world. For Michel Maffesoli this community is "neo-tribalism" (1996) and for Benedict Anderson it is an "imagined community" (1991). Zygmunt Bauman explains that the tribes of the modern world are formed as concepts and the members of these tribes support the symbolic traits of tribal allegiance (1991, 249). Bauman names these tribes as neo-tribes, following Michel Maffesoli's concept of neo-tribalism: "Neo-tribes are... the vehicles (and imaginary sediments) of individual self-definition" (Bauman, 249). Maffesoli himself argues that "the constitution of contemporary micro-groups in a network is the most final expression of the creativity of the masses" (1996, 96). We will now discuss, for our third finding, how Turkish guilds function as neo-tribes within the game and perform their Turkishness as their virtual identity.

4.3. Imagined Communities at SRO and Identity Practices of the Turkish Tribes

Following Benedict Anderson's definition of "nation" as "imagined communities"[15], we claim that within SRO Turkish players construct their

---

[15] Anderson describes a nation as "...an imagined political community and imagined as both inherently limited and sovereign" (1991:6-7). According to Anderson, a nation is considered as a community that is united by real or imagined markers such as history, language, traditions, and customs and linked with an imaginary homeland or a given territory. We claim that not only nationalist intelligentsia utilizes history, heritage, and myths to reconstitute "the imagined community" within the political discourse, but also through popular cultural narratives, in this case study the interface of digital game text, the digital game players do apply. Digital game text is turned to be a field for a political struggle, where the national identity and its collective memory are circulated. For the role of media and the popular culture in constructing the nation and its identical features see: Liza Tsaliki (1995) "The media and the construction of an 'imagined

new global and borderless imagined communities through forming guilds;
to indicate their belonging they apply symbolic signs such as flags,
emblems, images etc. and create borders between themselves and the
others. In the game, all the guild members share a "tag" on their avatars,
signifying their guild affiliation. On Turkish tribes on the Aege server, we
observe the use of "TR", an abbreviation for their guild names (i.e.,
OTTOMANS TR, Tr Grand Tr) that shows that these guild members are
from Turkey. Turkish players tend to buy as a pet a gray wolf, which is
considered as both mythical and mystic animal in Turkish ethnic legends.
On other SRO servers we observe guild names that refer to Turkish history
and the Ottoman Empire (e.g., KIZILELMA, GoKTuKLeR,
TuRKSuLTaNS), and to traditional and modern units of Turkish military
forces (e.g., KuVaiMILLIYE, KOLORDU TR, OZEL HAREKAT, 57
ALAY, MEHTERAn, SANCAKTAR, AKINCILAR). Some of the guild
names express the recent political climate in Turkey — for example the
guild called SARI ZEYBEK, on the Persia server, refers to the nickname
of Mustafa Kemal Atatürk, the first president and founder of the Turkish
Republic. Atatürk has an untouchable status in modern Turkish political
history, and is a symbol of Kemalist ideology, secularism and the unity of
nation state in Turkey.[16] The guild called AnTİ TeRoR, on the Eldorado
server, has a political stance and indicates the possible threads to the
nation state. Some of the guild names reproduce the stereotypes about
Turkish material culture, such as TuRK LoKuMu, which is a famous
sweet known as Turkish Delight, and Galatasaray, on the Greek server,
refers to a Turkish football club. Some guilds choose city names from
Turkey, such as İstanbul and Bursa.

We observe that guild members share the same social networks and
political stances in real life, making it easier to unite within the online
organizations. As mentioned, these Turkish tribes have even joined forces
in SRO against tribes hostile to Turkish players, and have developed a
global gaming strategy. Recently, Turkish tribes acted together against
hostility regarding Turkish military operations in northern Iraq. We think
that the simultaneous process of inclusion and exclusion operates within
these virtual organizations (Verdery 1996, 231), so that formations like the
guilds and unions within MMORPGs are indeed "imagined communities",

---

community': The role of media events on Greek TV". *European Journal of Communication*, 10: 345-370.
[16] For a detailed discussion of the status of Atatürk as a heroic mitos in Turkey see: Esra Özyürek (2006) *Nostalgia for the Modern: State Secularism and Everyday Politics in Turkey*. Durham: Duke University.

functioning rather like nations. Taking Anderson's definition of "imagined communities" (1991, 6-7), here nation is considered as a community that is united by real or imagined markers, such as history, language, tradition, and customs, and linked with an imaginary homeland or a given territory. Mass media, and now new media, function as means of empowering national identity and collective memory by circulating the stories about national myths and heritage.

We state that playing MMORPGs engenders national borders and national identities by circulating nationalist discursive practices among the guild members. Stuart Hall explains that:

> A national culture is a discourse, a way to construct meanings which influence and organize both our actions and our perceptions of ourselves. National cultures construct identities by creating meanings of "the nation", with which we can identify; these are contained in stories that are told about the nation, in memories which link its present to its past and in the perceptions of it that are constructed (Hall 1994, 201 cited in De Cillia et al. 1999, 155).

Turkish tribes utilize ethnic and nationalist symbols such as the Turkish flag, the portrait of the first president of the Turkish Republic, and the gray wolf to differentiate themselves from others and proudly express their Turkish identity to the global world of SRO. Symbolic activation of these symbolic repertoires by Turkish players reconstructs the imagined community at the cyberspace. By organizing fights against foreign tribes or narrating some ideological statements of the Turkish nation-state in SRO, we find that members of Turkish tribes are manipulated to share certain things in common against other players, such as common language, certain forms of culture and tradition, a specific history, an articulated feeling of belonging and of being at home (Verdery 1996). Turkish online players celebrate national days in SRO and by doing so contribute to producing embodied nationhood in this virtual world.

Turkish tribes construct "ethno spaces" for themselves within SRO. Anthony Smith explains the ethno spaces in this way:

> The land as historically unique and poetic landscape, as a decisive influence over historical events and as the witness to ethnic survival and commemoration over the longe durée: these are all components of a general process of 'territorialization of memory'… the poetic landscape is revered as an 'ancestral homeland' and the ethno space becomes an intrinsic part of the character, history and destiny of the culture community, to be commemorated regularly and defended at all costs lest

the 'personality' of the ethnic or regional community be impugned (1999, 151).

The members of SkY, for example, choose a distinctive location, a hill, from the SRO map, and assemble their tribe there, as we explained earlier. Thus SkY members illustrate a symbolic border for themselves, and construct a frame for self-identification. The members of the guild are required to act with respect while standing on the hill. For Anthony Cohen, a border contains community identity (1999, 8). As in real life, in SRO there are physically constructed mystical places and mentally accepted consensus over these places that act as borders between different guilds and their habitus. In this process, guild leaders efficiently employ the symbolic repertoire (Cohen 1999, 20, 57) that unites the members and differentiates them from the other players on the server, reproducing the collective identity.

The avatars are also an example of the use of a symbolic repertoire. In SkY, each member player has to choose an avatar cohesive with other members, and the guild leader organizes the selection of avatars. In Osmanlılar, the guild members choose an avatar from Turkish history especially from the period of Ottoman Empire; in other words, draw upon the collective memory with names such as "Yavuz Sultan Selim, Kanuni", "Kanuni Sultan Suleyman" etc.

We also observe within these virtual communities and within the Turkish tribes, that there is heroism. Blue King became a hero among the Turkish players on all the SRO servers because he reacts at the global level when negative opinions are expressed about the Turks. At the same time, he constructs good relationships with foreigners to promote Turkish culture and narrate the Turkish Republic's official history. He performs as an ideal player surrounded by virtues.

He also becomes an intellectual representative who thinks for and about the game. In other words, he is "above" the game. According to Anthony Smith:

> The intellectual is the interpreter, par excellence, of historical memories and ethnic myths. By tracing a distinguished pedigree for his nation, he also enhances the position of his circle and activity; he is no longer an ambiguous 'marginal' on the fringes of society, but a leader of the advancing column of the reawakened nation, the leaven in the movement of national regeneration (1999, 84).

Put in the words of Blue King:

I suggest that the game should not play with you, you should play the game. Don't allow Joymax to manage you, but you should guide the Silkroad. (Interview, August 30, 2007).

In real life, Blue King is a person who refers to nationalism and nationalistic ideology in everyday conversations. He talks about the global political and economical conditions and discusses the nation-state's position within this environment. In the online world, he emphasizes the necessity of the nationalist stance among the players: When he says, "Don't allow Joymax to manage you", it's a declaration of resistance to the Korean company. His habitus in the game is an obvious reflection of the real-life habitus, and his identity.

Conclusion

Guilds and unions are virtual public organizations where the dynamics of exclusion and inclusion operate simultaneously. "People symbolically construct communities, in order to transfer it into a source and stock of meaning and transform it to a signifier of their identity" (Cohen 1999, 134). Through constructing such virtual organizations, online players internalize the ethnic nationalist ideology that is comprised of certain habits of behavior and belief; everyday practices and routines that combine to make the social world meaningful, and thus natural (Billig 1995, 37). New media enable an easy and uncontrolled circulation of the heterosexist, homophobic, militarist and ethno-nationalist discourse in both global and local contexts.[17] This observation is not only specific to Turkish players; it can be seen in other cultures that produce and promote nationalist defense mechanisms. However, in this paper we observe the Turkish players' performance of the identity in the virtual world, and find that by these identity practices, Turkish players relocate their habitus, making the game world similar to real life, and come to see the game world as inconceivable without ethnically rooted guild organizations. For Turkish players, transferring the real-life habitus, especially social and cultural capital, provides secure game play, and makes easy to reach the player's goals within the game because of the solidarity among the guild members.

---

[17] For a detailed discussion, see: Bora, Tanıl. (2008) *Türkiye'nin Linç Rejimi*. İstanbul: Birikim.

In Turkey, mainstream media and the hegemonic political discourse
reproduce the anxiety that stems from the perceived threat to the national
unity and sovereignty[18], and the fear of the disappearance of the basic
elements of Turkishness. These menaces, real or imagined, legitimize the
community practices and collective actions of the Turkish tribes in the
online world. Nationalist rituals and the mythification of Turkishness are
embedded in everyday life and its routines. Recent research on the prime-
time news discourse on the mainstream television channels in Turkey,
carried by Esra Ercan Bilgiç (2008) shows that the discourse of Turkish
news reconstructs hegemonic Turkish nationalism, and addresses
homogeneity among the citizens of the Turkish Republic. The mainstream
news media's coverage overemphasizes the unity of the nation, the
national borders, the mythic status of Atatürk (Bilgiç 2008, 24-25).

Nationalism has become a popular stance among Turkish citizens as a
sign of political protest, so it is also natural to observe this pattern in the
online world. There was recently a popular practice among the Turkish
citizens who want to declare their support for the nation-state's unity,
Kemalist ideology, and Turkish nationalist discourse against the civil
rights of other ethnicities living in Turkish Republic. The popular practice
is to hang the Turkish flag, including the portrait of Atatürk, in apartment
windows as if to say "Turkish Republic is for the Turks". The flag
addresses an inclusion for the Turks and exclusion for those who are not
Turks. Moreover, the nationalist political slogan, "Either you should love
it or you have to leave", has been also circulated by some of the
mainstream media. This slogan is voiced by the young followers of the
Milliyetçi Hareket Partisi (MHP; Nationalist Movement Party) in the
public sphere, and youth spread the slogan with graffiti of a gray wolf, a
crescent, and text that reads "Ya türkçe, ya hic", which means "Only speak
Turkish" on the walls of the metropolitan cities in Turkey.

After acts by Kurdish separatists, Turks often hang flags and
mainstream media show a small flag in one of the corner of television
screens. Activities of the Demokratik Toplum Partisi (DTP; Democratic
Society Party), which is primarily Kurdish in nature, have led to some

---

[18] For a detailed analysis of the representation of national unity in media see;
Robins, K. (1996) 'Interrupting Identities: Turkey/Europe', pp. 61-86 in Hall,
S.and P. du Gay (eds) *Questions of Cultural Identity*. London: Sage; Negrine,
Ralph et al. (2008) "Turkey and the European Union", *European Journal of
Communication*, Vol. 23 (1): 47-68.

protests from the Turks.[19] For Turkish players in SRO, it seems "natural" to have a Turkish identity, to show nationhood through familiar symbols, and even react against virtual enemies. When the Kurdish separatists attacked Aktutun, a Turkish army station near by Iraq border, killing at least 16 soldiers, Turkish players at SRO walked from one city to another to show their respect for those who died. As a result, the construction of "us" and "them/others" is imprinted upon online games' virtual maps.

Flagging nationhood through guild tags is a construction of imagined community. The member players of the Turkish guilds and their leaders think they can speak for the nation, like national spokesmen, in SRO. For that reason, Turkish guild leaders playing online games develop virtual careers, choosing to establish highly disciplined techniques to rule their guild and develop the discourse that emphasizes the unity and solidarity of the guild members.

Bibliography

Anderson, B. (1991) *Imagined Communities: Reflections on the Origin and Spread of Nationalism*. London: Verso.
Aydın, Z. (2008) Milliyetçiliğin Çatı Partisi. http://www.turnusol.biz/public/makale.aspx?id=2122&pid=4&makale =Milliyetçiliğin%20çatı%20partisi (Access on November 13, 2008).
Bakardjieva, M. (2003) "Virtual Togetherness: an Everyday-life Perspective". *Media, Culture & Society*, 25, 291-313.
Barnes, S. B. (2004) "Issues of Attribution and Identification in Online Social Research". In M.D. Johns, S.S. Chen and G.J. Hall (eds.). *Online Social Research: Methods, Issues and Ethics*. New York: Berg. 203-22.
Bauman, Z. (1991) *Modernity and Ambivalence*. Ithaca, New York: Cornell University Press.
Bilgiç, E. E. (2008) *Vatan Millet Reyting: Televizyon Haberlerinde Milliyetçilik*. İstanbul: Evrensel Basım Yayın.
Billig, M. (1995) *Banal Nationalism*. London: Sage.
Bourdieu, P. (1990) *The Logic of Practice*. Cambridge: Polity Press.

---

[19] For a discussion on the rise of Turkish and Kurdish ethnic nationalist activities in 2008 see: Zafer Aydın's article. Aydın discusses the role of goverment in the accelaration of these two ethnic nationalist movements in Turkey. Zafer Aydın, "Milliyetçiliğin Çatı Partisi" http://www.turnusol.biz/public/makale.aspx?id=2122&pid=4&makale=Milliyetçili ğin%20çatı%20partisi. Accessed November 13, 2008.

Brubaker, R. (1993) "Social Theory as Habitus". In C. Calhoun, E. LiPuna and M. Postone (eds.). *Bourdieu: Critical Perspectives*. Oxford: Polity Press. 212-34.

Calhoun, C. (1993) "Habitus, Field, and Capital: The Question of Historical Specificity". In C. Calhoun, E. LiPuna and M. Postone (eds.). *Bourdieu: Critical Perspectives*. Oxford: Polity Press. 61-88.

Castronova, E. (2005) *Synthetic Worlds: The Business and Culture of Online Games*. Chicago: The University of Chicago Press.

Chen, S.L.S., G.J. Hall and M. D. Johns. (2004) "Research Paparazzi in Cyberspace: The Voices of the Researched". In M.D. Johns, S.S. Chen and G.J. Hall (eds.). *Online Social Research: Methods, Issues and Ethics*. New York: Berg. 157-75.

Cohen, A.P. (1999) *Topluluğun Simgesel Kuruluşu*. (Trans. by Mehmet Küçük). Ankara: Dost Yayınları.

De Cillia, R., Reisigl, M., and Wodak, R. (1999) "The Discursive Construction of National Identities". *Discourse & Society*, 10(2),1. 49-173.

Hine, C. (2005) "Virtual Methods and the Sociology of Cyber-social-scientific Knowledge". In C. Hine (ed.). *Virtual methods: Issues in Social Research on the Internet*. New York: Berg. 1-13.

Huizinga, J. (1970) *Homo Ludens: A Study of the Play Element in Culture*. Bungay, Suffolk: Paladin.

Jin, D.Y. and F. Chee. (2008) "Age of New Media Empires: A Critical Interpretation of the Korean Online Game Industry". *Games and Culture*, 3(1). 38-58.

Kivits, J. (2005) Online Interviewing and the Research Relationship. In C. Hine (ed.). *Virtual Methods: Issues in Social Research on the Internet* New York: Berg. 35-49.

Maffesoli, M. (1996) *The Time of the Tribes: The Decline of Individualism in Mass Society*. London: SAGE.

Mann, C. and F. Stewart. (2002) *Internet Communication and Qualitative Research: A Handbook for Researching Online*. London: Sage Publications.

Orgad, S. (2005) "From Online to Offline and Back: Moving from Online to Offline Relationships with Research Informants". In C. Hine (ed.). *Virtual Methods: Issues in Social Research on the Internet* New York: Berg. 51-65.

Sanders, T. (2005) "Researching the Online Sex Work Community". In C. Hine (ed.). *Virtual Methods: Issues in Social Research on the Internet* New York: Berg. 67-79.

Smith, A. (1999) *Myths and Memories of the Nation*. New York: Oxford University Press.

Taylor, T.L. (2006) *Between Worlds: Exploring Online Game Culture*. London: The MIT Press.

Verdery, K. (1996) "Whither 'Nation' and 'Nationalism'?" In G. Balakrishan (ed.), *Mapping the Nation*. London: Verso. 226-234.

http://www.joymax.co.kr
http://www.silkroadonline.net

Interviews

Nihat Anil Kesici, Blue King, the leader of SkY.
"Yavuz Sultan Selim", the leader of Osmanlılar.
"Aa", a participant in the online questionnaire.

CHAPTER FOUR

MOBILIZATION AND PEER-TO-PEER IDENTITY: AN INVESTIGATION OF BARACK OBAMA'S PRESIDENTIAL CAMPAIGN

YASMINE ABBAS

To organize a community you must understand that in a highly mobile, urbanized society the word 'community' means community of interests, not physical community. The exceptions are ethnic ghettos where segregation had resulted in physical communities that coincide with their community of interests, or, during political campaigns, political districts that are based on geographical demarcations.

People hunger for drama and adventure, for a breath of life in a dreary, drab existence. One of the cartoons in my office shows two gum-chewing stenographers who have just left the movies. One is talking to the other, and says, 'You know Sadie. You know what the trouble with life is? There just ain't any background music'.

But it's more than that. It is a desperate search for personal identity — to let other people know that at least you are alive. (Alinsky 1971, 121)[1]

---

[1] Michael C. Behrent (2008) "Saul Alinsky, la campagne présidentielle et l'histoire de la gauche américaine" in *La Vie des Idées*, http://www.laviedesidees.fr/Saul-Alinsky-la-campagne.html?decoupe_recherche=obama%20saul%20alinsky. Last accessed January 15, 2009. Saul D. Alinsky inspired both Hillary Rodham Clinton and Barack Obama (Clinton wrote a thesis about the community organizer; the thesis is available online at: http://www.gopublius.com/HCT/Hillary ClintonThesis.html. Last accessed January 15, 2009). Thank you to Thomas Watkin for the article.

Introduction

On a summer night of 2004, an American politician named Barack Obama gave a keynote address at the Democratic National Convention, held at the FleetCenter in Boston, Massachusetts.[2] A powerless "alien" with no right to vote in the United States of America — yet very concerned about the country's disastrous post-9/11 foreign policy — was watching television attentively.[3] I still hear a commentator saying something like: "This guy will go far". I remember thinking "How does he know?". This "guy", I learned, had opposed the "dumb war" that then had been raging for more than a year.[4] His discourse felt like a blessing — Barack means "blessed" in Arabic (Obama 2004, 104).[5] For sure, Obama's call for action was compelling because it was both democratic *and* inclusive. Events followed the extraordinary grassroots mobilization, and Barack Obama's historic nomination as the 2008 Democratic candidate for president of the United States; a nomination he accepted forty-five years after Martin Luther King Jr.'s "I Have a Dream" speech. After a landmark election, Barack Obama is now "POTUS".[6]

---

[2] Obama delivered his speech on July 27, 2004.

[3] According to the American Internal Revenue Service, an alien is "an individual who is not a U.S. citizen or U.S. national". http://www.irs.gov/ Last accessed January 15, 2009.

[4] October 26, 2002, at an anti-war rally in Chicago, IL, Obama's words were: "What I do oppose is a dumb war". Watch the video on Barack Obama's YouTube channel. Barack Obama joined YouTube on September 5, 2006; As of January 15, 2009, the channel had 149,713 subscribers and had been viewed 20,419,342 times.

[5] Excerpt from Obama, B. (2004). *Dreams From My Father*, New York: Three Rivers Press (p. 104):
"What did Marcus called you just now? Some African name, wasn't it?"
"Barack"
"I thought your name was Barry".
"Barack's my given name. My father's name. He was Kenyan".
"Does it mean something?".
"It means 'blessed'. In Arabic. My grandfather was a Muslim".
Regina repeated the name to herself, testing out the sound. "Barack. It's beautiful". She leaned forward across the table. "So why does everybody call you Barry?".
"Habit, I guess. My father used it when he arrived in the States. I don't know whether that was his idea or somebody else's. He probably used Barry because it was easier to pronounce. You know — helped him fit in. Then it got passed on to me. So I could fit in".

[6] POTUS is the acronym for President of the United States, and it has been used frequently in the blogosphere. Online communities also developed their particular

Both Obama's blurred identity — neither black nor white — and his innovative use of social networking during the campaign inspired me to elaborate on the interrelated concepts of mobility, identity and space. Obama's presidential campaign addresses three types of mobilities: first, a mental mobility related to cultural displacements — here we will develop the concept of the *hybrid*; second, a physical mobility that is literally the movement of an object or a body from one place to another (e.g., all the campaign paraphernalia created — this chapter included — and volunteers traveling around the United States); and finally, a digital mobility that relates to *neo-nomads*, participatory creation and digital affiliations.

1. Hybrids and Neo-nomads

Hybrids, people connected to different cultures, have emerged from the multiplication of travel and the resulting cultural encounters. Among the plethora of hybrids we find half-breeds, migrants and even cyborgs.[7] Hybridity is multiple and exists at micro and macro scales, whenever boundaries are crossed because of "the ability of individuals to avail themselves of several organisational options at the same time" (Pieterse 1994, 168). We are all hybrids to some extent. The practice of "crossing over" is what creates hybridity and semantically relates the hybrid to the neo-nomad.

The crossover derives from people's perception of belonging and establishes the grade of hybridism. "Obvious hybrids", those, whose crossovers are important, have a split identity. They are sort of "double agents" evolving in ecotones, which in biology describe the transitional areas between two different ecologies — the ecotone is itself a new ecology distinct from its ecological adjacency or constituent ecologies. Hybrids are attached to none, one, some, or all of the cultures from which they come. Subjects who feel displaced can develop an acute sensitivity toward people and places, feeling at times "strangers to themselves" (Kristeva 1991).

---

language: a "troll" (the word that dates back to the late 1980's) designated a "HCR" (Hillary Rodham Clinton) or a "McSame" (McCain) supporter that infiltrated and disrupted the Obama blog conversation. Schwartz, M. (2008). "The Trolls Among Us". *The New York Times*, http://www.nytimes.com/2008/08/03/magazine/03trolls-t.html. Last accessed January 15, 2009.
[7] Haraway defines the cyborg as "a hybrid of machine and organism, a creature of social reality as well as a creature of fiction" (Haraway 1991, 149).

Barack Obama was born at a time when miscegenation was still forbidden by law in many American states.[8] While at times a handicap, his "obvious hybrid identity" — which observers translated by asking "Is he black or is he white?" — ultimately strengthened the Obama brand and the ability of his campaign to mobilize people. Pieterse notes that hybridity in relation to politics is the "basis of bounding in collective action" because it eases the transcending of boundaries (Pieterse 1994, 173) "in recognizing multiple identities, [hybridity may] widen the space for critical engagement" (Pieterse 1994, 174). Yet communities need to be open to crossovers, accept differences while having an identity.

The hybrid is an analog version of the neo-nomad. Hybrids become neo-nomads when using technologies to reclaim a sense of belonging to places (Abbas 2001; 2006). The "true" nomads of Deleuze and Guattari, those in opposition to the State apparatus (designed to root you), "those who only assemble (*agencent*)", do not plant roots (Deleuze and Guattari 2003, 24). Neo-nomads use digital technologies to adapt to spaces, dwell-in momentarily and detach anytime and when necessary (they are efficient). Yet neo-nomads are not completely de-territorialized. Their actions leave traces. Their territory, rendered visible through occurrences and patterns of activity, is individual (they construct their own territories), though it exists inseparably from that of others. Neo-nomads adopt multiple identities and evolve in multiple ecotones as they belong to the "hypertext society" described by François Ascher:

> In the hypertext society, the individuals (words) change everyday of fields (texts) whose structures and rules (syntaxes) are different, and where they build various selves (meanings). The digital metaphor is all the more fitting as the society constructs and represents itself even more from the mobile networks, "real" and virtual relations that structure it. (2005, 8-9).[9]

---

[8] "Though the Supreme Court's 1967 decision in the Loving case struck down miscegenation laws, Southern states were sometimes slow to change their constitutions; Alabama became the last state to do so, in 2000". Martin, D. (2008) "Mildred Loving, Who Battled Ban on Mixed-Race Marriage, Dies at 68". *The New York Times*: http://www.nytimes.com/2008/05/06/us/06loving.html?_r=1. Last accessed January 15, 2009

[9] My translation of: "Dans la société hypertexte, les individus (mots) changent quotidiennement de champs (textes) dont les structures et les règles (syntaxes) sont différentes, et où ils construisent des sois (sens) variés. La métaphore informatique est d'autant mieux adaptée que la société se constitue et se représente elle-même davantage à partir des réseaux de mobilités et de relations "réelles" et "virtuelles" qui la structurent".

Being a neo-nomad is not a permanent condition, however. For example, in the context of the mobilization we are observing, many participants were first-time — and maybe last-time — neo-nomads. The common goal, to elect Barack Obama as "POTUS", drove people to experience all at once mental, physical and digital displacements. For example this first-time blogger posted:

> This is my first 'social networking' experience, and my first blog post... ever. For reasons undefined, I have resisted the temptation to join the 'social networking' revolution, but this is something that is important enough to draw me out of my (some may call) moderately old-fashioned shell.[10]

This chapter is an investigation of Barack Obama's political war machine. The subsequent spatial observations emerged in a very nomadic fashion, through exploring territories of thoughts, productions and practices, and hypertexting — establishing links, associating and collating data and ideas — a method very much aligned with today's social practices. For about more than a year I have been browsing online content related to the Obama campaign, collecting images, links of interest and words from various sites, supporters and essayists' blogs, social-networking and photo-management sites and online newspapers. The aim is to discuss the many different components of contemporary mobilizations.

2. Mobilization

The military semantic field includes both the words *mobilizing*, "to enable or incite (a number or group of individuals) to take collective action in pursuit of a common goal" and *campaigning*, "an organized course of action to achieve a particular goal", (Oxford English Dictionary online). Mobilizing comes from the French verb *mobiliser*, which by the first half of the 19th century already meant "render a body of troops ready for war"; and also "to make mobile; to render capable of motion or change of location". (Ibid.). The noun *campaign*, which originally meant "open

---

[10] "My Time for Change", blog post by Ryan Culbertson. February 3, 2008: http://my.barackobama.com/page/community/post/ryanculbertson/CPNb. Last accessed January 15, 2009. The activity tracker shows that this blogger has not been very active. 1 blog post, and seven groups joined as of today. Many blogs like this one start and end at the first blog post.

country" in French, entered English in the 17th century and then acquired its military meaning. The word *campaign* is "applied to any course of action analogous to a military campaign, either in having a distinct period of activity, or in being of the nature of a struggle, or of an organized attempt aiming at a definite result" (Ibid.). Mobilizing and campaigning thus involve tools and means of persuasion, which entail addressing — sometimes inventing — a struggle common to many. Putnam in part attributes the "massive [American] postwar civic renaissance" to the "mobilizing power of shared adversities" (Putnam 2000, 272).

Mobilizing or campaigning ultimately involves manpower — an army — organization strategies and tactics, displacements and momentary occupations, fields and actions and a clearly-defined common goal. Its success depends on speed. The more cohesive the group, the more responsive, fluid and fast the mobilization or campaign. Virilio writes: "the new military order is a speed order, a dromocracy" (Virilio 2005, 87). He is more concerned with the trajectory of the weapon — "the various means of penetration through space, through obstacles, through bodies" — than the weapon itself; with speed the object propelled gains a dangerous invisibility. (Ibid.). Today's mobilization relies on the speed of the internet to reach opponents, fact-check claims and disseminate messages. Barack Obama's political campaign used persuasive tools — for example, text messaging and Obama's powerful social-networking site (My.BarackObama.com, also called "MyBO") — to quickly move troops of organizers and volunteers to scout, canvass battlegrounds and enroll voters. These digital tools enable the Obama camp to rapidly adapt its strategies and tactically deploy or retrieve its infantry. While emails, text messages, blog posts or comments leave traces; they also gain certain invisibility because of the speed at which they move. Only their effect is visible.

Through the exploration of the three mobilities at play — mental, physical and digital — we will observe that mobilization today involves the co-creation of identities, peer-to-peer political enrollment (not only through social networking but also through the co-creation of objects), the precise deployment of objects, signs and people, the temporary occupation of spaces, and a series of characteristic actions such as surveillance and emulation.

3. Mental Mobility: Power and Control

Radicals should embrace power, wrote the community organizer Saul Alinsky, because "[p]ower is the very essence, the dynamo of life. [...] It is the power of active participation pulsing upward, providing a unified strength for a common purpose". (1971, 51). In our mythologies and popular cultures, hybrids (who are not always radicals) have a certain power that "pure breeds" — if such a thing exists — fear or admire: mermaids, half-woman, half-fish, attempted to end Ulysses' Odyssey; in the popular novel *Dr. No*, as in the movie named after it, the villain, half-German and half-Chinese, is an exceedingly powerful hybrid who couples the "worst" of East and West. Yet, hybrids are not always so powerful. In *Sartoris*, William Faulkner writes about a hybrid that Jackson, a character in the novel, wants to create. The new species, a "mutt", a hunting dog and a fox mixed, will, as Jackson hopes, inherit the greatest capacities of each species — the scent of the dog, and the speed of the fox. The result is pitiful because the genitors, or other "true species", deny the so-called "revolutionary" animal.[11] Hence hybrids are paradoxically powerful and powerless, negotiating acceptance with the two (or more) groups from which they are derived (Abbas 2001). It is not unlike for President Obama himself, a hybrid born from a black Kenyan father and a white American mother. It is perhaps even more complex, as his black roots are not "really" African-American: Even if Obama's "grandfather worked for the white man" in colonized Kenya, that ancestor was not a slave of the white American (2004, 405-406).[12] Obama is too often asked how could he possibly stand for "his people", if he does not belong. Identifying the hybrid as other is a strategy of the "pure breeds", themselves hybrids and displaced a long time ago, to gain power.

With a constant struggle to justify their identity — to feel grounded and to retain power — hybrids develop strategies to fit in. Obama committed 442 pages to guide us through his self-discovery (1995). The candidate for the highest position of the United States of America, the leader of the most amazing melting pot of all — a place one would think

---

[11] Faulkner, W. (1977) *Sartoris*. Paris: Gallimard.

[12] Excerpt from Obama, B. (2004), *Dreams From My Father*. New York: Three Rivers Press; pp. 405-406: "My image of Onyango [Obama's grandfather], faint as it was, had always been of an autocratic man — a cruel man, perhaps. But I had also imagined him an independent man, a man of his people, opposed to white rule. There was no real basis for this image, I now realized — only the letter he had written to Gramps saying that he didn't want his son marrying white. That, and his Muslim faith, which in my mind had become linked with the Nation of Islam back in the States. What Granny had told me scrambled that image completely, causing ugly words to flash across my mind. Uncle Tom. Collaborator. House nigger".

was created for hybrids — still felt the need to blend in. He uses design
and rhetoric to establish trust between him and his supporters. For
example, the graphic designer Michael Bierut comments on why the
Obama camp carefully calibrated the image of Obama using familiar
elements of everyday life:

> The challenge for someone named Barack Hussein Obama is that he's such
> an unprecedented figure in American politics — so much so that
> everything he's trying to do is, in a way, trying to make him look smoother
> and more normal. [...] I think he's using design in a way to make him look
> as normal, as comfortable, as inevitable as a brand can look in American
> life.[13]

Watching Obama sitting at the kitchen tables with American families,
physically present in American domestic spaces, calling potential voters
like other volunteers, celebrating Halloween like every other American, or
appropriating history surely helped assure voters that he is not different
(that he is legitimate), contrary to people's imagination.[14] If branding
helped Obama negotiate acceptance with all sides, his rhetoric drew us
back to the United States Constitution, addressing what is common to all
Americans, transcending racial and cultural boundaries and avoiding
partisanship. In his acceptance speech as the Democratic nominee for the
2008 presidency, he reiterated "That's the promise of America the idea
that we are responsible for ourselves, but that we also rise or fall as one
nation". Understanding the value of social capital, Obama confirms that
everyone is equal (including himself). This strategy to seek solidarity for
the struggle ahead aligns with Putnam's observation: "Inequality and
solidarity are deeply incompatible" (2000, 294).

The ecotone (*eco-* for environment and *-tone*, from the ancient Greek
word for "tension") is a particularly appropriate metaphor to describe the
habitat of the hybrid, an in-between space, a space in tension, a space of

---

[13] "Expertinent: Why the Obama 'Brand' Is Working" Blog post by Andrew
Romano. Wednesday, February 27, 2008: http://blog.newsweek.com/blogs/
stumper/archive/2008/02/27/how-obama-s-branding-is-working-on-you.aspx. Last
accessed January 15, 2009.
[14] Obama announced his candidacy in Springfield, IL., where Abraham Lincoln
lived until his election as a President of the U.S.A.. Obama was coincidentally
nominated on the anniversary of Martin Luther King Jr's "I have a Dream" speech.
Like his political idol, Abraham Lincoln, the President-elect took the train to go to
his inauguration, starting from Philadelphia, where the U.S. independence was
declared.

negotiation. The "third space" is not a new idea. Maureen Perkins, editor of the July 1998 issue "Third Space And Cross-Cultural Identities" of *Les Mots Pluriels*, reminds us that:

> The "third space" is a term which the cultural theorist Homi K. Bhabha takes from Frederic Jameson's Postmodernism, or, the Cultural Logic of Late Capitalism. Jameson talks of interstitial or in-between spaces and Bhabha expands the concept to signify expressions of hybridity. He urges the recognition of 'in-betweenness' as the means of avoiding 'the politics of polarity'. It is not necessary to choose one or the other pole, he suggests.[15]

Obama applies this concretely when he uses design and rhetoric to reach out to voters, while at the same time avoiding racial affiliations. His politics of the ecotone, augmented by information technology, has favored the temporary multiplication of social structures that spread Obama's branded identity into multiple others. Organizers and supporters met online and offline, as Asians for Obama, Latinos for Obama, Obamacans (Republicans for Obama), Quilters for Obama, A World Stand for Obama (A Facebook group), etc. The numerous groups are identifiable parts of the same whole. Groups of supporters apply their chosen identity to the canvas that is the Obama brand.

Although the then-senator carefully controlled the branding of his identity, he left his image for appropriation and diffusion. For example, Hope.Act.Change, is a virtual community that enables members to upload pictures related to Obama's mobilization: supporters at a rally, homemade campaign paraphernalia. These (mostly) color pictures aggregate in such manner that they populate every picture frame of a black-and-white video clip without losing the initial character of picture frame.[16] For example, take one picture frame of the video featuring Obama. Pictures uploaded by members aggregate into a pixilated portrait of Obama. Supporters create a

---

[15] Maurin Perkins quotes Bhabha, Homi K. (1994) *The Location of Culture*, London; NewYork: Routledge. In her editorial, Maureen Perkins also writes: "Across cultures and time we might point to terms such as half-caste, half-breed, mulatto, octoroon, métis, chabine. In the last one hundred and fifty years these terms have sprung from the notion of race, a concept hardened into rigidity by colonial powers anxious to strengthen their political and economic hegemony".

[16] The video clip entitled "Yes We Can" became an instant hit over the internet, and was soon adopted by the Obama campaign. It features Barack Obama and a crew of celebrities, friends of the singer will.i.am., who sing to Obama's discourse: http://www.hopeactchange.com. Last accessed January15, 2009.

collective mosaic, an evolving and growing composite portrait of the candidate. Obama became all of his supporters; supporters, together, became Obama and the message he embodies. The internet facilitated the co-creation of Obama's collectively imagined identity. "Who is Obama?" The question asked by Obama's opponents reflected the fact that Obama's identity was a coloring book left for supporters to fill in.

Yet, many creations that participate in the construction of Obama's identity also reveal individual or group self-identities. People contributed to his brand with the tools of production that they knew, also hoping to gather momentum and rise above the crowd.[17] As Saul Alinsky writes, the trouble with life "[Is that] it is a desperate search for personal identity — to let other people know that at least you are alive" (1971, 121). Obama's identity becomes a tool to achieve visibility, and thus strengthen one's own identity. Drawing for example a portrait of Obama is for many a way to showcase one's skills or oneself. The piece (a video, a painting) is indeed often exhibited online next to other work of art by the same artist, on the artist's website. However, in the prologue of his book *The Audacity of Hope*, Obama (again neither black nor white) writes that, because he is new to politics:

> I serve as a blank screen on which people of vastly different stripes project their own views. As such I am bound to disappoint some, if not all of them. (2004, 2)

This campaign has highlighted that even in the most individualistic societies, one's identity, the "I", cannot exist without the "we" — even for the sake of this mobilization, i.e., when the "I" is momentarily constructed. The "I" is created not only by comparing the self with that of others, but is also created with others, willingly or unwillingly.

---

[17] John Hart, Sameh Tawfick, Michael De Volder, and Will Walker experiment with nanotechnology: http://www.nanobama.com/ Last accessed January 15, 2009. Watch the *Battleground For Your Heart* video by Portal A Interactive who "produces original video content and brings it to an audience through innovative distribution strategies". http://portal-a.com/Home.html. Last accessed January 15, 2009. Listen to DJ Lighbolt GOBAMA MIX at: http://www.lightbolt.net/misc/gobama.html. Last accessed January 15, 2009.

4. Physical Mobility: Stitching Identities

In French, the word for furniture, *mobilier*, originates from the Latin *mobilis*, that which is moveable. In essence, a piece of furniture — a *meuble* — can be displaced. Yet because of the "system" in which it is embedded, a piece of furniture is more or less displaceable and more or less unique (Baudrillard 1996). For example, the heirloom is a piece of furniture that acquires its uniqueness because of the generations that owned it — especially when made before it became possible to mechanically reproduce objects. Time and memory participate to make the object belong to the family if not to contemporary interior design. Before gaining another life (e.g., sold as an antique to someone outside the family) the piece of furniture is rather immobile, part of a closed system. In comparison to and aside from the modern classics that have acquired a reputation over time, modern furniture is not unique and more mobile. They are not part of a particular setting; they are not tied by emotions to the closed circle of the household.

In *The System of Objects*, Baudrillard compares the furniture of the traditional interior to that of the modern interior:

> The primary function of furniture and objects here [in traditional interiors] is to personify human relationships, to fill in the space that they share between them, and to be inhabited by a soul (1996, 16).

And:

> The function [of the object of the modern interior] is no longer obscured by the moral theatricality of the old furniture; it is emancipated now from ritual, from an opaque ceremonial, from the entire ideology which used to make our surroundings into an opaque mirror of a reified human structure. Today, at last, these objects emerge absolutely clear about the purpose they serve (1996, 18).

Objects produced by Obama supporters are characteristic of our postmodern times in that they are both serial and unique, retaining characteristics of both the traditional and modern objects described by Jean Baudrillard. As the French author writes, they are "clear about the purpose they serve" while gaining a patina of strong identity — a uniqueness — because they are specially crafted (1996, 18). The objects produced by Obama supporters appropriate the standard images provided by the Obama campaign — the logo, slogans or even his portrait — and apply them to other serial objects like T-shirts or incorporate them into new objects of people's — or a community of people's — own making. One of the most suitable examples of a communal creation incorporating Obama's message is that produced by the Quilters for Obama group that has an online presence on MyBO.[18] The group describes itself as such:

> Quilters from across the country are coming together to make Blocks for Barack. [...] We are truly the Piecemakers for Change and Barack Obama is our leader.

The quilt becomes a model to discuss mobility and identity. A quilt is made of different pieces of cloth stitched together to form a carefully composed whole. One may argue that because of the stitching a quilt is just an aggregate of different pieces. Yet investigation of the production of the Gee's Bend community of "folk" quilters in Alabama reveals that fields of color formed independently of the stitching structure.[19] By matching colors, quilters crossed stitching boundaries and imagined new ones inseparable from each other due to the rhythm and the final composition.

In *A Thousand Plateaus: Capitalism and Schizophrenia*, Deleuze and Guattari discuss the difference between "smooth space and striated space — nomad space and sedentary space" (1987, 474). The "technological model", based on an observation of fabric and quilt, is one of the models the authors use to discuss "The space in which the war machine develops and the space instituted by the State apparatus". (Ibid.) They write:

> Patchwork, in conformity with migration, whose degree of affinity with nomadism it shares, is not only named after trajectories, but 'represents' trajectories, becomes inseparable from speed or movement in an open space (1987, 475).

In the case of the "Turning America Blue" quilt, the production of each block was distributed across the United States, as the quilters lived in different parts of the country. The choice of fabric and the craft remained that of the individual while at the same time followed a defined structure. For design consistency, quilters used the same pattern, the traditional

---

[18] The Quilters for Obama group page on MyBO: http://my.barackobama.com/ page/group/QUILTERSFOROBAMA. Last accessed January 15, 2009.
[19] In the fall of 2006, the first studio assignment given to architecture undergraduates at Wentworth Institute of technology was to analyze a Gee's Bend quilt of their choice, and infer a three dimensional space. See also: http://www.quiltsofgeesbend.com/. Last accessed January 15, 2009.

"Ohio Star" made with squares and triangles pieces, and the same color code — the color of the party. The quilt is also branded, adorned with the Obama camp slogan and logo. All of this is meant to retain control over the final composition and its intent. It works also as a metaphor for the United "Diverse" States of America.

The flyer explains that "26 women across states line" worked on the quilt "themed Turning America Blue 2008":

> It is made of 56 blocks: 55 star blocks (representing the voting entities of the primary: 50 states, 3 territories, Washington DC and Americans Abroad) around one block that is a cross stitch of the head of Barack Obama. These 55 star blocks were made by women from Hawaii to New York to Florida to North Dakota! [...] Our ethnic backgrounds are mixed, our ages range from 30s to mid-80s and our working lives couldn't be more diverse. [...] Despite the range of ages, range of sewing experience and differences in professions, these women worked as one to create a beautiful work of art where every block shines!

When seeking information about the group you find that it has been categorized under both "local" and "interests". The category "local" seems a little difficult to understand given the fact that production was distributed among different States and quilters — albeit all women — belong to different cultural and social communities. Yet quilting is a tradition deeply rooted in American history. By maintaining this tradition, quilters also participate to preserving an *imagined community,* to use the words of Benedict Anderson (1991). On one hand, the quilt, a product made by a scattered community of diverse backgrounds, becomes a unifying object, and the symbol of unity of a community of interest, where group members organized around a collective goal of electing a "leader" and because they like quilting. On the other hand, these quilters also meet temporarily, crossing classes and cultural lines, even if only for a particular period in time, e.g. the duration of the U.S. general election.

Returning to Baudrillard's "system of objects", the quilt that functions as a bed cover (an almost secondary function) and as a political vehicle also holds a strong identity because it is a symbol of unity — stitching different identities to make one. It is even offered as a lottery prize extending the community from quilters to lottery participants (both groups share a desire to help elect Barack Obama as president). Hence the postmodern object is a modern heirloom, one that belongs to everyone involved in its co-creation and at the same time unique not because there is only one of a kind, but because, as Baudrillard says, it "personifies human relationships" (1996). As a member of the group posted on her blog:

Hey Wow! Win a beautiful heritage Obama Quilt! It will be a great
heirloom for sure. A quilt made in honor of the man who has already
changed the way politics works. He is already one of the greatest figures in
American history.[20]

There are two other considerations to be taken into account concerning
the system of campaign paraphernalia: First, the mobility of these objects,
which supports mobility of the political message. The fact that they are
mobile enables the formation and deployment of campaign units. If the
quilt will adorn a lucky lottery winner's domestic interior, perhaps move
from one room to another, many other objects will travel long distances,
be downloaded, printed, move from hand to hand, be seen on public
transportation, while on the move, a bumper sticker on a car, a button on a
jacket, etc. Second, not only the abundance, but also the concentration of
these campaign paraphernalia is essential. In terms of advertizing across a
vast territory, where people travel long distances, the television screen is
not enough; signs have to be visible, on every surface, static or mobile,
physical or virtual — Obama advertises even on video games like *Guitar
Hero* and *Burnout Paradise*.[21] UCLA Professor of political science Tim
Groeling explains that signs in neighbors' yards can be more efficient than
advertising on broadcast media. If everyone in the neighborhood posts
similar signs, individuals living in the same neighborhood will more likely
understand that many people like a certain candidate, identify with them or
succumb to peer pressure.[22] When one individual supports a different

---

[20] "Hey Wow! Win a beautiful heritage Obama Quilt!" Blog post by Duane Kuehn.
August 1, 2008:
http://my.barackobama.com/page/community/post/duane/gG5kYV. Last accessed
January 15, 2009.
[21] "Obama Ads Appearing in Video Games". Blog post by Peter Mychalcewycz.
October 14, 2008: http://www.switched.com/2008/10/14/obama-ads-appearing-in-
video-games/. Last accessed January 15, 2009. Rutenberg, J., (2008) "Nearing
Record, Obama's Ad Effort Swamps McCain" in *The New York Times*:
http://www.nytimes.com/2008/10/18/us/politics/18ads.html. Last accessed January
15, 2009.
[22] In a report compiled by Grégoriadès, C., "Jardins, voitures, aux Etats-Unis tout
est bon pour afficher ses idées politiques" in *Le Monde*:
http://www.lemonde.fr/elections-americaines/portfolio/2008/09/12/jardins-voitures
-aux-etats-unis-tout-est-bon-pour-afficher-ses-idees-politiques_1094776_829254.
html, September 9, 2008. Last accessed January 15, 2009. Dr. Tim Groeling is an
Assistant Professor of Communication Studies at UCLA:

candidate from the majority, the pressure can get intense; signs are stolen and thus disappear from view. For example, this blogger writes that:

> If you can document gangs of McCain-ites sweeping through neighborhoods, trespassing on people's property and destroying signs, I would send the pics/video to every TV station in your state, and every major newspaper, as well. Then post it on Youtube.[23]

Spatially speaking, the concentration of similar signs permitted a sort of peer-to-peer political enrollment. The internet, like other older mediums, was also used to reclaim a spatial ordinance.

5. Digital Mobility: Identity Sharing

> I just received a FREE FLIGHT from a kind relative! That greatly reduces the cost of the trip, and increases my choices of destinations. I am considering going to Billings or Great Falls, a more conservative part of the state. So now I just need to be able to afford a motel, and a rental car, etc. The motel is the most important because I don't want to have to sleep in the car if I have the choice. My brother works for Enterprise Rental Cars so I only need $60 for 2 days of rental. Plus fuel which shouldn't be more than $50 unless we end up driving all over the place.[24]

The excerpt above was posted on ObamaTravel.org, a community website that enabled supporters to get funding for travel expenses related to campaigning for Obama. Sharing is extremely strong in this age of multiple mobilities, and crucial to mobilization. Supporters contributed to the campaign by giving away airline travel miles that dedicated volunteers — Americans and non-Americans — could canvass other battlegrounds. Campaign workers relied on the generosity of local inhabitants for lodgings — an indirect way of funding the campaign that is nothing new and is not included in fundraising metrics.[25] However, the internet makes

---

http://www.sscnet.ucla.edu/comm/groeling/web/Home.html. Last accessed January 15, 2009

[23] Blog comment by Michael in VA. September 20, 2008:
http://my.barackobama.com/page/community/post/stateupdates/gGgyz2/commentary#comments. Last accessed January 15, 2009.

[24] http://obamatravel.org. Last accessed January 15, 2009.

[25] "Jimmy Carter, who at one point was considered a long shot to win the presidency in 1976, depended on supporters in Iowa for a place to stay. Jerry Brown in his 1992 presidential bid earned a reputation as a messy houseguest,

staying with strangers easier and safer to organize. One can blog a request, join a group, and even check if a person has a criminal record.

While sharing space with strangers can be uncomfortable — someone else's house is never "home" — the process can also work in favor of shaping friendships. Yet if social networking permits the organization of meetings in the physical space, it yields to a second artificially created sociality. This does not mean that strong ties and deep friendship cannot emerge from meeting physically after having met online. It means rather that extending social networking from digital to physical space amplifies interactions. It boosts the probability of meeting new friends and augments the chance of building stronger ties — which also benefits fundraising. When it comes to social capital and philanthropy, Robert D. Putnam writes:

> Fund-raising typically means friend-raising. So the more involved I am in social and community networks, both formal and informal, the more likely I am to be asked. And I am more likely to agree if the recruiter is part of my network of friends. (2000, 121)

It is important to add that there are various degrees of friendship — one trusts some friends more than others — and that there is a probable correlation between the degree of friendship and the amount of a donation. For example, after creating an account on ObamaTravel.org,

> You send the word out to everyone you know that you have posted — usually in the form of an email that links to ObamaTravel.org.[26]

We may question if meeting in the physical space was at all necessary knowing how strong the determination of Obama supporters was. No chance was left out.

In contemporary mobilization digital social networking overlaps with physical spaces. On one hand, social networking helps expand the geography of the battleground — and reach as far as possible. On the other

---

leaving damp towels on the floor and his bed unmade. In this endless Democratic primary season, the need for lodging is no different — it's just more drawn out. Workers for Senator Hillary Clinton and Mr. Obama have found themselves living in a series of borrowed beds [...]" Excerpt from: Parker, A. (2008) "I'm a Campaign Worker. Can I Sleep Here?". *The New York Times*: http://www.nytimes.com/2008/05/04/fashion/04campaign.html?pagewanted=1&_r =2&ref=politics, May 4, 2008. Last accessed January 15, 2009.
[26] http://obamatravel.org. Last accessed January 15, 2009.

hand, social networking participates in drawing nearer the inhabitants of the same neighborhood, and in reinforcing a local culture of participation.

For example, the Obama camp launched a neighbor-to-neighbor tool that enabled supporters to "be able to immediately start calling potential supporters [undecided voters — those who have registered to vote but haven't registered with a party]" or "go door-to-door and talk to them directly". When supporters log into the neighbor-to-neighbor digital platform, after providing a permanent or temporary area ZIP code, they find a list of undecided voters located in the vicinity. They have two choices: to call them or meet with them. They do not need to worry about what to say, as the website provides precise recommendations. But each time they call or meet, they're asked to record the information and report back to the campaign.[27] Accordingly, the campaign — benefiting from myriad feedback loops — can adjust its strategy, pull out from an area or deploy more troops. What remains critical is both the importance of human scouting, and the database that structures sociality and spaces. In contemporary mobilizations, spaces and geographies exist because of the database organized and constructed with the help of the best scouts, from technology developers to people on the ground. Although mediated by a fill-in form, nothing yet can replace grassroots organizers' feel of the terrain (physical or digital) and their drive to mobilize others.

The younger generation embraced this culture of participation that may well characterize the 21st century because they saw a chance to "steer the boat". Politically speaking indeed, as Saul D. Alinsky writes in *Rules for Radicals*:

> If people feel they don't have the power to change a bad situation, then they do not think about it. Why start figuring how you are going to spend a million dollars if you do not have a million dollars or are ever going to have a million dollars — unless you want to engage in fantasy?
> Once people are organized so that they have the power to make changes, then, when confronted with questions of change, they begin to think and to ask questions about how to make the changes. (1971, 105).

It is the same for other forms of participation. The online communities that thrive happen to host dynamic members whose flow of participation is

---

[27] Videos on Barack Obama YouTube channel, last accessed January 15, 2009:
MyBO: Neighbor to Neighbor Phone Banking. September 9, 2008:
http://www.youtube.com/watch?v=2Oaj0CN72qA.
MyBO: Neighbor to Neighbor Canvassing. September 10, 2008:
http://www.youtube.com/watch?v=tt9JKIIs9Sw.

frequent, approved by other members, and gains reputation. Blue State Digital, the technology company that designed Obama's brilliant social networking platform, MyBO, understood this well.[28] To mobilize, they gave people (those who can tip the balance, in particular youth) the tools to feel empowered, to act, and to reinforce the "Obama brand". By that, campaign strategists also abide by Alinsky's sixth tactic for radicals:

> A good tactic is one that your people enjoy. If your people are not having a ball doing it, there is something very wrong with your tactic. (1971, 129).

Mentioning the original point-tracker system of MyBO, a tool that enabled users to collect points for actions taken to help the campaign, a blogger enthusiastically posted:

> I have been sucked in! This is crazy! They have turned this into a social networking site and a video game. I now have 73 points and am in 139,549th place — tied (only 1 point more to move up)![29]

Besides building the excitement necessary to incite people to act, the "watch" together with the "speed", "ranking", and "spread" of information are keys to this mobilization.

The Obama campaign masterfully watches what happened on battlegrounds, physical and digital. Like the "neighborhood watch" that Jane Jacobs observes in the American cities (Jacobs, 1993), the constant surveillance has been hugely influential for the life of the Obama community — supporters detect malfunctions, "trolls"[30] and smears. The campaign did have to update the activity tracker (albeit to the dissatisfaction of many users) to channel the enthusiasm toward effective campaigning:

> Unlike the old system, your actions — and your actions alone — now determine your activity level score. You will no longer constantly shift in rank based on other users' actions.[31]

---

[28] Talbot, D. (2008) "How Obama *Really* Did It: The social-networking strategy that took an obscure senator to the doors of the White House" in *MIT Technology Review*, September/October issue: 78-83.
[29] "A new kind of social networking!" Blog post by Paul de Jong. February 14, 2008: http://my.barackobama.com/page/community/post/pauldejong/CskL. Last accessed January 15, 2009.
[30] See footnote number 6.
[31] "Update on the New MyBO Activity Tracker" Blog post by Amy Hamblin. August 15, 2008:

The thrill of seeing that one's contribution matters can be intense, especially when the number of views on YouTube video ramps up, or when Obama's campaign team adopts it — supreme consecration that adds to the natural spirit of competition.

This is the case of the "Yes We Can" video clip by the entertainment artist Will.i.am and his celebrity friends, and the poster by the street artist graphic designer Shepard Fairey, which borrows references to the very popular image of Che Guevara and the iconic production of the pop artist Andy Warhol.

Embracing popular culture and reporting that the candidate is part of it (Obama's music playlist includes rap songs) facilitates the enrollment of the masses. But if consumers create — "crowdsource" — they also need to build consensus. Personal rewards are one form of incentives for people to engage because they are proof that their personal contributions matter. On another note, if we wrote about the personalization of campaign paraphernalia, we should also mention here the personalization of mass generated emails as a critical "human touch": Barack Obama, Michele Obama, David Plouffe and Joe Biden have all written to supporters. While the body of the email was the same for everyone, in most cases the electronic message started with "Dear (Your first name), etc.".

In widening its virtual real estate portfolio, the Obama camp offered various oases, virtual pieces of land where different communities of supporters could gather and recharge, places where they knew they would be heard or get attention because they are amongst members with common interests. To reach out to as many communities as possible, Obama was (and still is) present on inclusive platforms (platforms that are open to various communities) like YouTube and Flickr, or exclusive (for a particular community) like AsiaAve and BlackPlanet. This mobilization tapped into both relations of meritocracy and nepotism that social networking introduces. It strategically engaged emotions and practices of identification to successfully involve people to identify with the cause (the precise meaning of the "cause" even is deliberately confused).

Conclusion

By examining the complexity of mobility — through the careful deconstruction of the concept — I established how people co-create their

http://my.barackobama.com/page/community/post/amyhamblin/gG5Fyy.
Last accessed January 15, 2009.

identity based on that of the candidate, through tools, technologies and paraphernalia, spaces and actions, watching, emulating, enjoying, producing, etc. In fact in the three cases of mobilities, mental, physical and digital, mobilization dealt with establishing and constructing trust between Barack Obama and his supporters, through the momentary disintegration of boundaries, by allowing crossings, mixing, personalizing and appropriation of items and identities. Mobilization today is identity-sharing or about peer-to-peer identity. While Obama's identity offered various means of appropriation, supporters actively contributed their own identities as well. The political war machine temporarily transformed supporters into neo-nomads, a species that is not attached to a territory in particular, that plugs into and out of places — physical or digital — or situations (on demand), and whose mobility is highly monitored by communication technologies.

While this chapter wanted to bring readers to the realization that political mobilization shuffles identities temporarily, it also highlighted that because of technologies, today's mobilizations are never truly completed. The innocuous surveillance resulting from sophisticated use of technologies enables the Obama camp to adjust campaign strategies, cheer the troops and collect data on millions of supporters. People who have signed up online or in person are stored in databases indefinitely, in reserve for other future engagements. Whenever one opened an account on MyBO or bought some campaign paraphernalia through the official Obama website for example, s/he left traces, an email address, an address, a phone number, all of which was used (and could be used again in the future) to keep her or him focused on the objective — to win; to update her or him about the progress of the troops through a clever mixture of messages of hope and warning; and keep her or him motivated to engage, donate, fight against smears, and share information. In fact, while supporters projected their identities in the collective co-creation of Obama's identity (brand), they also willingly lost a little of theirs. The database will subsequently be used for calling people to more action. Mobilization requires supporters to lose a little of the "I", on demand.

History will tell if the momentum generated during this mobilization will hold with time. As a matter of fact, various internet platforms have now emerged calling for participation to press on issues that matter to particular interest groups.

Acknowledgment

Thank you to Dk Osseo-Asare, hybrid and neo-nomad.

Bibliography

Abbas, Y. (2001) *Embodiment: Mental and Physical Geographies of the Neo-nomad.* Master of Science in Architecture Studies Thesis. Massachusetts Institute of Technology.

—. (2006) *Neo-nomads: Designing Environments for Living in the Age of Mental, Physical and Digital Mobilities.* Doctor of Design Thesis. Harvard University Graduate School of Design.

Alinsky, S. (1971) *Rules for Radicals.* New York: Random House.

Anderson, B. (1991) *Imagined Communities: Reflection on the Origin and Spread of Nationalism.* New York: Verso.

Ascher, F. (2005) *La société hypermoderne ou ces évènements qui nous dépassent, feignons d'en être les organisateurs.* La Tour d'Aigues: L'Aube, Essai.

Baudrillard, J. (1996) *The System of Objects.* London, New York: Verso.

Behrent, M. C. (2008) "Saul Alinsky, la campagne présidentielle et l'histoire de la gauche américaine". *La vie des idées*: http://www.laviedesidees.fr/Saul-Alinsky-la-campagne.html?decoupe_recherche=obama%20saul%20alinsky. Last accessed January 15, 2009.

Deleuze, G. and Guattari, F. (1987) *A Thousand Plateaus: Capitalism and Schizophrenia.* Minneapolis, London: University of Minnesota Press.

Faulkner, W. (1977) *Sartoris.* Paris: Gallimard.

Foucault, M. (2001) *Dits et écrits II.* 1976-1988, Paris: Quarto Gallimard.

Haraway, D. (1991) *Simians, Cyborgs and Women: The Reinvention of Nature.* New York: Routledge.

Jacobs, J. (1993) *The Death and Life of the Great American Cities.* New York: Modern Library.

Kristeva, J. (1991) *Strangers to Ourselves.* New York: Columbia University Press.

Nederveen Pieterse, J. (1994) "Globalisation as Hybridisation". *International Sociology* 2 (9). 161-184.

Obama, B. (2006) *The Audacity of Hope.* New York: Three Rivers Press.

—. (2004) *Dreams From My Father.* New York: Three Rivers Press.

Perkins, M. (1998) "Third Space And Cross-Cultural Identities". *Les Mots Pluriels* 7. http://motspluriels.arts.uwa.edu.au/MP798index.html. Last accessed January 15, 2009.

Putnam, R. (2000) *Bowling Alone: The Collapse and Revival of the American Community*, New York, London: Simon & Schuster paperbacks.

Talbot, D. (2008) "How Obama *Really* Did It: The social-networking strategy that took an obscure senator to the doors of the White House". *MIT Technology Review*. September/October issue: 78-83.

Virilio, P. (2005) *Negative Horizon*. London, New York: Continuum.

http://blog.newsweek.com/blogs/stumper/
http://my.barackobama.com
http://obamatravel.org
http://portal-a.com/Home.html
http://www.gopublius.com/HCT/HillaryClintonThesis.html
http://www.hopeactchange.com
http://www.irs.gov
http://www.laviedesidees.fr
http://www.lemonde.fr
http://www.lightbolt.net/misc/gobama.html
http://www.nanobama.com
http://www.nytimes.com
http://www.switched.com
http://www.quiltsofgeesbend.com
http://www.youtube.com

WE SURF THEREFORE I AM

CHAPTER FIVE

THE IDEOLOGY OF THE SELF
IN LUDIC DIGITAL WORLDS

OLIVIER MAUCO

1. Digital Worlds as Ideological Utopian Devices

1.1. Ideological Travels in Utopian Spaces

Videogames are set up in an intermediate position between reality and fantasy. The producers' imagination is materialized in an "inter-world" (Sfez 2002, 138): images exist in an autonomous way, but are structured by both the producers who define them and the players who play with them.

While traditional games were a social activity defined by the group (Mauss 1926), videogames are different because of the production process: producers are not players. This dichotomy changes the nature of the ludic contract: When a player enters a videogame, he must submit himself to the structure of the game and the producers' conceptions. The game space is "cut from reality" (Huizinga 1958, 30), and to play is to accept all the rules of the system.

Because of this, videogame spaces are predestined and predetermined: liberty is an illusion, the player must follow the rules, but at the same time this imperative is both achievable and exciting. Within this "legaliberty" (Duflo 1997, 232) the player can act and accomplish his desires, but all of these are conditioned and offered by the game's producers. Unlike traditional games, videogames are pre-defined spaces filled with signs translating producers' ideas. They make sense to the player only as he also becomes a consumer.

To play a videogame is thus to play with signs in an autonomous space organized by the game's purpose. This characteristic makes videogame play a cognitive activity, a kind of bodiless travel. One of the main requirements is immersion: the technical apparatus, including the system and controllers, must be forgotten when playing. The screen is no longer considered a separation between player and game. Instead players "jump in [to]" (Microsoft's Xbox 360, 2006) videogame space, "living" their adventure (Sony's Playstation 3, 2006).

Game systems are promoted not only as objects, but also as doors to real worlds. Their marketing tries to establish a direct connection between player and game, erasing the console or computer. In this particular conception, the videogame should only be played: the activity should appear omnipresent and omnipotent. This is a naturalization process instituted by videogame creators and, more broadly, by all producers of digital technologies: the technology is presented as natural.[1] In this "expressionist" approach, the medium should no longer be visible and people should be linked directly to one another.

A videogame's world is a "universe of recognition", an autonomous rhetorical space where signs can be understood for themselves. This space can be compared to the non-place developed in the concept of "supermodernity": "a closed universe where anything makes sense as it is composed by a-symbolic and self-referent signs" (Augé 1992, 46). According to supermodernity theory, political and social institutions' loss of legitimacy and the growing number of repositories and references encourage us to construct our own universe of reference. From a pragmatic point of view, supermodernity is the theory of competitive "economics of beliefs" (Balandier 1992). This produces an ideological syncretism, with each one of us self-interestedly choosing aspects of different normative systems, mixing them into a melting-pot of beliefs. Videogames offer a strong normative frame, even if they can integrate multiple and contrary ideologies.

The utopian nature of ludic digital worlds makes this ideological syncretism possible. As "an ideological discourse with theoretical anticipatory value" (Marin 1973, 255), videogames propose an ideological experience in a utopian space. The topic is utopian in multiple ways: as a game (proper norms and *telos*), as an on-screen device (intermediate position between reality and fantasy), as a fiction of virtual worlds (political and social organization). Yet this utopia "deals with rationality"

---

[1] Influenced by Catholic thinkers in the 17th century, Western philosophy established an opposition between nature and culture, human and technology. In Eastern philosophy, however, technology is considered natural. For example, in Japan a city is considered to be part of natural evolution (Bercque 1997). The debate between the two positions applies to digital technologies, but is ideologically and culturally determined.

(Marouby 1990, 88) that is present in the code that structures the player's experience, in the game's norms, and in the ideological representations that legitimize a player's actions.

Utopian virtual worlds offer a mental experience, a kind of cognitive travel. They also propose a new way for understanding problems by establishing a system of rules, assumptions and laws designed to break with those governing reality. Players live in utopian worlds, and through the ideological organization of a videogame's world they discover an alternative government, new values, and novel kinds of social relationships. Through its norms and goals, a game "creates order, it is order" (Huizinga 1958, 30). Indeed, the game "carries out in world's imperfection and life confusion a perfect temporary and limited world" (Huizinga 1958, 30). Here a fundamental difference arises. The game is a parallel world, a momentary escape, a parenthesis cut off from the world but simultaneously within it. But contrary to games, a utopia can become a goal, a sort of guide for a political project. When videogames are used by producers to convey a political message they can also convey a social project as a "laboratory of social experience" (Mauss 1926).

Videogames propose an ideologically structured parallel world in a utopian space. According to Mannheim's analysis of links between utopia and ideology, videogames are a kind of mirror of social aspirations:

> Utopia is reaching more and more a close link with the historical and social situation of this world, this reconciliation is manifested not only in locating more and more its goal not even within historical framework, but in giving spirituality and raising to the social and economic structure immediately accessible. (1929, 100).

Then a videogame's topic is both a discursive space and a spatial discourse, meaning that the virtual world, the way it is organized, is itself an ideological discourse. The personal experience in utopian worlds, the way it will be entered and lived is ideological.

1.2. The Avatar in Procedural Ideological Systemic Spaces

Marxist ideology provides a structural framework by which to analyze a competitive topic. Competition (*agôn*) is the very essence of videogames. Since Marx, ideology has been understood as a superstructure maintaining the balance of power between the different classes and "creating a subjectivity of this domination" (Marx 1848, 32). The use of ideology in a videogame is possible because it is a closed system, cut off from reality. At the same time, games offer a utopian ideological experience, where many ideologies can be simultaneously presented. Ideology as a practice only exists and operates through the process of interpellation: "ideology sees individuals as subjects" (Althusser 1997, 302). This process links the individual to the system as it shapes the player's possibilities through avatar design and gameplay restrictions. Accession to victory will be as ideologically designed as what the player has won (peace, a cup, a princess, etc.).

A videogame is primarily a simulation of relationships (Frasca 2001). The player's posture is rather like a musician in an orchestra, playing the score and adapting his performance to that of others. The definition of ideology developed by Althusser enables us to understand the dynamic level, the procedural dimension: "[T]his is not their real lives, their way of real life, that men 'represent' in ideology, but above all their relation to these conditions of life which are represented" (Althusser 1995, 297). Videogames are political metaphors about such relationships, the real-world complexity of components; they formalize and model the balance of power. In their very essence they promote a general system of exchange of immaterial goods — on-screen signs.

On a second level, videogames define the player as an ideological subject within the system's rules. The rules of the game convey a specific message to the player: Every political representation faces many constraints, and conflict resolution is possible only through effective resource management. The meaning of the message is not only in its representation, but also in the interaction: "[P]rocedural rhetoric describes how political structures operate" (Bogost 2007, 75). For example, media representations of October 2005 riots outside Paris were critiqued through an amateur game, *Paris Riots*. The game's players have the role of a policeman who prepares for a fight and searches for rioters — but doesn't find any. This "non-game" postulates that events were not as dramatic as they appeared and that the media exaggerated the true situation (Mauco 2008). Videogame rules must thus be understood in terms of the laws governing ludic digital spaces as much as in terms of the ideology mobilizing the player.

Ideology in videogames is systemic. It produces classical forms of discourse within audiovisual dimension, and a new kind of production of the utterance through the action, a "procedural rhetoric" (Bogost 2006; Bogost 2007). The ideology is produced not only by words, but also by acts performed within a predetermined framework. As an ideological system with in-game interpellation process, a videogame produces new political conceptions and can be considered as a "machine producing subjectivity" (Guattari 2007, 24).

What is interesting about videogames is that multiple subjectivities can be produced according to different kinds of producers. All the post-modern debate about the "hyperreality of cyberspace" (Poster 1998) seems to be limited in the case of ludic digital worlds. The ludic component is a way to concentrate player attention, offering a normative *telos* that produces a strong focus on the subject in a rational reduction of this reality echoing producers' ideologies.

1.3. The Self as a Multi-Level Communication Device

We could summarize life in videogames under a cybernetic conception:

> [T]o live effectively is to live with adequate information. Thus, communication and control belong to the essence of man's inner life, even as they belong to his life in society. (Wiener 1954, 18).

In a structural sense, videogames are communication games in which a player manipulates on-screen signs as he navigates through the patterns, like a rafting boat on a wild river. In another way, videogames are utopian spaces that propose ideological experiences. The link between cybernetic space and utopia enacts itself through the player's figure: the avatar. An avatar is not only a character to play by and with, the narrator of utopia, but also a medium through which a player communicates. The avatar is the central regulatory device, crystallizing and focusing player interactions within the game system. That is why the player's identity through the avatar figure is no more than a sign of all his past communications and actions.

Most game stories offer tales of peaceful places disturbed by enemies: *Loco Roco*, a kidnapping; *Zelda*, a peaceful village; *Guild Wars*, before the Charr invasion; *Bioshock*, before the plane crash; *Far Cry*, the initial hero's holidays. The goal is to restore the peace, to return the initial order, and the best way to play is to adapt to the environment. Communicating effectively means manipulating signs without disturbance. To experience utopian space means to submit to utopia's rules.

Most studies of virtual worlds tend to define them as panopticons (Mendizabal 2004, 115), with a centralized, omniscient authority. It is true to say that game developers are able to regulate the worlds as both monitors and creators. For example, if one kind of profession or class is stronger than others, developers might modify their characteristics to balance the game. If a player is rude, irrelevant or has an attitude contrary to the ethic of the game (included in the end-user license agreement, or EULA), he can be easily banned. But all this is only true in the utopian space, within the game, cut off from reality. Being banned from the game means that the player's avatar is not able to play anymore, but the player can create another and return. The avatar is the border, the point of passage between the player and the game, the reader and the utopia, the individual and the machine.

Through the ludic dimension that enables play within the game, what appears to be an illusion of liberty is more like a wasteland waiting to be conquered. This notion resembles John Locke's point of view: Everyone should be free to choose the normative system that rules his own life as long as it exists in the private sphere. It is the same with videogames: The multiplicity of universes should be an opportunity to sustain player liberty. Conversely, game systems always have a classical structure: player/avatar/system. The avatar is the "eidetic body" (Mendizabal 2004, 129) through which the game system gives the player an identity. In a utopian world, an avatar should be totally normalized. It is partially done in videogames, but the social and individual factors, the player's knowledge and habits, skills and culture are filters.

Because the self in videogames is partially determined, we should revisit Foucault's opposition of spectacle and disciplinary societies (Foucault 1975, 252-253). Videogames are both because technology enables the synthesis of antagonisms, as "utopia can link opposites" (Marin 1973). The dichotomy between the individual and the avatar is somewhat problematic as the spectator is an actor, the consumer a producer. The player is the "spect-actor" of this drama controlled by software; he must control in order to win, consenting to his illusion as he co-produces it. Because the player can travel through worlds as diverse as there are games, his avatar will always be in flux (a warrior, a space ranger, a football team, a god, a secret agent, a cartoon, etc.). What remains constant is the way he interacts with the system.

Digital utopian worlds are thus extensions of individual interiority. As the avatar is no more than a sign, as the body is not important, as everything is a matter of cognitive communication in a sign-based system, this liberation in the "field of possibilities" is the consecration of communication and libertarian ideologies that are socially produced.

2. Multi-level Ideologies: Libertarianism and Communication Imperatives

2.1. Entering "Brave New World": Self Reborn

Within a videogame, each element is expected to interact with the player's choice. It is a contextual game placing the player in a hostile environment (traps, gaps, enemies, etc.) to which he must continuously adapt. Actions are not created by the player but chosen from what is essentially a predetermined set of options. Programmers try to simulate a sense of freedom, but everything is calculation, the result of mathematical formulas.

The avatar in videogames is the entrance point by which the player can interact with the game. Not unlike Buddhists' "god reincarnated on earth", the player is reincarnated in the digital world. Two kinds of avatar can be observed. The first is more akin to a character out of classical fiction, one designed by the game producers, a puppet the player manipulates. The second is constructed by the player through software that allows him to create an ideal character. While the pre-built character allows game publishers to deals in licenses and franchises (*Mario*, *Sonic*, *The Prince of Persia*, *Solid Snake*, etc.), the second of avatar becomes increasingly important: it offers a way to develop a player's immersion (and incarnation) by making him (or another of his "selves") the hero of the adventure. Most games propose to construct a character, especially role-playing games like *Oblivion*, *World of Warcraft*, *Conan*, *Dofus* or social digital worlds such as *Second Life*, *There*, etc.

The digital avatar is not a god's reincarnation but an individual investment determined by a player. The body is only a representation, just as the carnal dimension is only a coded sign. The construction of a player's avatar represents a simulation of freedom. The more the available combinations, the less deterministic the game feels. Bodily construction in videogames is a "hyperchoice" (Ehrenberg 2000), however. Self-sublimation would make the player choose a strong warrior, an attractive woman, or a wise magician; others might choose an ugly character for shock value. The choices made are influenced by two logical threads: self-representation and social issues through gender, appearance, racial and professional choices.

Gender: Sexual identity does not always match player identity, as a study revealed: 57% of game players engage in gender swapping (Hussein and Griffiths 2008, 52). Playing a woman in on-line games can constitute a strategy in a male-dominated environment to obtain help or be more easily chosen for a multiplayer quest. Because on-line games are also social spaces, some players told us that it was a way to experiment with sexual fantasies and to fulfill their desire to change their sexual identity.

Appearance: Players spend a considerable amount of time in body construction because it is the most personal part of the process. This conception of the body resembles that of the body-object, "the body becomes the sum of different parts" (Detrez 2002, 48). This is linked to technical and in-game constraints: body animation and figuration is an assembly of interactive parts, the middleware's ability to render complex 3D graphics within the game's variables. If the program can only offer a small number of criteria, the probability that a player will encounter his digital double increases.

Race: Players can often choose to be human or something more exotic like an alien, elf, or troll. Choosing a race is as much an aesthetic choice as a gaming preference, even if different races can offer the same gaming experience. The discriminating factor is not the in-game races, as most are heroic-fantasy shared imaginary (Orc, Elves, etc.), but skin color. For example, players can be less helpful with black avatars than white ones (Eastwick and Gardner 2009). Such racism is more explicit in political contexts: Members of the extreme-right National Front party in *Second Life* ask an avatar why it is black (Mauco 2007). Such actions illustrate how real-life beliefs and stereotypes can be transferred into digital worlds.

Profession: When the player chooses his class, he is choosing to belong to a particular occupation such as a warrior or a magician. Each profession offers different gameplay and sets up a system of individual actions specific to the profession. For example, warriors are made for close combat, with great strength and a high level of resistance. Magicians, while physically weak, are designed for long-distance combat, with powerful zone skills. So depending on the specifics of their characters, players will experience a different kind of game, as a striker and defender will not play the same way in a soccer game.

The self here is a "digital hexis" (George 2008), meaning the act to be in digital world. As a negotiated space between individual interiority and digital environment, this digital hexis describes the process of investment initiated by the player, the way he will conquer the digital territory and how he will exist in it. Nevertheless, videogame ideology reverses this process, as the self will not only be "the act to be"; the self will exist by acting, action will determine the being: "[I]dentity is what makes the singularity of different ways of existing through one same and unique frame of references" (Guattari 2007, 93).

2.2. Communication Ideology Imperatives in Interactive Action

Together with the creation of the avatar's body, communication is omnipresent in videogames. If computer code science is a mathematical language, it also pervades the conceptions of programmers. This approach is similar to that of those who understand the human being as an information process, where genetics is merely an almost endless line of code. This figure announced the *Homo comunicans*, the man who communicates as it has been developed in Norbert Wiener's works.

The body in Wiener's works is a communication device that implies that the body's essence is more a matter of organization than composition: "the physical identity of an individual does not consist in the matter of which it is made" (Wiener 1954, 101). The nervous system is a matter of input and output, the brain an analogue to a digital device. What becomes important is the way the message is treated according to the taping process, the order of sequences decoding the message.

> The biological individuality of an organism seems to lie in a certain continuity of process, and in the memory by the organism of the effects of its past development. This appears to hold also true for its mental development. In terms of the computing machine, the individuality of a mind lies in the retention of its earlier taping and memories, and in its continued development along lines already laid out. (Wiener 1954, 102)

Self-presentation in a digital world is driven by these conceptions: the body as the player's sign of presence is also an interactive device that enables him to communicate with the machine. When the player controls an avatar, he interacts both with the machine and with the game. As a computer artifact, it incarnates the input-output: pressing a button produces a movement. As a gaming artifact, what you have done, have lost or have won, is shown on-screen and incorporated in the avatar's appearance. Self-incarnation is a sign structured by communication and game.

As the game progresses, the avatar's appearance will be enriched by armor, weapons, and other objects won during the game. This part is important in on-line and off-line role-playing games: most quests will offer rewards, so if everyone accomplishes his duty, everyone would get the same object. The collected items are new capabilities for the player to communicate with his environment: new spells, new combinations of shots, etc. Moreover, acquiring a new item is the condition to get to a new level, to enter a new world. It can be the main goal of a game, especially in adventure and role playing games: In *Zelda: A Link to the Past*, the hero must get the Triforce in order to fight Ganon; in *Oblivion*, the king's amulet must be reconstructed. The ludic component introduces a random process: computer program generates rare items, kind of player holy grail.

All this will "generate a status inequality" (Castronova 2006, 107) whose corollary is a top-player oligarchy. As shown, this "civilization process" (Elias 1997) encourages the lower classes to imitate the upper classes, encouraging the aristocracy to develop new tastes and habits. So it is in digital worlds: Top players are recognized by the sword or the armor they wear and this is soon imitated by those below them. Introducing a new feature can modify a game's equilibrium, encouraging players to spend time seeking out new items ("farming") to preserve their superiority. But this inequality of status can also be understood in terms of communication skills, as some players will benefit from a wider range of ways to interact with the game system. Moreover, getting a rare sword is not just a gaming and communication issue; it is also a social process inside a game device that allows player to enter the selected class of top-level players. What an avatar wears reveals the player's level and abilities; it is a sign of recognition and a distinctive label of valor.

Since the 1950s transparency ideology has become more and more efficient; this rising idea breaks classical conceptions of man as a creature whose self-identity was once considered an autonomous private sphere. One postulate changed man's conception: crimes and atrocities committed in secret during World War II, and "secret partly takes roots in this self interiority" (Breton 2004). The solution sets the figure of a transparent modern man who could not hide, guided by his impulses. To do this, it became necessary to present a human being turned outward, totally transparent and reactive. This point is interesting, because as long as the self is defined by an external context, it is possible to regulate and influence man's interiority. In a larger perspective, the human self is no longer a matter of being but a problem of acting: In videogames the self is the player negotiating a place as he meets the adaptative environment.

Most videogame missions involve delivering a message or getting information. For example, in *Guild Wars* the player has to travel from one point to another to inform a lord of the crisis and to offer help. It is the same process in *Oblivion,* where the hero has to reach local kings and transmit the new emperor's needs. In *GTA IV*, Niko Bellic must assure the successful transmission of information. In *Ghost Recon Advanced Warfighters*, the commando must destroy enemy communication resources getting good information from an advanced communication device. Even if communication seems to drive these spaces, a player's characteristics, his psychological history, personal career, and ludic and social capital are components of his subjectivity as the game strives to produce a normalized identity through his bodily representation. The most interesting issue is that this body, as the interface between the player and the machine, is a sign waiting to be invested with player aspirations. That's why the game's technological determinism is efficient through the normative devices and yet limited by individual identity "in real life".

The player's body is a place of utopian aspirations, marking "both a devaluation of the body and a revaluation of thought, first of rational thought" (Breton 2004, 56). He is the incarnation of the subject figure in videogames. It is a "body-sign" externalized, purely mechanical, under a process of rational choice, although subject to the desires of the player:

> The *Homo communicans* is a being without interiority and without a body, who lives in a society without secrets, a whole turned to the social, which exists only through information exchange and, in a society made transparent through the new machines (Breton 2004, 50).

A player's survival does not depend on the state of his avatar's body, but on its gauge of life. This gauge corresponds to a number of points: As soon as the life gauge falls to the zero point, the player is dead, the game is lost. To avoid losing, there are healing potions or spells. The distinction is one between the body and the life of the player, however, because the number of life points is independent and may increase as the player gains experience. The externalization of the body translates into a deep denial of corporeality within the video game. In ludic digital worlds there is a passage from the "techniques of the body" (Mauss 1936, 366) to a technological body driven by an unnatural rationality. As the body in communication ideology is absent, it will be replaced by a technological artifact, an envelope that must not be fulfilled but animated. The player breathes life into it through manipulation, negotiating between the code and the norms.

2.3. Ideologies of the Self: Psychic Economy and Libertarianism

Videogames postulate an individual experience of digital worlds through the avatar, a communication device opposing an individual to the system. Freedom is the rule, self-satisfaction the goal. Videogames are libertarian in many ways: self property, private property, action and use of violence. Libertarian ideology postulates that everyone is their own master, but in videogames your avatar is both yours and the programmers'.

Many juridical debates are dealing with issues of property: does the avatar belong to the game creators or to the player as ludic and social identity?[2] The player's avatar is not only a game character; it is also an interface focusing his social networks, a way to be identified in those spaces. No one else can use a player's avatar; providers can be sued if they cannot secure access according to the *End-User License Agreement* (EULA) agreements and legal protections.

Videogame stories frequently consecrate this personal property: the hero must defend himself against the world. The main example is the *Grand Theft Auto* series, in which a player must raise a little gangster and help him rise to the top of the social ladder. In an extreme case, lost of property might create a true drama, such as Shawn Woolley's 2001 suicide after being robbed of his possessions in *EverQuest*. But personal property remains a utilitarian point of view (Mauco 2006), as everything composing individual environments, material or immaterial, should be determined as individual's rights as a user, not a gamer. In videogame scenarios, preserving or regaining personal property can be one of the most important motives: a princess kidnapped in *Mario*, a sacred item, magical swords. Most games offer the opportunity to accumulate possessions so as to become stronger. This conception connects private property with the use of violence.

Contrary to most discourse about videogame violence, the player does not initiate violent acts without suffering from an original aggression. Many stories begin with a murder, a crime which must be repaired or revenged. In *Guild Wars* the world has been destroyed. In *Oblivion* the emperor was killed. In *Grand Theft Auto* you were betrayed. The use of violence against the player legitimates the use of violence against the environment. Even in the controversial *Carmaggedon* series (1997; 1998), in which the player kills through auto races, the use of violence is enabled by a totalitarian government that allows this kind of fight to happen.

As developed in the previous section, the man of action is almost always the main subject of videogames. Playing is acting; fighting against the world is a player *leitmotif*. Self-identity is no longer a matter of existence, but of acquisition and action. What a player has done will determine what he is: hero or loser. In *Oblivion*, one of the main quests given by the emperor ends with this line: "Stop talking; what is important

---

[2] For a good review of the juridical debate on avatar status see:
Lastowka, G. and Hunter, D. (2004), "The Laws of Virtual Worlds" in *California Law Review* Vol. 92, Berkeley.
Fairfield, J. (2005) Virtual property, *Boston University Law Review*, Vol. 85.

is to act". In *GTA IV*, consumerist critics exaggerate their ideology through in-game publicity parodies (be a millionaire, get rich and clever, act like a man, etc.).

As observed by Alain Ehrenberg, "The limits between the allowed and the forbidden, wanes in favor of a tearing between possible and impossible" (Ehrenberg 2000, 14). Videogames are domains of possibilities, but to play is to submit to a game's rules. They are one of the most efficient ways to avoid contemporary "self-indetermination" (Ehrenberg 1995, 307). To extend Elias's theory, videogames are a temporary technological apparatus of the self that enables self-control and fulfills this supply of individual and social norms. As videogames internalize technology, they are a powerful technology that channels "psychic economy". At the same time, they can be considered as an extension of the inner self, which can be defined as "out from any public determinism [...] and the citizen's interior deliberating space" (Rangeaon 1995, 109). As a cognitive process, the player, acting through the avatar, is a bodiless mind evolving in this digital solipsistic space. Even if these ideologies are not commonly shared by policy makers, videogames should be considered autonomous political projects, "satisfying expression and society ideals" (Huizinga 1958, 28), that produce new subjectivities strengthened by the digital communities' social pressure. If today they are entertaining utopian runaways, tomorrow they may lead to political hope.

Acknowledgement

I would like to deeply thank Ian Bogost from the Georgia Tech, for his precious help and Thomas Gaon from the Digital World Observatory in Human Sciences (OMNSH), for his advice.

Bibliography

Althusser, L. (ed.) (1970) "Idéologie et appareils idéologiques d'Etat". *Sur la reproduction.* Paris: PUF. 269-314.
Augé, M. (1992) *Non-lieux. Introduction à une anthropologie de la surmodernité.* Paris: Seuil.
Balandier, G. (1992) *Le Dédale. Pour en finir avec le XXème siècle.* Paris: Seuil.
Berque, A. (1997) *Japan Cities and Social Bonds.* Northamptonshire: Pilkington Press.
Bogost, I. (2006) *Unit Operation: An Approach to Videogames Criticism.* Cambridge: MIT Press.

—. (2007) *Persuasive Games*. Cambridge: MIT Press.

Breton, P. (2004) *L'Utopie de la communication : le mythe du village planétaire*. Paris: La Découverte.

Caillois, R. (1998) *Les jeux et les hommes*. Paris: Folio.

Castronova, E. (2006) *Synthetic Worlds: The Business and Culture of Online Games*. Chicago: The University of Chicago Press.

Detrez, C. (2002) *La Construction sociale du corps*. Paris: Points Seuil.

Duflo, C. (1997) *Jouer et philosopher*. Paris: PUF.

Ehrenberg, A. (1995) *L'Individu incertain*. Paris: Hachette.

—. (2000) *La Fatigue d'être soi*. Paris: Odile Jacob.

Eastwick, P., and Gardner, W. (2009) "Is It a Game? Evidence for Social Influence in the Virtual World". *Social Influence* 4 (1). 18-32.

Elias, N. (1990) *La dynamique de l'Occident*. Paris: Pocket.

—. (1997) *La Société des individus*. Paris: Pocket.

Foucault, M. (1984) *Histoire de la sexualité. Le souci de soi*. Paris: NRF.

—. (1975) *Surveiller et punir*. Paris: NRF.

Georges, F. (2008) "L'Hexis numérique: Sémiotique de la représentation de soi dans les dispositifs interactifs". PhD thesis. Paris I Panthéon Sorbonne University.

Guattari, F. (1992) *Chaosmose*. Paris: Galilée.

Guattari, F. and Rolnik, S. (1984) *Micropolitiques*. Brasilia: Les empêcheurs de tourner en rond.

Huizinga, J. (1998) *Homo Ludens*. Paris: Gallimard TEL.

Marx, K. (1848) *L'Idéologie allemande*. Paris: Folio.

Mannheim, K. (2006) *Idéologie et utopie*. Paris: MSH.

Marin, L. (1973) *Utopiques : jeu d'espace*. Paris: Minuit.

Marouby, C. (1990) *Utopie et primitivisme*. Paris: Seuil.

Mauco, O. (2006) "Les représentations et logiques politiques des jeux vidéo. L'intériorisation des logiques collectives dans la décision individuelle". In Genvo, S. (ed.). *Le game design de jeux vidéo : approches de l'expression vidéoludique*. Paris: L'Harmattan. 117-135.

—. (2007) "Les tentatives de politisation des modes virtuels. Analyse comparée de World of Warcraft et de Second Life". Paper presented at the *Congrès for the Association Française de Sciences Politiques*, September 5-7.

—. (2008) "La médiatisation des problématiques de la violence et de l'addiction aux jeux vidéo". *Quaderni* 67. 19-31.

Mauss, M. (1926) *Manuel d'Ethnographie*. Paris: Payot.

Rodrigo Mendizabal, I. (2004) *Maquinas de pensar. Videojuegos, representaciones y simulaciones de poder*. Quito: Universida andina Simon Bolivar, Abya Yala, Corporacion editora nacional.

Poster, M. (2008) "Virtual Ethnicity: Tribal Identity in an Age of Global Communications". In Jones, S. (ed.). *Cybersociety 2.0: Revisiting Computer-Mediated Communication and Community*. Thousand Oaks: Sage. 184-211.

Ruyer , R. (1950) *L'Utopie et les utopies*. Paris: PUF.

Turkle, S. (1995) *Life on the Screen: Identity in the Age of the Internet*. New York: Simon and Schuster.

Wiener, N. (1988) *Human Use of Human Beings*. New York: Da Capo Press.

CHAPTER SIX

"WHATEVER I AM, WHEREVER I AM, HOW DOES IT MATTER?... WHY DOES IT MATTER?" — EGOCASTING IN-BETWEEN IDENTITIES

FRED DERVIN AND TANJA RIIKONEN

Introduction

As more people move around the world and settle in foreign countries, the number of intercultural narratives has increased immensely. Though it is not really an innovation in itself, the emergence of "in-between identities" (Bhatia 2002), i.e. feelings of being dual or multiple with regard to one's national or ethnic identity, is more and more common in these narratives. This is evidenced by immigrants or members of various diasporas who share their experiences of living abroad in various personal and public spaces; be they through mere telephone calls, e-mails, (un)published autobiographies, interviews in newspapers and magazines, documentaries, films, etc. In our technological worlds, new opportunities for sharing such experiences, including Web 2.0 and Web 3.0, have developed over the last decades. Access to these opportunities depends, of course, on the migrant's financial means and technological *habits*. For the researcher, this gives her/him a great opportunity to easily collect "data twenty-four hours a day across the globe" (Joinson 2005, 21).

This contribution looks at a special case of narrating one's experiences of mobility and identities through the personal use of podcasting in cyberspace. Podcasting[1] is a form of technology used to supply audio (or

---

[1] The origin of the naming of the technology is unclear. Officially, it combines iPod (the Apple player) and Broadcasting.

video) programs over the Internet. It can be considered as a major contributor to Michel Foucault's *technologies of the self* (1988, 18). Foucault (1988, 27) demonstrated in his book *Technologies of the self* how "(...) by the Hellenistic age, writing prevailed and real dialectic passed to correspondence. Taking care of oneself became linked to constant writing activity. The self is something to write about, a theme or object (subject) of writing activity". The increase in *taking care of oneself* in postmodernity through the use of new technologies bears a strong resemblance to the Hellenistic technologies of the self (cf. Turkle 1995). References to podcasting, through the phrase *egocasting*, which refers to broadcasting that is solely centered on presenting, shaping and talking about the self (cf. Allard 2005), seem to confirm this hypothesis.

For the researcher working on intercultural communication and the construction of national, ethnic and religious identities, personal podcasts are excellent data as they are not "created" or "touched" in any way by the researcher her/himself, as is the case of e.g. interviews, and are therefore 'authentic'. In order to uncover the specificities of the construction of selves through such technology, the article will attempt to analyse the emergence of positions in discourse, their organization and reorganization, within this specific computer mediated context, through the adoption of a dialogical perspective (Bhaktin 1979/1986; Marková et al. 2007) and a linguistic-pragmatic adapted version of the theory of *Personal Position Repertoire* (PPR thereafter), as developed by the psychotherapist Hubert J.M. Hermans (2001a). Episodes from three podcasts related to the topic of migration and identity will be examined. The study therefore belongs to a branch of research that applies the theories of positioning and multivoicedness to intercultural contexts in order to tackle unstable, unfixed and liquid identities (Bauman 2000) and diversities, which are at the center of contemporary worlds.

1. Positioning and Multivoicedness

1.1. On Researching the Self and Identities

In terms of research, the notions of *self* and identity have been the subject of "a veritable discursive explosion in recent years" (Hall 1996, 1). The way researchers have been looking at them has moved away from solid conceptions or from what Michel Maffesoli has described as the "fantasy of the unicity of the self" (1997).[2] In other words, the existence of a core, objective and immutable self has been challenged by many scholars across disciplines. This is not a new development, given that philosophy, since Ancient Greece and through Socrates, Plato, Heraclitus, had already proposed that the individual is always in the process of becoming. The recent explosion of the conception of self and identities as being fluid, fragmentary and contingent has resulted from the proposition of related terminologies such as, *inter alia*, Protean (Lifton 1993), saturated (Gergen 1991), multiple (Rosenberg 1997) narrated or storied (Sarbin 1986) and liquid (Bauman 2001). Our chapter is based on this understanding of the self and identities.

Based on this paradigm, many theories across various scientific fields, such as *social identity theory, optimal distinctiveness theory* (Brewer 1991), *intersectionality theory* (Collins 2000) but also the more linguistically orientated *narrative studies* (de Fina et al. 2006), *theories of enunciation* (Marnette 2005), or *intercultural hermemeutics* (Dahl et al. 2006) can be used in the analysis of the expression, construction and enactment of identity. This paper will explore a linguistic approach to identity.

A review of the research on the topic of identities in this field shows that various approaches are used by researchers (Benwell and Stokoe 2006) and that numerous terms such as "position", "role", "personality", "category", "subject" and "agent" are used as a substitute (Benwell and Stokoe 2006, 6). Research has been done on most 'common' identities such as gender, age, national identities, and migrant identities. Two approaches will be explored in this chapter: we firstly adopt dialogism, which emphasizes that "humans live in the world of others and that their existence, thought and language are thoroughly interdependent with the existence, thought and language of others" (Marková et al 2007, 1). Secondly, we concentrate on the method based on the organization of personal repertoires of internal and external positions in discourse, as proposed by the Dutch scholar H.J.M. Hermans (2001a). Through the selected approaches, we shall look at the concepts of multivoicedness and positioning. References to French theories of enunciation will also be made, as they are very close to these theories and can act as a tool when attempting to linguistically identify such phenomena.

---

[2] Though some scientific approaches to identity and intercultural communication still configure their research methodologies on an essentialist solid paradigm (cf. Abdallah-Pretceille 1986, chapter 2).

1.2. Positioning

Positioning is a concept which has been widely introduced in narrative studies (Bamberg 2004) and is defined as "the discursive process whereby selves are located in conversations as observably and subjectively coherent participants in jointly produced story lines" (Davies and Harré 1990). Inspired by the work of M. Bakhtin, H.J.M. Hermans (2001b, 337) proposed a theory of the *dialogical self* by which to study the self as a fluctuation of positions. According to the therapist, the *I* functions as a process of positioning and repositioning (Hermans 2004), which is dependent on the presence of others. The current contexts of *hypercommunication* and multiple encounters that are made possible in our society have an impact on positioning as "increasingly we find ourselves in a situation of 'mediated dialogue'" (Hermans 2004, 305), whereby individuals' repertoires of the self are rendered more heterogeneous, hybrid and "subjected to larger 'position leaps' than ever in history" (Hermans 2004, 307). In other words, the presentation of the self (selves) varies according to contexts and continuously changes as "one cannot be a self on one's own" (Taylor 1989, 36). It is also important to note, along with Talamo and Ligorio (2001, 112), that "each person is also carrying his or her own story and his or her multiple selves in the interaction".

These various positions can be approached from two angles: they are either internal or external (Hermans and Dimaggio 2007). Internal positions form the different parts of the self (*I* as a lecturer, *I* as a passionate person, *I* as a neighbour...), while external positions "refer to people and objects in the environment that are (...) relevant from the perspective of one or more internal positions" (Hermans 2004a, 252). External positions in one's discourse can therefore be adopted by in-groups, helping to examine selves and operate a disclosure of oneself. It is also through differentiation from out-groups that people identify.

According to Hermans and Dimaggio (2007), various interactive acts can take place between all these positions in discourse: internal positions between themselves (*I* is talking to *I* and confronting e.g., two positions, which is the case when dealing with virtual voices or self-talk (Goffman 1978), e.g., I said to myself...), internal positions can dialogue with external ones (*I* is arguing with a colleague) and external positions can dialogue together within the *I* (two individuals' interaction is enacted in somebody's else speech). Choosing a *self* to exploit/explore in interaction is related to a specific situation and the significance of this situation. As such: "playing different identities is then a resource that participants use to give relevance to their argumentations during the discourse in interaction"

(Talamo and Ligorio 2001, 112). Finally, all these positions can vary in their level of identification. It is also important to note that boundaries between internal and external positions can be fuzzy, with some positions, as we will see later, not always being identifiable. In a previous study, Dervin (2007; 2008) has shown how, in intercultural communication, many unidentifiable internal and external positions cross the interlocutors' discourse (e.g., by means of the pronoun *on* in French – which can correspond to the generic and impersonal *one, you, they...* but also to personal referents in English –, free indirect represented speech...). He has demonstrated how these positions allow interlocutors to use various discursive strategies to construct their identities.

Let us now explore the notion of *multivoicedness*, which is attached to positioning.

1.3. Multivoicedness

1.3.1. Strategic Presence of Others in Discourse

The notion of multivoicedness derives from the works of Michael Bakhtin (1981) and his theory of polyphony, which has inspired numerous theories, such as that of the French linguist Ducrot, the praxemic movement (Montpellier, France), ScaPoline (Scandinavian theory of linguistic polyphony)... According to the Russian author, discourse is filled with an uncountable number of voices: visible entities, which can be easily identified (as in e.g., *Paul told me he was happy*)[3] and unidentifiable "invisible guests" (Watkins 1986) (as e.g. the voice of the *doxa* or *common sense*, but also "professional jargon, authorities of various circles, sociopolitical ideologies (...)" (Hermans 2004)[4]). As such: "The personal voices of other individuals or the collective voices of groups enter the self-space and form positions that agree or disagree with or unite or oppose each other. Along these lines, real, remembered, or imagined voices of friends, allies, strangers, or enemies can become transient or more stabilized positions in the self-space that can open or close itself to the globalizing environment" (Hermans and Dimaggio 2007). As various voices are multiplied in postmodernity (technology has a major role to play in this trend — cf. *infra*), every individual's voice can be under the influence of many ideas, thoughts, words and sentences from very

---

[3] Though there's no guarantee regarding the authenticity of the discourse as it might be altered to fit one's purpose and/or misinterpreted.
[4] Cf. also Paveau, 2006 and her theory of pre-discourse.

different and even sometimes contradictory sources (Hermans 2004, 305). This is why Bhatia (2002, 73) argues that voices and positions can also be conflicting in one's discourse.

1.3.2. Types of Represented Discourses

The presence of otherness in discourse (*others* but also *one's own* otherness) can be identified through what is usually referred to as reported speech, but which we will label represented discourse (Johansson 2000, 78) as this term appears to be closer to reality[5] (one never knows if a discourse has really been uttered in a particular way as it is decontextualised). Canonical and non-canonical forms of represented speech are found in the literature. *Direct represented speech*, whereby someone directly takes somebody's words and includes them in their own speech by showing boundaries between both discourses (through the use of verbs such as to say, to tell,... and other marks (Mochet 1986, 127), is the most explicit form of dialogism (Verine 2005, 188). In this type of discourse, at least two speakers are present. On the other hand, *Indirect represented speech* incorporates the voice of an *other* into that of the speaker. Pronouns, verbs and deictics from the represented discourse are transferred to the *hic et nunc* of the speech (Marnette 2005, 23) and introduced by *verba sentiendi*. In this sort of represented discourse, one speaker is involved but two enunciators and one unique context of enunciation can be found in this type of discourse.

On top of these two canonical forms of represented discourse, one finds their free forms where the boundary between the speaker's discourse and the discourse that is integrated is fuzzy and possibly more difficult to identify. Various researchers have also included the following in this kind of discourse: the use of the conditional tense in the media (Dendale 1992), the use of incises such as "apparently" (Fleishman and Yaguello 1999), metadiscourse and modalities (Marnette 2006, 31). Finally, the concept of self-quotation (Rabatel 2006; Maynard 1996) or "a quotation by oneself of utterances that are presented in discourse as uttered before by the speaker" (Rabatel 2006, 81) is increasingly attracting greater attention from linguists.

Several elements have an impact on the apparition of such discourses in interaction. First of all, the genre (i.e. the type of interaction and means

---

[5] Rosier (2005, 17) lists the following neologisms that have been proposed to refer to reported speech: "imported speech, deported speech, evoked discourse, quotational disjunction...".

of interacting: a letter to a friend, an e-mail, a formal interview…) may lead to various identifiable/unidentifiable voices and positions being introduced in interaction. The context of interaction (at a supermarket or in a meeting…), the power relations that are established between the interlocutors, the identities that interlocutors impose on each other (Pavlenko and Blackledge 2004, 21), their familiarity, emotional and mental states of the interlocutors, what is at stake in the interaction, pre-discourse (or "frameworks of knowledge, beliefs and practices" Paveau 2007), etc. also play a role in the introduction of voices. This is why positions and multivoicedness are actually co-constructed by the interlocutors and do not just depend on one speaker (Shotter 1999, 77).

In this paper, we will focus on the canonical forms of represented speech and concentrate on the presence of identifiable and unidentifiable exterior positions. We will nonetheless take *self-quotations* into consideration as we argue that this type of represented discourse can be categorized as external positions (the speaker "dissociates" themselves as s/he defines her/himself by using her/his own exteriorized voice).

2. Selves and Identity

2.1. Previous Research on the Construction of Selves and Identity

Research on the expression and construction of identities is an emerging branch in many major scientific fields. Let us start with general studies carried out on new technologies and identification. In 1995, Sherry Turkle published one of the first books about the internet and the impact of its use on the expression of identities and games of identities. She demonstrated how users in the 1980s and 90s mixed and played with identities in the use of e-mail and Multi-user domains. Since the early 2000s, research has boomed in psychology (cf. the psychosemiotic approach proposed by Hevem and Vincent 2004), language learning and teaching (synchronous chats, Thorne 2003), gender studies (Herring 1996; Huffaker and Calvert 2005; Rellstab 2007), queer studies (Rak 2005), etc. Various technologies have been used for collecting corpora: chats, SMS, iTV SMS Chat, videoconferencing, avatars in metaverses, etc. The technology that has attracted researchers the most is blogging.

Though studies on the expression of identities have been the focus of various fields of linguistics (Ewins 2005; de Fina et al. 2006; Benwell & Stokoe 2006), few researches have devoted themselves to the study of the expression and construction of immigrant identification through new technologies. Our previous study (Dervin & Riikonen forth.), which examined identification in two genres of podcasts (an academic talk-show and a personal diary) based on discussions on immigration, and Dervin's study of the construction of self and otherness in a podcast produced by mobile academics, are the only ones based on technologically-produced oral corpora (Dervin 2007). This makes our study pioneering but can also be seen as a call to use such data for analysis.

2.2. Podcasting: Technical Considerations

Podcasting is a technology that allows unlimited personal creations to be posted on the Internet. Anyone can post any of their productions on a website (e.g., iPodder.com or Podcast.net) or a music software platform (e.g., Apple computer's iTunes, Quicktime or Windows Media Player). Subscribing to a podcast or downloading it entitles users, in theory, to listen to the programs of their choice, when they want, where they want, and how they want. Any digital audio player (mp3 players, USB players, iPods...) or computer (Windows, Linux or Apple) can play podcasts. With very simple technology (e.g., a simple microphone plugged into a computer), podcasters can record "shows" on just about anything: life stories, reviews, conferences, discussion, news... just about anywhere: over the (mobile) phone, on a plane, on the streets... They can be monologues or conversations between different people which have been recorded in different spaces-times. Like radio shows, podcasts can be edited or recorded live and contain various sources: music, recorded speech... by the podcasters or "guests". Podcasts in themselves are not *live* as they need to be uploaded to a music software platform or website to be downloaded. They are therefore components of asynchronous communication.

Similar to a weblog, but oral in its form, a podcast is usually linked to a website (the podcast's *relational anchor,* as it can bring together podcasters and listeners) where listeners can comment on the episodes in writing (by means of a "comment" function), send in documents to the podcaster (either by e-mail or through a website) and send mp3 files to the podcasters who might use them in their own shows. This makes podcasts extremely interactive, contributing to podcasters' virtually constructed identities as they become showcases of the *self.* This is why they seem to correspond to the technologies of the self as defined by Foucault (1988, 18): "technologies of the self, (...) permit individuals to effect by their own means or with the help of others a certain number of operations on their own bodies and souls, thoughts, conduct, and way of being, so as to transform themselves in order to attain a certain state of happiness, purity, wisdom, perfection or immortality". Rory Ewins (2005, 373), in his analysis of weblogs, expresses what podcasts could potentially be doing to their creators: it is "a form of self-administered therapy, allowing one to work through the issues in one's life day by day, and can play a significant role in identity formation".

Another aspect of podcasting is that it can allow its producer(s) to expose themselves to potentially anyone who has an interest in their podcast and who owns the (readily available) technology to listen to their episodes. Like other media, such as television, a podcaster typically is unaware of who listens to his productions (though s/he may have his/her "followers"). According to Hermans and Dimaggio (2007), this novelty is a factor which makes podcasting meaningful in research terms:

> The process of globalization implies not only an increase in the number and heterogeneity of addressees and their various cultural backgrounds but also the number and heterogeneity of audiences that are implicitly present in the speech of everyday life.

In a sense, podcasting contributes to the dramatization of both the self and the selves, which in turn become constructions.

Finally, podcasts have different formats, amongst which we have identified the following: monologues (one speaker, either live or edited, improvises, self-reflects or reads a text), monologues accompanied by extra documents (as above plus music, messages sent in by listeners or friends), *big brother* style podcasts (someone continuously records what they do and say), interviews (two or more speakers in a studio or outdoors), talk-show (like the example one but more professional, with jingles…), etc.

We will now explore the specificities of the dramatization in podcasts. We shall try to demonstrate how the presence of external positions (but also indirectly internal positions) can contribute to acts of self-examination and positioning in three podcasts.

3. Analysis

3.1. About the Corpus

Our analysis is based on episodes from three different personal diary-like podcasts: Fusionview[6], Nik-in-Paris[7], and Generation 1.5.[8] The three recordings differ from, and are similar to each other, in many ways. All three podcasts are monologues and we chose to analyse them because of their reflective and very personal nature. Let us give some information concerning each podcast to start with. First of all, Nik-in-Paris was recorded live and includes "natural" unedited noises (from ambulances to phone calls). The author even records his podcasts on the street, while shopping, on his way to work... The analysed episode was probably recorded at the podcaster's home. Fusionview, on the other hand, was edited after the recording. In Fusionview, listeners can hear some editing effects (pauses and scratches) at least twice during the episode. As for Generation 1.5, the show doesn't include editing noises but does include clear pauses in the podcaster's speech. The following analysis is based on one entire episode of Fusionview and Generation 1.5, while the episode from Nik-in-Paris is only a short extract which concentrates on the expression of the podcaster's in-between identification.

The first podcast, Fusionview, was edited by Yang May Ooi who is originally from Malaysia and has lived, studied and worked in Britain most of her life. In the specific episode that we analyse below, she is responding to a message that a Malaysian writer left on her website after listening to her podcast:

> This is the first time I am listening to a podcast here I had a culture shock when I heard your voice. Is this English sounding voice Young May's? I ask myself. Of course it is why should I be surprised as you have been living in the UK for years it is just when I look at your very Chinese pix I couldn't reconcile it with the very English accent.

This message triggers an 8.41-minute monologue in which Yang May Ooi discusses what she calls her "split personality" as she feels that she is both English and Malay - which corresponds *par excellence* to the "in-between" identities that we are concentrating on in this paper.

---

[6] http://www.Fusionview.co.uk
[7] http://www.nikinparis.com
[8] http://www.podbazaar.com/view/126100789566373927

The second podcast is similar to the first one. Generation 1.5's episode *What tribe am I?*, is a 21.58-minute monologue recorded by Yesha, who was born in India and has been living all her life in America, growing up in New York and New Jersey and working later on in San Francisco. The name of the podcast, Generation 1.5, refers to the idea of an immigrant youth who has moved to a new country early in their lives and has evolved between two or more "cultures". The analysed episode *What tribe am I?* includes the podcaster's diary entries from 1976-1994. This podcast thus differs from the other ones in the sense that multivoicedness is more marked than in the others (at least textually). The reason for Yesha's reflections on her identity is an internet-based discussion that she had had on the meaning of her Indian identity:

> In a recent internet conversation, that got a little heated, someone asked me "what does Indian really mean?" when I insisted that I was Indian... I said: "great question"... and he said: "no, really, I wanna know, what does Indian mean to you?"... and I still said: "great question". I've been thinking a lot about that since then...

In response to this enacted chat-conversation, Yesha presents some extracts from her diary about notable events from the past concerning her identity and self-construction as an Indian living in America. Before reading the entries, Yesha discusses the use of various terms attached to her identity:

> One interesting thing I have noticed and heated discussion of the word Indian and Desi[9], is that Desi is in a diaspora, well, I guess Indian Desi is in a diaspora, really can't win when it comes to the word Indian because if we use the word Desi to describe ourselves, many people would take umbrage of that and say: "just say what you are, if you're Indian, say you're Indian"... however, if I do use the word Indian to describe myself, many Desis from the home country would say: "You're not Indian, you're American"... I guess I can't win... well...

This reflection is the starting point for her in-between identity construction in the podcast.

---

[9] Desi refers to "the homeland" in Hindi and Urdu, i.e. India here. For Cullity (2002, 409), "global desi" is a combination of "how the global and the local, the cosmopolitan and the traditional, modernity and tradition, are all inextricably bound together in a hybrid (...)".

The third podcast, Nik-in-Paris, is a diary-like personal podcast (duration: 6.37). In the excerpt, Nik also reacts to a comment left by a listener about his accent in English. Though Nik says he is half-English, half-Brazilian, the listener asserts that Nik sounds French. From there, Nik questions his own identities, his in-betweenness (English, Brazilian, French but also other identities related to places in Britain). The listener's words are also introduced by Nik, as follows:

> Leo writes to me and says by the way I still think that you have a French accent while the British one is still (…)ful.

Nik constantly asks for reactions from his listeners on this issue during the episode. This podcast differs from the other podcasts as Nik puts forward a range of identities which is not limited to two (in Ooi's case: Malay and English; Yesha: Indian and American) but includes as many as five (Brazilian, Scottish, French, "Cambridgean", Welsh).

All in all, we see that the three episodes emerge from what others have said and asked the podcasters and serve as answers, that, as we will see later, do not offer clear-cut responses. The inclusion of external positions (be they one's own voices from the past, the voices of others or unidentifiable voices) and represented speech included in discourse is not innocent, but in fact rather meaningful. What we will be looking at in what follows is the intervention of external positions in the three episodes and the impact that they have on what the speakers are uttering. We take into consideration voices which are identifiable and unidentifiable (or fuzzy) in the three documents. Fuzzy voices are either generic voices or voices that are difficult to specify as they can represent a large group of individuals or an unspecified person.

Podcasters	Nik-in-Paris	Yang May Ooi	Yesha
Identifiable External positions	-a taxi driver -the guys who picked me up at the airport -Bruno (the podcaster's partner) -my parents -my mum -my dad	-A Malaysian writer -Hugh Grant in the film *Four Weddings and a Funeral* -An English girl -the Podcaster's English friends	-an aggressive 9-year-old girl -little John, or maybe it's Tony -my anthropology professor - my family - my friend Elaine -a forgotten friend Judy -Mrs N. is my tenth grade's English teacher -Madonna -Miss Universe
Fuzzy External Positions	-Scotland people -in England (…) people -in France (…) people -British -what I'm told (passive voice)	-Malaysian people who listen to the podcast -"we" (Malaysians?) -"you" (The listener? Malaysian writer? A generic you?) -French people and German people -The English -people -Nobody -'you'	-South Asians, Pakistanis, Sri Lankans, Bangladeshis, Desis, Indians -many Desis from the home country -other people from the South Asian diaspora and from the home countries... -An American -"you" -many people

The table shows that all three corpora include both identifiable and fuzzy external positions. The identification of the voices is, of course, not always straightforward. For example, in May Ooi's episode, the podcaster enacts a dialogue with "an English girl" that she met when she was a child, but Ooi doesn't give any details about who the girl really is. Yet, this categorisation is based on the fact that if the voice is referring to one person that the podcaster has tried to specify in one way or another, it is considered as identifiable. In other words, identifiable voices refer to a person who can potentially be reached and identified, such as Nik's *mum* and *a taxi driver*, Ooi's *Malaysian writer* and *English friends,* and Yesha's *anthropology teacher* and *Madonna*. These identifiable voices make the episodes more personal in nature, and can serve as authorities in the construction of identities (again the fact that one chooses an external position to support one's claims may not be arbitrary). On the other hand, non-identifiable voices, which have been identified in great numbers in the podcasts, tend to be more broad and nonspecific: personal pronouns (*you*), representatives of countries (*The English, South Asians*, so-called 'imagined communities'), generic words (*people, nobody, many people*) and impersonal markers such as the generic "you" (Ooi and Yesha) and the use of the passive voice (Nik: "What I'm told..."). A selection of the external positions presented in the table will be used for the analysis which follows.

Having now identified positions used in the podcasts, we will examine three principal roles that the external positions play in the speakers' discourse: imposing identities, contributing to the speaker's discourse of becoming and to the construction of in-between identities.

3.2. Imposing Identities

In all three corpora, we identified a way in which the external positions impose identities on the speakers. All three podcasters had different emotional reactions concerning these imposed identities, generally involving either confusion, acceptance or rejection.

3.2.1. Confusion and Multiplicity

In the first excerpt, the imposed identities that Nik presents emerge from his identification based on different accents that he attributes to himself. As previously stated, Nik is binational (Brazil-England), has moved around a lot within Britain and has been living in France for ten years. After defining himself as an *outsider*, Nik lists a series of external positions that contribute to this state:

> I always feel a bit of an outsider because for instance *Scotland people would say* I was English because they heard my accent and it sounded English to them it wasn't definitely Scottish in any case and euh when I was in S... in England I was even more surprised when *people said to me* I had a Scottish accent so in way the accent made me feel different and when I am in France I speak French and *people say* I have an accent I don't necessarily sound like an English person speaking French *that's what I am told* but *they can tell* I am not French you know *they say* you have got an accent when you speak so that makes me feel different again

In this excerpt, we can identify various kinds of fuzzy external positions, which have an impact on the description of imposed identities. These positions, or voices, are expressed in the form of indirect represented discourse and are accompanied by various tenses which give them a generic tone: the conditional in *Scotland people would say I was English*; and the present in *people say I have an accent* (i.e., French people). In three cases, the external position *people* refers to imagined national groups (i.e., places where Nik has lived): Scotland, England and France.

Generally speaking, an accent can be perceived differently by people who share the same language (native and non-native speakers), depending on the context and the "images" or "masks" that interlocutors put forward or impose on each other. Moreover, as N. Pepin (2007) has demonstrated, accents can serve as discursive ploys in interaction. In his book on French migrants in Switzerland, he has shown how French migrants *identify* through alternative use of Swiss and French accents. The reason why accents can be interpreted as imposed identities in the podcast is that they have an influence on Nik's emotions: "in England I was even more surprised when people said to me I had a Scottish accent so in way the accent made me feel different". Nik's feelings show that he doesn't really agree with the definitions of his accents (cf. the use of "surprised", "different", "outsider"), which makes him feel like a stranger to himself. The imposed nature of these identities comes to the surface in Nik's discourse through yet another device: the passive form in a different external voice, *that's what I am told*. This passive form of an external position is a very strong form of imposed identity because it can be said to exclude the speaker's responsibility and action in deciding upon who s/he is.

Two other excerpts show the strength of Nik's feelings when people associate him with Frenchness and doubt his Britishness. In order to demonstrate this imposed identity, Nik introduces two identifiable voices in his discourse, *a taxi driver* (accompanied by *or something*) and *the guys who picked me up at the airport* (when he went to a wedding in England a year prior to the recording):

> what really shock me is about a year ago I went back to the UK and I think it was *a taxi driver* or something like *they said to me* you know you've got... where you from? And I said well I am from the UK but I am living in France and they said I heard... well because I heard your French accent and I thought you are French

> and then it happened again when I went back to Coventry just recently for the stag party, *the guys who picked me up at the airport they also said* you know they thought I was French because of my accent so hum it's kind of weird because it makes me feel as if a www it's a link with the UK that has been cut off I don't know maybe it's just in my head

With these two voices, the podcaster is defined by blending direct and indirect represented speeches of external and internal positions, whose contents correspond precisely to what the listener who triggered this episode wrote. In the narrative on the taxi driver (note the fuzziness in "it was a taxi driver or something"), Nik enacts a dialogue he had with this person. In representing the dialogue, Nik self-repairs when he introduces the first voice of the taxi driver: "you know you've got... where are you from?". The self-repair could indicate that Nik wishes to insist once again on the fact that he is from the UK and that he lives in France, instead of admitting and/or reintroducing the idea straight away that he has a French accent in English. The second excerpt contains confusion and negative feelings: Nik appears to be shocked and asserts, in a very emotional way, that "it's a link with the UK that has been cut off". In other words, external positions, which emphasise his non-Britishness, deprive him of his solid declared "identity".

3.2.2. Imposed Identities Accepted

In Yang May Ooi's podcast, as many as three voices are inserted, each serving to impose identities: two generic and unidentifiable voices (*the English* in general and *Malaysians who are listening to the podcast*) and one identifiable voice (her English friends when they were visiting Malaysia together with her). These voices are linked to both her appearance (she looks 'Asian') and her accent (she sounds "English").

In the first unidentifiable position, Ooi explains how English people only see her as Chinese when they first meet her. She says:

> when I am with the English and when I am talking to them *they may think* when they first see me *oh she looks different she is Chinese* but then when I start talking they actually seem to forget what I look like and they start to respond to me as if I am just you know who I am and that's the important thing (…)

The podcaster seems to be aware of this imposed identity and includes a direct represented speech of the imagined "English" to express what they must be thinking when they see her ("oh she looks different she is Chinese"). If we refer back to the comment that triggered this episode, it is easy to see that the same argument was found in the Malaysian writer's discourse (cf. the "Chinese" face in her comment). So in a way, Ooi is telling the Malaysian writer that even English people get confused by her. Eventually, Ooi explains that, thanks to her voice (she calls it her *English voice*), this imposed identity (that of being non-English) is reviewed by the

English. She explains the change of attitude by saying "they start to respond to me as if I am just you know who I am" while she asserts at the end of the episode that she doesn't actually know who she is and that she has a split personality. This is the first example of a series of contradictions in the podcasts.

While the English external voice positioned her as Chinese, her native in-group's voice is also included in the episode, imposing an identity on her: that of a non-Malaysian speaker of English. At one point, she comments on her Malaysian English, as she has been mimicking this type of English several times in the episode, to show her Malaysian side (she says she uses this kind of English with her parents and friends back in Malaysia). She addresses Malaysians who are listening to the episode and says:

> as you have heard I have done the Malaysian accent earlier on in this podcast and I suppose maybe that the Malaysians who are listening to this podcast would say [takes on a Malaysian accent] *that's not a real Malaysian accent* in my ear it sounds more Malaysian than English and of course it is not a Malaysian accent of someone who's lived in Malaysia all this time but of course it is a Malaysian accent of someone who's lived in England who remembers back to the time I lived in Malaysia.

In this excerpt, Ooi is dialoguing with her "peers" and defending herself against potential criticisms of her Malay-English accent. Once again, she imagines an utterance that she forces into other people's minds: "that's not a real Malaysian accent" and responds to this by dissociating, through the use of *someone* (internal positions): "it is a Malaysian accent of someone who's lived in England who remembers back to the time I lived in Malaysia". Is the criticism something that she has heard before? Is she reusing an external voice from her past experience that questioned her identity?

Finally, May Ooi resorts to the direct and identifiable voice of some her English friends' during a joint trip to Malaysia. She explains:

> they told me afterwards when someone asked *where is Yang-May?* and one of them said *oh she is outside being Malaysian* and I have always remembered that because being Malaysian to me meant being out there you know having a good time having a laugh making a lot of noise which when I am in my English persona perhaps I don't make that much noise perhaps I am quieter perhaps I would be sitting with my English friends having a chat.

In this excerpt, she firstly enacts a dialogue between external positions (cf. "someone asked" and "one of them said"). This dialogue allows her to introduce an interpretation and a discussion on what her Malaysian and English 'personas' are. The difference between this last imposed identity ("she is being Malaysian") and the first two is that Ooi questions the first two (they question who she is or who she thinks she is) while she seems to accept her English friends' identification.

3.2.3. Calling Imposed Identities into Question and Rejecting Imposed Identities

The third podcaster, Yesha, shares the same duplicity in questioning her "in-betweenness" and presents many voices in the podcast, which can be seen as constructing imposed identities. In what follows, we shall analyse two voices that are potentially identifiable and refer to one specific person. These voices are *a little John* or *maybe Tony* and *my anthropology professor* and they emerge in the second diary entry that she reads. Unlike the excerpts supra, a sense of unfairness and impossibility to defend oneself against the way external positions impose an identity on the podcaster can be felt. The first example dates back to her childhood and school years and deals with religious beliefs:

> the teacher tells everyone: "let's take a minute to pray, I want everyone to close their eyes and pray the God"... I shut my eyes tight, I know about prayer... at my Saturday school I learn the Gita, I learn about the Vedantic philosophy and Swami Vivekananda's ideals about character building education, so I shut them tight and pray to the God that I haven't believed in so strongly since... and then the minute is over and *little John, or maybe it's Tony* pipes up: "Mrs. Zoenso, why did Yesha close her eyes, she doesn't believe in God, she's Indian!"... I don't remember Mrs. Zoenso having a good answer to him, I don't think she said anything.

The end of this extract is based on an enacted conversation between two external positions which contribute to imposing an identity on Yesha. The podcaster gives the impression that she had a very passive role in this conversation as she recounts the dialogue as a mere "witness". The last sentence of the excerpt, which goes back to the *hic et nunc* of the podcast, serves as a conclusion and shows that Yesha was surprised at her teacher's reaction as she wasn't capable of responding to the identity imposed to her as an "Indian who cannot pray God".

In the second excerpt, Yesha recalls the time when she was older and becoming more aware of her in-between identity. The represented conversation enacted below is based on a discussion between Yesha and her anthropology professor about her cultural conscience:

> (...) for the first time I become aware that I'm an American as well as an Indian, until now... I truly have thought of myself as been on the outside, an Indian in America, but *my anthropology professor* asks me to see him after I write a paper discussing my culture: "this is a good paper, some good insights, but why do you call yourself Indian, you're American, you grew up here", "I thought you had to be white or black to be an American..?", "no, you're American", "but I'm not, I was born there in India", "Yesha, You've lived in this country since you were one, and now you're eighteen... you're American, like it or not", "then why don't I feel like it?", I don't think I like it, I'm bewildered... but slowly I accept it that maybe, perhaps, I'm American too... a little...

This is a very good example of how other people can influence someone's identity construction. Yesha's professor is insisting that she is American because she has grown up in the US, while Yesha doesn't see herself as an American because she thought that "you had to be white or black to be an American". In other words, though Yesha is solidifying *Americaness* by limiting its representatives to black or white people, she does not accept her professor's imposing voice by insisting on her being born in India ("but I'm not, I was born there in India"). Yesha's use of the represented speech of the professor "you're American, like it or not" is presented in a very peremptory way, leaving her without the choice of reflecting on her identity but evoking nonetheless strong feelings in her: "then why don't I feel like it?", I don't think I like it, I'm bewildered... but slowly I accept it that maybe, perhaps, I'm American too... a little". When she returns to the person that she is at the time of the recording, these feelings lead her to draw the conclusion that she has changed her mind and accepted that she is also "a little" American.

As we saw before, the major impact of imposed identity on the podcasters is that either they accept these identity constructions from the 'outside' or they deny, criticize or respond to them through negative feelings. In the next section, we will examine the discourses of becoming which refer to the ways podcasters narrate their identity formation.

3.3. Discourses of Becoming

In all three podcasts, the speakers describe how they have become who they are in their own ways. Discourses of becoming are very important in order to self-construct, given that, according to the post-modern definition of identity, identity is storied and narrated.

In Nik's podcast, he describes who he is/who he has become through narrating his "mobile" past. He introduces the positions of his parents, their backgrounds, his Britishness and "the problem" of moving around the United Kingdom during his childhood to provide arguments for his in-betweenness, as well as the fact that he speaks English in a French accent. Self-quotations (*as I said; I'd always assumed*), which reintroduce previous speech presented in the episode, allow him to insert these positions in his discourse:

> I have always been well *as I said* my mum's Brazilian and my dad's English and I grew up in the UK so up until now *I'd always assumed* that I had a British accent and I think it probably I definitely had one and then euh the problem was when I was growing up well it is not really a problem but what happened was when I was growing up my parents moved every four years or so and they moved like to different regions of the United Kingdom

Nik reminds the listener (as he had done several times before in the episode) that his mother is Brazilian and his father is English and that he grew up in the UK. Though these are omnipresent pieces of information (in the episode, in previous episodes, on his weblog...), the podcaster seems to be reintroducing these elements to provide further evidence and authority to his accent being British (despite demonstrating to himself indirectly that there is no such thing as a British accent, as he gives a list of accents such as Scottish, Cambridgean, Welsh... later on in the episode). His becoming "British" through recounting his past seems to help him to support his claim to a British identity.

In Yang May Ooi's episode, the Malaysian writer's comment (that she reads at the beginning of the episode) was the starting point for questioning her own identities. The beginning of the episode introduces various narratives on how Ooi managed to become "English" or how she acquired, what she refers to as an "English voice". Her answer to the writer's comment, which simulates a dialogue, is as follows:

> Yes, Lydia I have been living in this country for ages but I didn't always speak like this I suppose because I have been surrounded by English voices I was at school here at university my friends were generally English at work I speak in English, I write in English so I guess it's quite natural I sound English

Ooi's explanation shows that she considers that the presence of external positions such as "English voices" and "friends" has allowed her to become a "copy" of the *English* and speak like a native. In a way, this contributes to the phenomenon of auto-solidification that Ooi seems to be using quite a lot in the episode. Given the diversity of accents, lexicons and errors which characterise native speakers of English in England, one can question the fact that Ooi is giving the impression that there is only one type of English (this is similar to what Nik does in his episode). She in fact develops this limited vision of Englishness throughout the episode. So her discourse of becoming appears as a mere transition from one identity (that of a Malaysian speaker of English) to another (Ooi "sounding English"). Later on, she asserts that she can actually juggle with both.

In the rest of the narratives on how she learnt to speak English like an "English" person, Ooi explains her motivations for wanting to sound English. She introduces a story from her childhood from when she came to England:

There was one time I was telling someone about my school about my work and I was good at English but I wasn't good at *saits* and she said:
– [imitating interlocutor's English accent] *you're not good at saits?*
– [taking on her Malaysian accent] *You know I not good at saits-la*
– and she said
– *what saits? I don't know that subject*
– *you know saits like maths, chemistry, and biology and things like that-la*
– *Oh* she said *science*
– *ja-la science.*
You know it's been a long time since that conversation and I remember it I remember exactly where I was I remember what the girl looked like because it was very traumatic for me I felt so embarrassed I felt that I was having to repeat myself I felt like an idiot that's pretty hard

This long narrative includes a represented dialogue between her and an English classmate, which shows how "foreign" she was and sounded in that situation. The external position (that of the English girl) leads to Ooi introducing one of her internal positions for the first time: her Malaysian voice from the past (which will come back later on in the episode but within her grown-up voice). The introduction of both positions allows Ooi to draw conclusions ("it was very traumatic") and justify why she sounds English.

In the third podcast, Yesha constructs her discourse of becoming at the beginning of the podcast during the introduction to the diary entries. Yesha's discourse of becoming includes all the potential "masks" that she has and that she associates with her identity. She starts by grouping the external positions that represent nationalities and ethnic groups in her home country:

> I'm Indian, originally from India and... *I grew up calling myself* Indian... however, in the last few years *I felt myself many times substituting* the word Desi where *I used to use* the word Indian... not in all cases, of course, *if I'm just talking about* my family's culture, or traditions specific to us, *I may even get more specific and use the word Gudrati...* but I find that the word Indian can be very restricting, especially when *I'm trying to refer to* experiences that are shared by many, if not all *South Asians...*

In this excerpt, a series of self-quotations demonstrates how Yesha has adopted various words and phrases that she has used throughout the years to create and categorise her *self/-ves*: "I grew up calling myself" + Indian, "I felt myself substituting the word" + Desi, "I may even get more specific" + Gudrati, "I'm trying to refer to" + South Asians. These positions are used to introduce a discourse of becoming across multiple spaces-times (when she grew up, in the last few years, India, South Asia...). Yet, this multi-referencing to times and relative localities is contradicted by other external positions in the rest of her podcast:

> one interesting thing I have noticed and heated discussion of the word Indian and Desi, is that Desi is in a diaspora, well, I guess Indian Desi is in a diaspora, really can't win when it comes to the word Indian because if we use the word Desi to describe ourselves, *many people* would take umbrage of that and say: "just say what you are, if you're Indian, say you're Indian"... however, if I do use the word Indian to describe myself, *many Desis from the home country would say*: "You're not Indian, you're American"... I guess I can't win...

In this example, Yesha uses two unidentifiable external positions (*many people* and *many Desis from the home country*) in order to describe the difficulty that she has faced and that she still faces, from various sides, in defining herself and using some of the words and phrases presented before. Actually, in reference to the previous section, these voices can also be seen as imposing identities on her ("If you're Indian, say you're Indian"; "You're not Indian, you're American"). Yesha's discussion is linked to the use of different terms, *Indian* and *Desi*, which includes different groups of people, different points of view and stakes, different (nested) places and localities.

3.4. "Whatever I am, Wherever I am, How does it Matter?" Concluding on one's Self/selves

In this section, we concentrate solely on the conclusions that the podcasters draw from the demonstration of their in-betweenness that they deliver in their podcasts. All three podcasters explicitly conclude that, in one way or another, they have an in-between identity. They also question the existence of clear boundaries between these identities. As such, at the very end of each podcast, the podcasters insert a macro-sequence/proposition (Adam 1985, 48-52), which is reminiscent of Labov's coda in his macro-model of narrative (1972, 365). Adam proposed calling this type of sequence 'evaluation' or 'the moral' (ibid.). We shall see how this model can be applied to all three podcasts and what indications they provide us with regarding identification.

The first podcaster, Nik, reflects on the definition of his identity through the accents that he attributes to himself or that are attributed to him. He introduces an unidentifiable external position *people* to draw a conclusion about who he is:

> so I am coming to the conclusion (...) I am coming to is that I probably
> have an indefinable mix of accents there is a little bit of Scottish for *people*
> who recognize that there is a little bit of English there is a bit of French and
> I know when I speak Portuguese when I speak French I have a Portuguese
> intonation from the way I speak Portuguese so maybe it's just a mish mash
> accent mish mash accent I don't know it's kind of confusing for me

As we can see at the end, Nik feels that he has *a mish mash accent* which means to him that people can recognize many influences of different hybrid accents in his speech (cf. the external position). Yet, the podcaster expresses his feelings and uncertainty towards this identity: "I don't know it's kind of confusing for me ". In a way, we can say that Nik tries to define his identity through otherness ("there is a little bit of Scottish for people who recognize that") but that he is not capable of defining his own identity. This is probably because he doesn't acknowledge his multiple in-betweenness and the fuzzy nature of identity, but tries to explain them instead.

The second podcaster, Young Mai Ooi, also has difficulties in defining herself in the last macro-sequence - though her discourse is less unstable in a way. Responding to her English friends' direct represented discourse "she is outside being Malaysian", and having talked about her Malaysianness and Englishness, she concludes that she has "a split personality":

(...) *she is outside being Malaysian* [English friends' speech] and I have always remembered that because being Malaysian to me meant being out there you know having a good time having a laugh making a lot of noise which when I am in my English persona perhaps I don't make that much noise perhaps I am quieter perhaps I would be sitting with my English friends having a chat so then that's why I think that I have a split personality I am English but also I am Malaysian-la which one is the real me? Very difficult to say

When one compares Nik's and Ooi's identity construction, Ooi solidifies herself to a greater degree and solely oscillates between two identities (cf. "split", i.e. Englishness and Malaysianness) and that is why she suggests that she has "a split personality". The difference between Ooi's and Nik's conclusions is that Ooi tries to form her own definition of her identity. As we can see, she *solidifies* Malaysianness and Englisness in her discourse. Being Malaysian to her means "having a good time" and "making a lot of noise", which is in contrasted with her English "persona": "perhaps I don't make that much noise perhaps I am quieter perhaps I would be sitting with my English friends having a chat". In spite of this tentative definition of her identity, in the end, Ooi admits the impossibility of a clear definition of identity: "which one is the real me? Very difficult to say". This is why Ooi's definition remains open. Though she tries, she admits that she cannot name *the real me*.

The third podcaster, Yesha, also defines her in-betweenness at the end of the episode. Like Ooi, Yesha's reflections on identity are based mostly on two solidified identities (Indianess and Americaness) in her diary entries. At the end of the podcast, Yesha draws this conclusion:

I do have reasons to be angry, I wish I had met different influences in my childhood, they shaped me through hurt for years, and yet, now it's different... they are just ghosts, I can choose to be angry or I can choose to get on with my life and laugh... I let go, I'm Indian from India, and American from America, either way, whatever I am, wherever I am, how does it matter?... why does it matter?

Though this excerpt doesn't contain any clear external voices, we suppose that her repetition of phrases such as "I'm Indian from India, and American from America" are pure confirmations of the external voices of e.g. the anthropology professor or Desis that she mentioned earlier, as these two identities need to be defined in contrast with other individuals. The major difference between Yesha and the two other podcasters is that she definitely leaves it completely open and questions the use in giving a delimited definition: "either way, whatever I am, wherever I am, how does it matter?... why does it matter?". Yesha's identity definition can be seen as the archetype of the postmodern liquid identity: it is a process which is never complete and ever changing.

Conclusion

This chapter has been one of the first attempts to examine the construction of identities within the context of egocasting (i.e. broadcasting about one's *self*) and intercultural in-betweenness through dialogism. Based on a linguistic dialogic and multivoiced approach to identification, we have demonstrated that external voices (one's own and those of others') contribute to constructing selves and questioning them. Though our corpora were very similar in their formats (the questioning of identification was triggered by an *other,* many voices and positions were introduced to question, argue for and bring to light identities, a coda admitting to in-betweenness concluded each podcast...), there were differences in the ways the podcasters accepted the identities that were put forward in the episodes. May Ooi is probably the only one who used external positions to construct who she thinks she is (both Malay and English) without rejecting the ways these external positions perceived her duality. On the other hand, Nik didn't really contradict the various voices that he introduced to describe his feeling of "foreignness" with regard to his "Britishness" but expressed his confusion at them. Finally, Yesha was more skeptical about (and sometimes rejected clearly) what external positions said about her and concluded that choosing one's identity when in in-betweenness is but useless.

As any other social experiences, podcasts are based on dialogicality and multivoicedness. Of course, these phenomena are not just found in technologies of the self such as podcasting. Yet, this act of computer-mediated communication does undoubtedly contribute to the contemporary multiplication of voices in the definition of identities (anyone in the world can download, listen and react to such podcasts, Hermans 2004, 304) and the ability to *"create ourselves as a work of art"* (Foucault 1997, 262). Consequently, as part of a self-construction, egocasting in-betweenness can itself be a matter of shutting out the unease and confusion felt after the speaker realises how others want to define and pigeonhole him/her.

Through their easy availability, podcasts allow anyone's voice to become part of the attire of the contemporary nomad individual (Abbas 2008) as they can be listened to by potentially anyone, anywhere (Abbas speaks of the invisible "technological tapestry" that is around us, cf. Wifi technology) and at any time. *Otherness* has thus become readily available "on request", can be easily contacted (by e-mail or voice-mail left on weblogs that accompany podcasts) and is therefore potentially omnipresent (one can listen to podcasts while walking down the street, be moved by them and self-reflect, something which was impossible two decades ago). In a way, while a mere radio producer would have never had the opportunity to be stimulated by just about any listener on the planet, now podcasters cannot but be influenced by what other people have to say about their shows – across multiple spaces and times (in fact, some podcasters often spend time at the beginning of their programme reviewing and answering comments received from listeners worldwide on their website). This makes podcasts the space of dialogicality *par excellence,* a form of technology that we could sum up as *a collage of voices.*

Bibliography

Abbas, Y. (2008) Environnements néonomades, système écologique? In Dervin, F. & A. Ljalikova (eds.). *Regards sur les mondes hypermobiles : mythes et réalités.* Paris : L'Harmattan. 19-36.

Abdallah-Pretceille, M. (1986) *Vers une pédagogie interculturelle.* Paris : Anthropos.

Allard, L. (2005) Express yourself 2.0! Blogs, podcasts, fansubbing, mashups... : de quelques agrégats technoculturels à l'âge de l'expressivisme généralisé. Freescape: Biblio du libre. http://www.freescape.eu.org/biblio/article.php3?id_article=233

Bakhtin, M. (1981) *The dialogic imagination: Four essays by M.M. Bakhtin.* Austin: University of Texas Press.

Bamberg, M. (2004a) "Narrative discourse and identities". In Meister, J.C., Kindt, T., Schernus, W. and Stein, M. (eds.). *Narratology beyond literary criticism.* Berlin; New York : Walter de Gruyter: 213-237.

Bauman, Z. (2001) *Liquid modernity.* Cambridge: Polity.

—. (2004) *Identity.* London: Polity.

Benwell, B. and Stokoe, E. (2006) *Discourse and identity.* Edinburgh: EUP.

Bhatia, S. (2002) "Acculturation, Dialogical Voices and the Construction of the Diasporic Self". *Theory & Psychology* 12. 53-75.

Cullity, J. (2002) "The Global Desi: Cultural Nationalism on MTV India". *Journal of Communication Inquiry* 26. 408-425.

Dahl, Ø., Jensen, I. and Nynäs, P. (eds.) (2006) *Bridges of understanding. Perspectives on intercultural communication.* Oslo : Unipub.

Davies, B. and Harré, R. (1990) "Positioning : The discursive production of selves". *Journal for the Theory of Social Behaviour*. http://www.massey.ac.nz/~alock/position/position.htm. Last accessed April 17, 2006.

De Fina, A., Schiffrin, D. and Bamberg, M. (eds) (2006) *Discourse and identity*. Cambridge: Cambridge University Press.

Dendale, P. (1992) "La polyphonie comme notion épistémique". In De Mulder, W., Schuerewegen, F. and Tasmowski, L. (eds.). *Enonciation et parti pris. Actes du colloque de l'Université d'Anvers* (5, 6 & 7 Février 1990). Amsterdam/Atlanta: Rodopi. 105-120.

Dervin, F. (2007c) "Podcasting and intercultural imagination: Othering and self solidifying around tapas and siesta". *Culture, language and representation* 4. 67-91.

—. (2008) *Métamorphoses identitaires en contexte de mobilité*. Turku : Université de Turku.

Dervin, F. and Riikonen, T. (forth.). Itsen teknologiat: tutkimus identiteeteistä kulttuurienvälisissä podcasteissa. In Tanskanen, S.-K., Johansson, M. and Helasvuo, M.-L. (eds.). *KIELI VERKOSSA. Johdatus tietokonevälitteiseen vuorovaikutukseen*. Helsinki : WSOY.

Ewins, R. (2005) "Who are You? Weblogs and Academic Identity". *E-Learning*. Vol. 2 (1). 368-377.

Fleischman, S. and Yaguello, M. (1999). Discourse markers across languages? In Moder, C.L. et Martinovic-Zic, A. (eds). *Discourse accross Languages and Cultures*. Amsterdam: Benjamins. 129-147.

Foucault M. (1988) *Technologies of the self: A seminar with Michel Foucault*. Amherst: The University of Massachusetts Press. 16-49.

—. (1997) *Ethics, Subjectivity and Truth*. London: Allen Lane.

Goffman, E. (1978) "Response cries". *Language* 54 (4). 787-815.

Hall, S. "Who needs identity?" In Hall, S and du Gay, P. (eds.) (1996) *Questions of Cultural Identity*. London: Sage Publications. 1-17.

Hermans, H.J.M. (2001a) "The construction of a personal position repertoire: Method and practice". *Culture & Psychology* 7. 323-366.

—. (2001b) "The dialogical self: toward a theory of personal and cultural positioning". *Culture & Psychology* 7. 243-281.

—. (2004) "Introduction: the dialogical self in a global and digital age". *Identity* 4(4). 297-320.

Hermans, H.J.M. and Dimaggio, G. (2007) "Self, identity, and globalisation in times of uncertainty: A dialogical analysis". *Review of General Psychology* 11(1). 31-61, available at: http://www.dialogicalscience.com/Hermans%20&%20Dimaggio%20(2007).pdf

Herring, S. "Posting in a different voice: gender and ethics in computer-mediated communication". In Ess, C. (ed.) (1996) *Philosophical Perspectives in Computer-Mediated Communication*. Albany: State University of New York Press, Albany. 115-145.

Hevem, V.W. (2004) "Shreaded identity in cyberspace: weblogs & positioning in the dialogical self". *Identity* 4 (4). 321-335.

Huffaker, D. A. and Calvert, S. L. (2005) "Gender, identity, and language use in teenage blogs". *Journal of Computer-Mediated Communication* 10(2). Article 1.
http://jcmc.indiana.edu/vol10/issue2/huffaker.html

Johansson, M. (2000) *Décontextualisation du discours. Discours représenté dans l'interview politique médiatique*. Turun Yliopiston Julkaisuja/Annales Universitatis Turkuensis. Turku: Turun Yliopisto.

Joinson, A. N. "Internet behaviour and the design of virtual methods". In Hine, C. (ed.) (2005). *Virtual methods: Issues in social research on the Internet*. Oxford: Berg. 32-34.

Lifton, R. J. (1993) *The Protean Self: Human Resilience in an Age of Fragmentation*. Chicago: The University of Chicago press.

Maffesoli, M. (1997) *Du nomadisme - vagabondages initiatiques*. Paris: Livre de Poche.

Markova, I., Linell, P., Grossen, M. and Salazar Orvig, A. (2007) *Dialogue in Focus Groups: Exploring Socially Shared Knowledge*. London: Equinox Publishing.

Marnette, S. (2005) *Speech and Thought Presentation in French: Concepts and Strategies*. Philadelphia, PA, USA: John Benjamins Publishing Company.

Marnette, S. (2006) "Je vous dis que l'autocitation c'est du discours rapporté". *Travaux de linguistique* 52 (1). 25-40.

Maynard, S.K. (1996) "Multivoicedness in speech and throught representation: the case of self-quotation in Japanese". *Journal of pragmatics* 25. 207-226.

Mochet, M.-A. (1986) "Des citations dans l'entretien". *Cahiers du français des années 80* 2. 123-169.

Paveau, M.A. (2006) *Les Prédiscours*. Paris: Presses Universitaires de la Sorbonne Nouvelle.

—. (2007) Discours et cognition: les prédiscours entre cadres internes et environnement extérieur. *Corela*. Available online: http://edel.univ-poitiers.fr/corela.

Pavlenko, A. and Blackledge, A. (eds.) (2004) *Negotiation of identities in multilingual contexts*. Clevedon, UK: Multilingual Matters.

Rabatel, A. (2006) "Autocitations et autobiographie dans *Du sens*, de Renaud Camus". *Texte.* 39-40.

Rak, J. (2005) "The Digital Queer: Weblogs and Internet Identity". *Biography* 28 (1). 166-182.

Rellstab, D.H. (2007). "Staging gender online: gender plays in Swiss internet relay chats". *Discourse & Society* 11 (18). 765-787.

Rosenberg, S. "Multiplicity of selves". In Ashmore, R.D. and Jussim, L. (eds.) (1997) *Self and identity: Fundamental issues.* New York: Oxford University Press. 23-45.

Sarbin, T.R. (1997) "The Poetics of Identity". *Theory Psychology* 7 (1). 67-82.

Shotter, J. "Life inside dialogically constructed mentalities: Bakhtin's and Voloshnikov's account of our mental activities as out there between us". In J. Rowan and Cooper, M. (eds.) (1999). *The plural self.* London: Sage. 71-92.

Talamo, A. and Ligorio, B. (2001) "Strategic identities in cyberspace". *Cyberpsychology and Behavior* 4 (1). 109-122.

Taylor, Ch. (1989) *Sources of the self: the making of the modern identity.* Cambridge: Harvard University Press.

Thorne, S. L. (2003) "Artifacts and Cultures-of-Use in Intercultural Communication". *Language Learning & Technology* 7 (2). 38-67.

Turkle, S. (1995) *Life on the Screen: Identity in the Age of the Internet.* New York: Simon and Schuster.

Verine, B. "Dialogisme interdiscursif et interlocutif du discours rapporté : jeux sur les frontières à l'oral". In Bres, J., Haillet, P. P., Mellet, S., Nølke, H. et L. Rosier (éds.). (2005) *Dialogisme, polyphonie : approches linguistiques. Actes du colloque de Cerisy.* 2-9 septembre 2004. Bruxelles : Duculot. 187-201.

Watkins, M. (1986) *Invisible Guests: The Development of Imaginal Dialogue.* New York: Analytic Press.

IDENTITY GATHERING

CHAPTER SEVEN

COLLECT TO CONNECT IN THE MOBILE AGE

CATI VAUCELLE

Introduction

As children in our home country we collected everything that made us explore and understand the world and its habitants (Singer 1990): international stamps, rocks, samples of sand from every beach, pen pals from all around the world, or leaves from every tree. If we were on a family trip, we would compile a summary of the journey with cards, pictures, flyers and fragments of bottles. We played competitive games by trying to find the most unique rock on the beach and came up with rules that made the most sense for the rarest discovered shellfish. We cherished these gathered treasures that the family house protects for us, even after we left home. Living away from our homeland, we are separated from our past. Limited in what we can carry on, we need to leave behind our keepsakes, prompts to souvenirs and thoughts that ground us in our emotional memory. We are orphans of a country that we left for another one, cities that we explored but also abandoned (Kristeva 1994) while their souvenirs evade with time. We are a generation of nomads, neo-nomads (Abbas 2006), carrying the summary of our house on our back, making sacrifices in deciding what to keep and what to leave out. This results in a selection of memento directed by a mobile life. Robert Opie, collector of advertising and packaging, claims that as part of the collecting instinct, one has to be prepared to tolerate the physical space taken by the collected objects (Elsner and Cardinal 1997). Now that we become mobile, physical things must go. We cannot keep up with the collection of artifact souvenirs.

I am investigating this new breed of collectors that emerged with neo-nomadism. I observe the collection in its digital form that serves the purpose of connecting us to one another. I analyze the process through which one collects to connect in social networks. I introduce the impact of these new collecting habits on the self and present a striking characteristic of the modern collector, the tendency for narcissism while pretending to connect on social networks via gift giving.

1. The Digital Collection

Digital cameras are here for us to take overwhelming numbers of shots of the same location. The internet keeps our emails. Online services host our pictures and video fragments. Video games allow us to collect avatars, connect remotely with peers and construct our new identities in a virtual world. It seems that the digital is welcoming a new generation of collectors. The digital object is appropriated, collected, hacked, transformed, possessed and shared. Anyone can capture a memento with a cell phone, or multiple shots of the same scene that end up being accumulated on the computer hard disc.

Online tools, such as Flickr, precipitate the act of collection, inviting anyone to be a collector. Flickr users collect pictures, diligently select their favorites, organize them into groups, and share them. The audience navigates and searches for specific shots, comments and sometimes annotates directly on the photographs. Our digital collectors — or neo-collectors — save things for later, re-edit and re-stage collections to show their treasures to chosen audiences and decide whether or not to make them public. Collectors have to decide who to invite and who to leave out. Some collectors decide to never show their collection to anybody. In the physical collection, the collector saves one object from the whole with an attempt of classifying it and naming it. In the digital world of objects, the objects appear to be accumulated while additionally they can be thematically organized. Our collections take shape by identification and categorization, while we look for similarities and nuances between objects. The collection begins at the moment of discrimination (Levy et al. 2006) and the digital collection starts when people select their digital media, edit and beautify them, organize them into specific groups and present them as part of thematic "sets".

2. The Physical Collection Expanded via Digital Means

The digital realm can also directly participate in the physical collection. Online trading systems, such as Ebay, are designed to invite collectors to share, sell, and exchange their collected material. What can be found, now that Ebay has been available for over 10 years, is that people collect almost anything. Social networks also call for the collector instinct by reinforcing the need to share contextual information as part of a "user profile": people collect friends, pictures, movies, songs, links and blogs to present themselves. While Del.ici.ous offers the abilities to collect links, StumbleUpon reinforces the idea of "dénicheur" — a term from French art in the 20's — the one that hunts. Here the *dénicheur* hunts for digital links, links that will become popular as the World Wide Web (WWW) grows. For the digital link "accumulator", systems are designed to bridge very different content and allow an automated organization of the gathered material. In the blogosphere, by specializing and discriminating, the blogger collects information and curates media geared towards a specific topic. As much as a curator for a museum is a collector of artifacts, a blogger represents a new generation of curators by collecting and ultimately exchanging information.

Both as children and adults we invest in the evocative qualities of the display for the collection (Putnam 2001). From the stamp book, to carefully designed velvet boxes for rocks, we present each piece as if it were in a museum. The digital realm has not explored this dimension yet: organization and labeling both take place on a very simple online page. The experience of digitally capturing the everyday and making sense of it through the physical act of collection could be combined. The digital could inform the physical. The physical could ground us deeper in our surroundings, and they both could exist independently from one another (Vaucelle 2008).

The key to bind the physical act of collection and the digital opportunity of representation is metadata. Imagine a scenario where the object discovered grows references beyond the thing held, and the thing seen. The digital world can tie to an infinite number of features of the object, only limited by the technologies used to analyze and link the data. However, even simple features gain new meaning through tagging the collected object by investigating metadata such as location, temperature, personal labeling on gathered objects. This investigation would challenge the exclusivity of digital and physical opportunities of interaction, and provide an experience where the physical process of collection is completely married to contextualization via digital means.

The world is being slowly overlaid with and in turn transformed by a virtual one, conveniently allowing us to keep going while being able to look back onto our digital collections. We bring our memories online: we scan pictures from the past to be "saved" and also shared, we digitize music, movies, books and we are working on ways that we can integrate more of our natural senses within this space. We make sure every existing physical object has its existing phantom online. It is a transition state as if we knew that our physical world was about to end, we feel we will never get it back (or get back to it) again. As Roland Barthes put it, "the Photograph mechanically repeats what could never be repeated existentially" (Barthes 1981). The online digital space does something more: it makes sure this existential repetition is being shared with everybody. Nobody can be forgotten nor can we forget: everybody is connected through thematic collections of data organized by locations, genre, or even a type of friendship connection. One can easily construct a new self (Turkle 1995), idealized through the careful selection of representative images, using descriptive tastes and links for personality reinvention, manipulating social network connections to pretend to belong to a chosen group. Sharing photographs ensures an identity validation and/or reinvention through the co-observations of carefully selected images. It is as if users start the collection in the physical world for the purpose of the digital collection, grabbing objects, landscapes, colors, and expressions to later digitally capture them. The digital collected object can also exclusively exist in the digital world, e.g. Facebook's popular digital gifts.

3. The Impact of these New Collecting Habits on the Self

3.1. The Narcissist

Observing how users digitally collect and connect, a trend seems to occur within modern collectors. In this back and forth between idealized and controlled image reflected on online tools, the self is never challenged. It is less about others and objects than it is about a constructed self. The modern collector collects herself to a point that glorifies her alter ego and makes sure this ego is never threatened. This narcissist plays with a myriad of images to admire herself and contrasts her appearance through imagery in different scenes, different contexts, surrounded by different persons. Her online friends exist exclusively to witness her existence.

On Facebook, contests are here to reinforce the idea that the narcissist receives a devotional attention. Contests take the form of a comparison between friends. Online friends are invited to express the qualities of a person, and the narcissist takes part in the contests that can channel the unconditional love of her admirers. The narcissist will look at her online profile to accentuate her self-reflected, self-promoted image, including descriptive characteristics within a personal profile, e.g. the books currently being read, along with her "exceptional" movie and/or music tastes. The narcissist selects her friends, similarly to how a collector discriminates between objects, albeit to assure a validity context for her identity reinvention. For a narcissist, a friend list is exclusively composed of admirers, the ones who will never threaten her. The narcissist will not be engaged in online role playing games, because being someone else by projecting herself onto someone else's life is devoid of interest for a narcissist.

Instant communication messaging systems are her ultimate means of communication. Even though all modern players use instant messaging, the narcissist particularly benefits from such a system because she does not need to develop, be attached, or confronted by a relationship. With instant messaging, she can drop out of any conversation without explanation and avoid any confrontation; she can pretend to be busy or "idle", or she can jump in to receive any required self-support. The super image of the narcissist is maintained. The digital realm works as a portable mirror whose feedback can be used to exclusively enhance the prodigal narcissist. In the digital realm, her represented self is entirely under her control.

3.2. Gift Giving

While these new collecting habits call for the narcissist in us, they also reflect our instinct to collect. In the sensibility of the collector, Charles Randall Dean explains that collecting might even predate people. He shares the following story of a dog he met who is a collector:

> I was on the beach recently and saw a woman walking with her Scottie dog and he had a rock in his mouth. And I said, "That's so nice that your dog is bringing a rock back from the beach for you". She said, "oh, this is not for us. This dog collects rocks". And she said he would spend fifteen of twenty minutes on the beach looking around for a rock that resembled the ones he already had, which were roughly hamburger shaped, and put them under the bed. (Randall 2006, 86)

Our pets collect rocks on the beach while we collect bits of flowers and thumbnails of friends on our computer. It seems that we all collect by instinct, but that we also use the act of collecting to connect to others. In the digital world, online users send "virtual" gifts to one another, motivated by opening the availability of a new series of digital gifts in return. The digital gifts can be growing flowers, animals or more recently any growing "things". These digital gifts are collected somewhat in the spirit of how postcards, sent by family members and friends, used to be collected. Facebook application developers keep producing various digital gifts, means to enhance a profile, personalized photo and music albums, aggregations of tastes and personality contests. The collected digital-gifts imply reciprocity, a reciprocal exchange in which the object is tied to the giver (Mauss 1990). This relationship is enhanced with tools that directly link to the giver.

In the role-playing realm and in massive multiplayer games such as World of Warcraft, the ability to gather, collect and equip avatars with their virtual objects contributes to the game addiction. Players spend hours not only to try to upgrade their avatar's gear to the highest rank, but to equip them with all of the coolest pets that the game has to offer or all of the tabards that can be encountered within the game. The player who possesses the rarest riding mount with which to equip her virtual character is acclaimed. In massive online role playing games, another dimension accompanies the progression within the game, the one of collecting a series of elements, serial gathering facilitated through quest completion and exchanges with other players, e.g. to build a specific outfit, a player needs to exchange rare items with players and depend on others to finally possess the item. Through these virtual exchanges rise connections between players, connections that might affect the player's everyday life, with the feeling of having "friends".

It seems that our attachment to physical objects is being projected into this hybrid space. It is as if the new generation instinctively uses the digital collection to catalyze virtual connections. Collecting and connecting go hand-in-hand in social networks and eventually influence the everyday interactions of users. I have explored how gift giving is an inherent part of being a collector today. I will now investigate its language.

3.3. The Form and Language of the Digital Collection

3.3.1. Communication Cues

Non-verbal communication cues might differ among cultures and might have changed with digital communication. Forty years ago, the distance between individuals drastically affected the dynamics of space interaction (Hall 1973). Now that we travel by plane and reach destinations further away from our natal home, we are more sensitive to the dynamics of non-verbal communication and the dynamics of space interaction might have changed. We absorb most of these social interactions in our everyday routines. One of the virtues of the virtual space is to not interact through body language, as if we intrinsically avoid miscommunication and connect with persons we might not be able to connect to without confrontation and misunderstanding in the physical realm. We are now connected instantly to the other side of the planet and the myth of teletransportation is virtually achieved.

3.3.2. Connection

The virtual world allows us to be perpetually connected to one another, connected but out of touch. While cell phones inspire us to be contacted at any point in time, the online realm forces us to never disappear. Engines such as Google can sentence us to an electronic death. In that case, we cease to exist online and we cease to be found. This type of digital extreme measure has implications both in the physical world – we cannot easily be contacted and found – and the virtual world – we disappear digitally. We can now get jobs in rich countries, advertise small companies, and develop a sense of omniscience through the ever growing information on the WWW. With the WWW, people who are less likely to meet can finally meet. Children with atypical interests can finally find other children with the same hobbies. The digital space might become the land for the discovery of other cultures. People meet others from different countries via social networks. It is the ultimate place for meeting habitants from unknown places, cultures and perspectives.

3.3.3. Perspective Taking

It is rather banal to say that with the internet we can be more connected. What is interesting is how the styles of our connections change. Our collection extends ourselves by discovering the world and its particularities. Stamps are a good example of how a child discovers places through the lens of a stamp she later shares with peers. Our digital collection might equally allow us to challenge our point of views, interacting and sharing collections with a much wider audience. The ability to take perspectives is a complex skill that does not necessarily mean putting oneself in someone else' shoes. This following quote illustrates this point; not only we cannot know what someone else feels, but we also cannot know that someone cannot know about someone else's life.

One day Soshi was walking on the bank of a river with a friend. "How delightfully the fishes are enjoying themselves in the water", exclaimed Soshi. His friend spoke to him thus, "You are not a fish, how do you know that the fishes are enjoying themselves?" "You are not myself," returned Sohsi, "how do you know that I do not know that the fishes are enjoying themselves? (Okakura 1906, 66)

Trying to understand someone's life results in a process, an iterative back and forth between discovering, trying to understand, being challenged and reflecting on someone else's life, perhaps never understanding it correctly, but that is not the point. What matters is the process that brings people in opening themselves to new perspectives.

The digital space can be perceived as a space where one can lose track of reality, but it can also be used to sharpen perceptive skills by challenging new ideas, visions and ways of thinking. By connecting to someone else, one can relate and create bonds. By creating links, one can project onto someone else's life and later empathize. By communicating with habitants from all over the world, one can perceive things differently. Navigating on the Internet, discussing role-playing platforms, managing guilds and groups of peers requires a "mindful" state. This mindful state is exposed by being opened to novelty, being alert to distinction, being sensitive to different contexts and being aware of multiple perspectives. The widespread failure to recognize the insights that can be found in all different perspectives may itself constitute a disability. Thus, being confronted to individuals in a dynamic of communication that becomes unpredictable, such as through the WWW, might teach children to adapt themselves to new situations rather than being trapped in their conditional learning. At the heart of many theories of intelligence is a belief that it is possible to identify an optimum fit between the individual and his/her environment. Even navigating through the internet requires an education to *New Technologies*. It is not a matter of fitting ourselves to an external norm; rather it is a process by which we give form, meaning and value to the world (Langer 1998).

3.4. The Implications of a Digital Body

3.4.1. From the Digital Collection to the "Digital" Body

The digital offers a variety of tools and algorithms that impact remembrance and facilitates organization of media. The digital now offers terabytes of data storage capacity carrying for us unlimited digital collections. It acts a bit in the way the family house does for us: we know, may it be illusionary, that it will always be there for us, wherever we go and whenever we want.

We are able to capture the life of a person, through pictures, video, speech recordings and her interconnections with others. The Human

Speechome Project from the MIT Media Laboratory analyzes the language development of a single child, by recording, storing, visualizing, and analyzing communication and behavior patterns in several hundred thousand hours of home video and speech recordings. The goal of Lifelogging is to record and archive all information in one's life: text, visual data, audio, media activity. It can even collect bio information from sensors that one wears. Our digital body motivates us in exercising. For example avatars and weight-loss calculators on virtual models encourages us to run.[1]

Soon we will be able to have a digital copy of oneself, a copy that will coexist online starting from birth and that will be able to perpetuate its existence after death. This copy will evolve independently from us, based on our original complexities, and will interact with other digital selves.

3.4.2. Things are Getting Lost with Dematerialization

While expanding our experience, some things get lost along the path to de-materialization. We connect to our world using our senses. Every one of our senses is a knowledge shopper that grounds us in our surroundings (Ackerman 1990): with touch, one feels the texture of life, with hearing one perceives even the subtlest murmurs of our existence, with vision one clarifies their instincts. But human senses are not only about perception. We use gesture to apprehend, comprehend and communicate. We speak to ultimately translate and exchange with others. We visualize, record, and playback events using our memory to reflect on our history and to be immersed in experience. We as children and adults are engaged in everyday pretense and symbolic play. We embed and later withdraw from the world, using imagination to project ourselves into situations (Singer 1990). Our mental constructs are necessary to reach a deeper understanding of our relationship with our environment (Ackermann 2004). With the computer, the relationship between distance and proximity, direct communication, corporeal versus indirect and mediation is transformed (Gauthier and Moukalou 2007).

While fifty years ago children progressively learned how to build toys under their grandfather's supervision, now they think they can be champions in Karate without moving a finger. While in the twentieth century kids were gathering outside, creating groups and risking their identity by confronting others, now they can stay home while contacting

[1] http://www.fpgamerunner.com/index.php and http://myvirtualmodel.com/cs. Last Accessed July 30, 2009.

the entire planet. As much as people cannot grow without interpersonal connection, without separation they cannot relate (Ackermann 2004). As Kegan said, cognitive growth emerges as a result of people's repeated attempts to solve the unsolvable tension between getting embedded and emerging from embedded-ness (Kegan 1982). "Dwelling in" and "stepping back" are equally important to get the cognitive dance going (Ackermann 2004). The measure of the cause and effect of each gesture that goes through an iterative process by gathering in locations and spaces is reduced now that children communicate and play in virtual chat rooms.

This virtual world that we trust, and on which we spend half of our day, does not connect to all of our senses: at best, the visual and auditory senses are triggered. The entire body package is not being invested. It is as if we privilege a communication in which the body is absent. While our skin stands between us and the world, our hands feels intuitively and precisely what it touches and grounds us deeper in where we stand (Ackerman 1990). The virtual disconnects us from our physical existence. Joysticks designed to vibrate, when one bumps into a virtual car, are ironic. It is as if this video game controller says "Remember! You had a body! Let me show you how it feels!" and everybody loves it. We are in a transition stage where we are too afraid to invest in our limited physical life and in which the virtual space makes things so much easier: no limitation of space and time, no reality check, no identity threat — we can be who we want to be without actually being the one we want to be.

3.4.3. Our Powerful Human Machine!

Technology brought us a means to organize ourselves, to schedule our time, and to "synchronize" ourselves with one another. However, humans are intrinsically linked to the rhythm of life, not to a planned calendar. People are tied together and yet isolated by hidden threads of rhythm and walls of time (Hall 1983). Time is treated as a language, organizer, and message system revealing people's feelings about each other and reflecting differences between cultures. Through repetition, learning, depth of understanding and rhythm occur and affect our entire being. Synchrony in life seems strangely related to rhythm in music. The pattern of our movements can translate into a beat. Without this rhythm, we are not synchronized and we lose our contact with life. When humans interact in the virtual space for a long period of time, they might become unsynchronized. It seems that the digital potential of remembering, of allowing us to communicate with the entire planet, and of being always connected, found and synchronized, seems to rely too much on computation and not significantly on human's potential. Why doesn't the digital space allow us to make use of our human possibilities rather than replacing our incredible memory with more powerful hard disk space and clever task management software, replacing our subtle intuition and sense of deduction with automatic pattern analysis and behavior prediction? It seems that the virtual world makes us dream that we are heroes by enhancing all of our senses, senses that we could exploit in physical reality. In role playing games we are equipped with sonic hearing, super vision, abnormal strength, and ultra sensitive noses. We are able to achieve all sorts of quests, relying on our never-ending lives. The virtual space is a pale copy of a dream of ours to be super human, yet we keep forgetting that we are a powerful machine. Our potential is being projected in virtual worlds, losing track of our capabilities. With the rise of our virtual selves, are we becoming unsynchronized with life?

Conclusion

I investigated a new generation of collectors, their digital collection, the tools that support their collections, and explored how they collect to connect in the digital space, alternating between exhibiting their narcissism and their need for sharing. I analyzed the form and language of the digital collection presenting how people communicate, connect to others and challenge their point of view. Transitioning from the digital collection to the emergence of a motivating digital body, I urge for a software connection to materialization. Novel software interfaces could benefit from rethinking their link to materialization, because even though the digital world gives us power, it disconnects us from our physical body. We need to connect to the world using our senses and to have the benefits of technology without losing our connections to the body. Technology needs to bridge to our senses, grounding us in our surroundings. It's only through being grounded in experience that we can give birth to new ways of living. The digital body creates opportunities but loses something in dematerialization. Focusing on the senses, situated at different points of the physical body, can create new points of entry for interaction. The missing piece between the digital and physical body is grounding. The link between the dematerialized digital body and sensory opportunities is grounding, this by creating a shift in perspectives, from a new discovery of the environment to playing with our senses. Software and hardware design should not just passively deliver information or stimulate the senses, it should actively construct a relationship between digital and physical body in the individual.

Bibliography

Abbas, Y. (2006) *Neo-nomads: Designing Environments for Living in the Age of Mental, Physical and Digital Mobilities.* Doctor of Design Thesis. Harvard University, Graduate School of Design.

Ackerman, D. (1990) *A Natural History of the Senses.* New York: Random House, Inc.

Ackermann, E. (2004) "Constructing knowledge and transforming the world". In Tokoro, M. & Steels, L. (eds.). *The Future of Learning.* Amsterdam: IOS Press. 15-35.

Barthes, R. (1981) *Camera Lucida — Reflections on Photography.* New York: Hill and Wang.

Baudrillard, J. (1996) *The System of Objects.* London, New York: Verso.

Dunne, A. (1999) *Herzian Tales: Electronic Products, Aesthetic Experience and Critical Design.* Cambridge, MA: The MIT Press.

Elsner, J. and Cardinal, R. (1997) *The Cultures of Collecting.* London: Reaktion.

Forty, A. (1992) *Objects of Desire: Design and Society Since 1750.* London; New York: Thames & Hudson.

Gauthier, J. M. and Moukalou, R. (2007) *De la guerre des boutons a Harry Potter: Un siecle d'evolution de l'espace-temps des adolescents.* Bruxelles: Mardaga.

Hall, E. T (1973) *The Silent Language.* New York: A Doubleday Anchor Book.

—. (1983) *The Dance of Life: The Other Dimension of Time.* New York: Doubleday.

Kegan, R. (1982) *The Evolving Self.* Cambridge, MA: Harvard University Press.

Kristeva, J. (1994) "Toccata and Fugue for the Foreigner". In *Strangers to Ourselves.* Columbia University Press. 1-40.

Langer, E. J. (1998) *The Power of Mindful Learning.* Cambridge, MA; New York: Da Capo Press.

Levy, F., Randall, D. C., Horowitz, G. Stone-Richards, M. and Subkowski, P. (2006) The sensibility of the collector. In *Roundtable Journal of the Philoctetes Center for the Multidisciplinary study of imagination.* Vol 1 (2).

Mauss, M. (1990) *The Gift: forms and functions of exchange in archaic societies.* London: Routledge.

Okakura K. (1906) *The Book of Tea.* New York: Fox Duffield Publisher.

Putnam, J. (2001) *Art and Artifact. The Museum as Medium.* London; New York: Thames & Hudson.

Singer, D. and Singer, J. (1990) *The House of Make Believe: Children's play and the Developing Imagination.* Cambridge, MA: Harvard University Press.

Smith, M. and Morra, J. (2006) *The Prosthetic Impulse: from a posthuman present to a biocultural future.* Cambridge, MA: MIT Press.

Subkowski, P. (2006) "On the Psychodynamics of Collecting". *International journal of psychoanalysis.* 87. 383-401.

Turkle, S. (1995) *Life on the screen.* New York: Simon and Schuster.

Vaucelle, C. (2008) "The everyday collector". Published in the *Proceedings of Ubicomp.* Tenth International Conference on Ubiquitous Computing, ACM Press.

CHAPTER EIGHT

NEW TECHNOLOGIES OF THE SELF AND SOCIAL NETWORKING SITES: HOSPITALITY EXCHANGE CLUBS AND THE CHANGING NATURE OF TOURISM AND IDENTITY

MICHAEL O'REGAN

Introduction

Muecke (2006, 36) notes how Buckminster Fuller, the designer who gave us such mobile habitable environments as the Dymaxion house (houses which could assembled on site; suitable for any environment), pointed out that "humans were born with legs and feet, not roots, and that our primary natural advantage as a species is mobility". Although a constant in the world of modernity, mobility has acquired new dimensions in the late modern (postmodern) context — a constant movement of images and people (Lash and Urry 1994) — and "staggering developments in communication and transportation" (Cresswell 2006, 20), which have changed "our apprehension of space, time and subjectivity" (Simonsen 2004, 43) creating and stretching new and existing social, cultural, economic networks, unleashing and accelerating various mobilities (Bechmann 2004). Cresswell (2006, 45) argues "[n]ot only does the world appear to be more mobile, but our ways of knowing the world have also become more fluid" which possibility might not just change the world but ways of knowing it. Therefore, it can safely be said that the concept of mobility reflects tendencies in postmodern society (Nielsen 2005), where routes in combination with roots have become a defining feature of social life, identity-making and cultural belonging (Aas 2007). Indeed, Bauman (1998, 2-3) surmises that "[m]obility climbs to the top of the uppermost among the coveted values and the freedom to move, perpetually a scarce and unequally distributed commodity, fast becomes the main stratifying factor of our late modern or postmodern times". While mobility takes place for many reasons and is found at many scales and in many forms (migrant, tourist, academic), one popular form is leisure mobility (travel and tourism) which has been increasing in volume and scope in recent decades (Urry 2007), given the modern subjects search for authenticity which Oakes (2006) argues can only be fleetingly satisfied by a self-induced and self-controlled mobility. Morgan and Pritchard (2005, 29) argue that "[t]ourism is largely concerned with considerations of being, meanings and identities" important given that "identity is no longer a matter of occupying an already given subject position" (Diken and Laustsen 2001) and so increasingly, mobility — the spatial flows of people to a geographic region (an integral aspect of tourism) is intertwined with a reflexive search for recognition in order to create or build an identity.

Within tourism, Urry (2002, 9) notes that "[t]ourists show particular fascination in the "real lives" of others that somehow possess a reality hard to discover in their own experiences", seeking authenticity in other times, other places and other people's lives. Postmodern theorists leave the impression that tourists "seek out only the exotic, authentic 'other' and experience every destination through a detached 'gaze' that rarely engages the 'real' (i.e., uncommodified) aspects of the place" (Williams and Kaltenborn 1999, 214), having become socialized into consuming by gazing. This habitual and unreflexive gazing, MacCannell (1999) argues means no one escapes the systems of attractions; no one exempt from the obligation to go sightseeing except the local person. MacCannell (2001, 383) argues that

> [a]ny thought one might have entertained about getting to know the life of the native peoples as it is actually lived... becoming identified with the remoteness and mystery of the place, quickly give way to the realization that the dominant element in every tourist landscape are the tourists. The others one meets in tourist settings are other tourists and local workers whose job it is to serve tourists.

While this may be so, he argues that it does not diminish the desire to go beyond the role of being a "mere" tourist, as individuals search for encounters with "locals" is a key reason to travel for many. This is especially true for non-institutionalized travelers such as backpackers who are characterized as aiming to go beyond the façade of the tourist industry, avoiding "tourist traps" in the search for alternative experiences (Huxley 2005) and seeking "authentic" backstage cultures and peoples. Yet, even the most noble of travelers (Urry 2002, 87) are inhibited by various constraints, with Huxley (2005) arguing that other backpackers, economic asymmetry, imbalanced relationships and lack of time create barriers between tourists and "locals". Economic Asymmetry, Huxley argues, is an imbalance which causes the unequal access to economic capital while imbalanced roles and relationships between host-guest and the distinction of their roles also create barriers. While the "guest" is in a position of leisure, able to simply gaze upon their chosen destination, people, and culture, the "hosts" are working and must perform their expected everyday duties (MacCannell 1999).

Huxley (2005) also suggests that as backpacking has become increasingly commercialized and packaged into conventional routes and formats with "opportunities to engage with aspects of local culture behind the tourist-trap façades become increasingly difficult" raising the question as to whether tourists, even when non-institutionalized and immersive can submerge himself or herself in the more local processes of daily transportation, movement, dwelling and everyday life. Even the most immersive oriented of travelers "can never be fulfilled within the context of tourism" (Jansson 2002) with Maoz (2006, 234) noting that many backpackers forgo any deep and close understanding of the locals and their culture, instead settling for "instant authenticity wrapped in a nice package". Hutnyk (1996, x) argues in such respects "alternative travel" can be "criticized as an illusion of 'nice' cottage capitalism, soothing ideological anxieties while extending commercialization and the tourism industry". The result, according to Urry (2000) is that modern tourism is "institutionalizing" the rights of outsiders to look into its "real lives" of others for the exclusive use of tourists, delivering access to "backstages" while locals, even those involved in the tourism industry seek to protect these backstages (Quinn 2007). While these experiences enable an increasing number of travelers to satisfy their goals by gaining some passing experience of local cultures, Edensor (2001, 78-79) proposes these postmodern staging's proffer a "dystopian future for tourism where every potential space becomes increasingly intensively stage-managed and regulated as part of the commodification of everything" creating what Boorstin called "pseudo-experiences" or "satisfaction with superficial experiences of other peoples and other places" (MacCannell 1999, 10). This is "self-perpetuating system of illusions" and spectacle disregarding the "real" world (Urry 2003, 10) with tourism operators selling or arranging "local experiences" while concealing the commercial nature of the exchange resulting in choices that ultimately constrain personal growth, and wider social and cultural affordances such as self-exploration and self-development.

At the same time as this increased commercialization and institutionalization, the distribution and impact of new "technologies of the self" are challenging the conventional practices and credentialed experts (guidebooks, commercial hospitality, tour guides) within travel and tourism. These technologies appear destined to become powerful tools in forms of individual subject-making, serving as counterweights to the conventional tourist industry. Individual appropriation of new technologies offer tools to individuals to explicitly act to fashion their identities by regulating their bodies, their thoughts and their conduct in new ways, assembling wider networks of relations around themselves. These technologies change the apprehension of time, space and subjectivity, as individual users in a bottom up approach create and inhabit emerging social, cultural and economic networks, unleashing and accelerating various leisure oriented mobilities that change our understanding of tourism, and even making the term tourism, as widely understood increasingly obsolete.

This chapter reflecting a post-disciplinary agenda investigates one such new media network called Couchsurfing, a social networking site that has attracted over one million users since 2004. Drawing on a theoretical, physical and intellectual engagement and immersion within the symbolic and material landscapes of mobility and practice to which Couchsurfers relate to, inhabit and belong, I seek to investigate a medium that offers its members an arena to reflexively develop and sustain an identity through which they fashion themselves within a collectivity of like minded others. Linked to an ethnomethodological approach, this chapter unpacks from the inside, a little understood and under researched mobile grouping. As a member of Couchsurfing since 2005, this research is positioned within the embodied and situated practices that participation in the site generates, my immersion combined with online and offline participant observation and semi-structured interviews with fifteen members of the network forming the basis of this chapter. While I have both accepted visitors into my home as a "host", I have also "surfed" to others' homes many times since 2005. The interviews took place during a Couchsurfing event called "London Calling" in London during June 2006 and an annual hospitality exchange event called "Winter Camp" which took place in Istanbul, Turkey, in December 2007. These internally organized events regularly take place all over the world and can attract anywhere from two to 700 participants without any publicity.[1]

1. Technologies of the Self

New forms of "connected travel" has emerged out of cumulative technological changes since the late 90s and continues to alter the tourist scapes as access to virtual space and tools for self-representation becoming omnipresent and ubiquitous given that the internet and other mobile communications technologies are actually becoming increasingly integrated into travel practices. Germann-Molz (2006) argues that there is a growing convergence between travel and the internet which is reconfiguring corporeal travel practices, given that "travellers are travelling *on* the Internet, but also *with* the internet" (Germann-Molz 2006, 378, original emphasis) inscribing new social realities for travelers. Research shows that the internet and other mobile communications technologies are becoming progressively more integrated into corporeal travel practices (Wang et al. 2002; Wang and Fesenmaier 2003) acting as a platform for a diverse range of everyday activities from travel planning, review sites, travel blogs through to the incorporation and use of "social networking" sites that technologically enable a travel life that is global in nature (O' Regan 2008). Mobility related technologies, especially information and communication technologies are increasingly having symbolic and material resonances for the way people aspire to and perform their particular imaginative and spatial geographies. Given travel and tourism related motilities provide powers to stage one self and develop identities, individuals are activating "Technologies of the Self" (Foucault 1988) providing grounds for individuals to strive for authenticity both individually (and necessarily) with the help of others.

Foucault, having predominantly focused on technologies of power, in later life became interested in human agency and the role individuals play in turning him or herself into a subject. Technologies (or "practices") of the self, a technology of unquestioning obedience is traced by Foucault within Greco-Roman philosophy in the first two centuries A.D. of the early Roman Empire and also within Christian spirituality and the monastic principles developed in the fourth and fifth centuries of the late Roman Empire (Foucault 1988) to describe the methods and techniques through which we constitute ourselves by regulating our bodies, thoughts

---

[1] http://www.couchsurfing.com/meetings.html

and conduct to search for truth from within oneself. Foucault defines technologies of the self as those

> which permit individuals to effect by their own means or with the help of others a certain number of operations on their own bodies and souls, thoughts, conduct, and way of being, so as to transform themselves in order to attain a certain state of happiness, purity, wisdom, perfection or immortality (1988, 18).

Technologies of the self then, are specific techniques constituted in real practices that shape people's lives, through which individuals assist themselves in becoming self-transformed, self-directed, self-managed in the face of others who bear witness to such self-transformation. They comprise strategies and tactics that arise not only in knowledge and power fashioned by organizations outside of the actor but also from the creation and deployment of knowledge of their own making.

Each historical time frame is marked by its own technologies of the self (early radical guidebooks, letters, diaries, blogs, Web 2.0); each instrument helping the individual fashion a self in connection to an outside world. Subjectivity is no longer characterized only as a reified construct of power, given that individuals are able to transform their own subjectivities through techniques of the self. Individual's traveling with the internet can now activate technologies of the self from diaries to blogs (travelogues, weblogs), to recast an identity and give agency. Lovink (2007) observes that blogs are primarily used as a tool to manage the self — the embodied and physical self, a means to tell stories of their experiences and express agency while traveling, a "personal narrative" addressed to real and imaginary others (van Dijck 2007) written for oneself and an audience in mind. Germann-Molz (2006) in her study of "round-the-world" travel blogs found authors used their blogs to forge connections and feelings of home, but also used their sites to open up the possibility for interaction, highlighting their geographical proximity and availability when arranging meetings with friends, family and locals. For Germann-Molz (2006), blogs are a rich environment for self-expression and self-representation as individuals can communicate their mobility to a potential global audience, broadcasting certain performances that validate their travel style, while hiding other behaviors that might reflect badly on their membership of a social grouping such as the family unit (Nardi et al. 2004; Viégas 2005) or the imagined community of other travelers. Individuals are not free to fully define their own identity through blogging given their availability, visibility and accountability to their audience. While some travel blogs are written on stand-alone individualized domains, the majority are located within travel portals (i.e. travelpod.com, travelblog.org) where users using specific travel related tools that both orientate the writer and direct the reader to the writer's subjectivities. With Germann-Molz's (2006) study, it is unclear as whether there was a real audience following the authors or an imagined audience but together, each individual writer and reader enter a discursive realm, agreeing to a pragmatic pact that recognizes the author's subjectivities. Expressing their individuality, these blogs provide the means for individuals to "be seen or to see themselves through the lenses of others" (van Dijck 2007, 68). Their choice of such travel communities highlights their use, not just as a means of identity construction but also as a communal means of expressing, sharing and even "synchronis[ing] one's subjective experience with those of others, to test one's evaluations against the outside world" (van Dijck 2007, 72). Germann-Molz (2004, 262) found that

> [m]any travellers post... invitations on their websites and then 'receive guests' throughout their trip making possible new kinds of interactive social connections 'both in person and at a distance' the authors deriving mobile sociality, carving out 'moments of connection and sociality within mobility' forging a 'sense of community and belong precisely through the mobility — whether online or on-the-road (Germann-Molz 2004, 178-179).

Yet, most studies have found that reciprocity is not a standard feature of blogs (Viégas 2005; Nardi et al 2004; Van Dijck 2007) with comments or feedback rarely given to blogs of short duration with bloggers keen to keep the audience, if any, at arm's length (Nardi et al 2004) through anonymous posting and the deletion of negative comments. Once travel is over, blogs rarely get updated and are even deleted as the *liminoid* phase of travel expires with any accumulated capital also expiring. Lovink (2007) argues that the "[t]he essence of a blog is not the interactivity of the medium: it is the sharing of the thoughts and opinions of the blogger" that signals the need "to connect, either to someone or something else or to oneself" (van Dijck 2007, 67-68).

While travel blogs are certainly a technology of the self, it is not a technology of affect or a social tool; the writers being subjectified by the community they write within (Viégas 2005) and their real and imagined audiences they write for. They have little potential to build a social network beyond those they already have (unless by linking or blogrolling to other travel blogs) and can in effect, act to limit the individuals' mobility and their ability to continually produce and distinguish themselves. The presence of family, friends and co-workers acting as a social network can subtly enforce coercive power on the authors as they downplay certain activities while still performing the role of the intrepid travelers by taking a position that must pursue popular tourist activities their audience will enjoy. While blogging can be either "liberating" or "repressing" technologies of the self with regard to the production of stories of self and travel (Crossley 1999), travel blogging is not a model to overcome the limits of tourist subjectivity and discourses or provide opportunities to break with normalizing touristic type practices. It does however highlight how digital "technologies of the self" help individuals strive for "authenticity" both as individuals and as part of imagined communities, even though the blogger may not act as a tool to meet or know fellow members of that community. In addition, travel blogs highlight how individuals are transformed and empowered by others or with the help of others; the fact of belonging to specific social networks represents a key element of self-identification, self-representation and development.

In summary, travel blogs as an "old" technology of the self might hamper individuals, given the perceived presence of certain audiences, which can regulate and impede upon individuals using their bodies and minds to regulate and facilitate their own conduct (Foucault 1988, 18; Nardi et al. 2004) and rather than facilitate bodily associations with unknown others there is a sharp author/reader divide. Blogs are characterized as much by an obligation to known others (with many blogs being initiated by others according to Nardi) as by any articulation primarily to one's self. Acting primarily as a means to self-fashion an identity and as a bridge to known others, blogs tie individuals (families, friends) together for the duration of the trip, its major component is continual and sustained writing. Rather than a means to connect or encounter unknown others as part of a complex social and culture game, the development of their online identity is simply to take of oneself, "mediating between us and ourselves... transforming the content and scope of our self-dialogue" (Hermans 2004, 305) the uploading of entries lasting primarily only as long as the trip, their limited functionally not allowing for persistent identities or new relationships (Pahl 2000); the trip ending with few traces of their selves in informational spaces remaining once blogs are either deleted or archived without any further update. The more recent proliferation of social networking websites however, offer the potential for users to develop more persistent identities which can be maintained over both periods of mobility and fixity; whether the individual is "at home" or "away" helping individuals produce themselves as "proper subjects" through co-constructors and thereby bringing about significant changes to personal mobilities; conventional and normative leisure mobilities; knowledge and identity construction; socialization and self-expression.

2. Hospitality Exchange Cubs and Couchsurfing

Oakes (2005, 52) notes that while the tourist is driven to seek authenticity, he/she "remains constrained by modernity's inability to satisfy that search with anything more real than the mirage of touristic space". For some individuals though, travel and tourism are still undertaken as a socio-cultural secession from safe networks, physical corporeal mobility, a means to bridge connections and encounter unknown others, experiencing humans through a re-articulation of the global and local — to live amongst those they visit at a destination and share back regions with them (MacCannell 1999). When Casey Fenton, a software programmer from New Hampshire (USA) found a cheap last-minute ticket to Iceland, he wanted to experience a "real Iceland" through the people who lived there and rather than booking a hotel or hostel, he hacked into the University of Iceland student directory, and spammed 1,500 students with requests for advice and guidance receiving more than fifty replies. In January 2004, Casey along with other (co)founders started Couchsurfing.com, a social networking site, whose premise on the surface, seems simple: if you need a place to stay, this social networking system enables you to identify and find someone to give over sleeping space in their home for free. The site remains non-profit and is supported entirely by website member donations and an address verification system. While Couchsurfing was not the first "hospitality exchange site" it has become the largest, its membership over one million,[2] its beginnings now project folklore, often featured in news articles; a mobility related activity that became a key "focus" (Scott 1981) from which the network has developed, providing the shared understanding, beliefs and norms for participation. The understanding that participation will lead to face-to-face contact and prolonged and intense interaction with other members shapes the dynamics of the network creating what Du Gay (1997, 15) calls a "semantic network" — which he describes as a network of shared meanings and practices associated with its own discourse. Like many social network start-ups, it started out being used by friends of the founders and grew organically through word-of-mouth. As a social

---

[2] http://www.couchsurfing.com/statistics.html

networking site, it draws together, serves and connects a geographically dispersed network of strangers based around a shared interest and practice, a medium by which participants draw purpose and which suggests rather than directs a new way of life. Using an internal messaging system, individuals (called surfers) can contact potential hosts and request a "couch"; part of a narrow code of vocabulary specific to the site; an example of how "a symbolic code can aid in the identification of who belongs to a certain social space and who does not" (Yus 2005, 89). If a request for a couch is granted, then a process of information exchange occurs with the host sending out details of where to meet, an address, transport options and usually a mobile phone number for micro-coordination. Rather than being either online or offline, the process by which hospitality is "exchanged" is a complex dance of face-to-face encounters, scheduled meetings, telephone calls, emails that ultimately leads to face-to face contact and overnight stays that normally last between two and seven nights (Biaski 2007).

Membership on Couchsurfing is free although verification of personal details (real name and address) for a fee is increasingly encouraged. Like the majority of social networking sites, when an individual joins, they are required to build a semi-public profile, using their real name and address and fill in personal information as well as pictures and interests. The profiles, similar to those used on Facebook and MySpace serves as a digital representation of one's identity, but unlike most networking sites, where you first connect to known others by "friending" them, there is no function on Couchsurfing that allows individuals to comment on other users' profiles or start "friending", or inviting unknown others to view your profile. While Myspace and Facebook are primarily designed to sustain and maintain an already known network of (former) friends, colleagues and family, Couchsurfing is made up of dispersed strangers. The fixed profile categories are quite rigid, sparse and hospitality explicit, requiring users to highlight whether they can offer hospitality (couches, a coffee/drink), what they can offer guests, their language skills, past and future travel plans and personal interests. There is little freedom to add third party plugins (video, flash) or applications and while individuals can "hide" personal data such as age or birthday, the profiles default position is public. While the profile allows users to express salient aspects of an identity (Boyd 2008), commitment to that identity can only be created and maintained through highly visible testimonials, vouches and (friend) connections, which can only be obtained by offline participation in the Couchsurfing project. Once the hospitality exchange takes place; both the host and guest rate the experience as positive, neutral or negative, as well as write personal testimonials of each other. These reputation testimonials or trust features are public to the whole community and serve to define the individual and their place within the project. Interaction, participation and feedback from others are a perquisite, which directly influences the possibility of a new user pursuing an offline social life through the site and realizing their own mobility projects while being on the move.

There is a limited amount of mediated interaction, with live chat being withdrawn from the site in 2009 while "virtual reputations" are clearly marked, utilizing a large computer icon and are undoubtedly and visibly subordinate to "real world" testimonials. The project urges users to use the reputation system carefully to rate others only after real world interaction, thus bestowing reputation on them after completing a "hospitality transaction". Online technology-mediated reputation systems based on transactions that are socially contextual from Couchsurfing to Ebay have become to play a pivotal role in society and everyday lives, the accumulated evidence over time as to one's character and personality; the number of vouches and reputation testimonials establishing a person's status, trustworthiness, consistency, commitment and participation that's difficult to fake. Positive feedback after a number of hospitality exchanges makes it more likely individuals will be more accepted by potential hosts in the future, while members of good standing can also apply to become a Couchsurfing "Ambassador", a status role that highlights continual and active participation.

In summary, the primary means of expression isn't the profile per se but mobility, expressed in the couches, connections and reputations which are visible to all; not only "an expression of an individual's mental model of exterior relations, but an explicit performance of a social network intended for consumption by others, whether visible or invisible during the performance creation" (Boyd 2007, 155) and which like blogs, makes them accountable to their audience. Travelers traditionally characterized as immersive (such as backpackers) must continually communicate and re-establish themselves by continually communicating their 'road status' (Sørensen 2003) verbally to others through conversation, photographs, blog entries, status exchange and communication. This was because "no fixed mechanism can convey the individual's road status and no continuous social relations can confirm and transmit previous ascertainments of it" (Sørensen 2003, 857). Yet, I argue that the reputations garnered on Couchsurfing carry a permanent archive of past contributions and actions, acting as permanent reminders, a particular narrative and a consistent identity. Profiles, not only represent the individual, their cosmopolitan disposition but they also continually represent the individuals themselves in the context of their mobility as well as their (global) potential for mobility in the context of the global, even when temporally and relatively immobile.

Couchsurfing having risen out of the individualization of self, allows dispersed strangers to become "visible to themselves" (Livingstone 2005) and others even if geographically dispersed; both a "technology of the self" given their members come to rely on it to express a subjectivity but only because of a mutuality of or expectation of reciprocity. While the individualization of motivation has created the global network power of Couchsurfing, it also creates a type of collective global agency that sustains and circulates commonly recognized (although contested) understandings, traditions, norms, identities, values, direction, interest, practice, interaction style and purpose; that only become visible through participation in and through the medium. Conradson and Latham (2005) ask for recognition and understanding of the wider networks of relations that people seek to assemble around themselves. They argue that it becomes clear that "it is not just individuals who develop and evolve through the opportunities that friendship networks afford them; this is also true of the relations that constitute the networks" (Conradson and Latham 2005, 295).

From its founding, participation has not been market based but user led as each individual acts on principles other than economic profit, as stories of trust and intimacy continually circulate across differences in individual socio-economic background, ethnicity, motivations and self-interest. Couchsurfing can address countless strangers rather than a community that existed a priori, around a particular discourse, a medium where identity is performed and not formed in, providing tools where individuals in a self-organizing and reflexive manner can address themselves and each other as part of a social network. This network values a non-institutional sociability and hospitality, cultivating a reflexive awareness of one's identity and lifestyle (Binkley 2003) which for many are continually produced in a sense of "deep play" (Geertz 1973) that was once only available to a minority of individuals who rejected their homeland in order to shape an alternative expressive lifestyle (artists, therapists) within a cosmopolitan culture of expressive individualism (D'Andrea 2006). In Couchsurfing, each person is a node in a global network, with each individual helping to sustain the activities of the others through mobility and fixity, contributing to their own identity whether at home or on the road. Individuals then are increasingly responsible for their own experiences, without scheduled events, routes, or fixed places of co-presence and sociality, which can be interpreted as an expression of a new form of control over subjectivity.

This "de-routinization" (Southerton and Tomlinson 2005) of temporalities and spatialities is replaced by the agency of travelers themselves and the user-generated content and identities they themselves produce with like-minded others, altering, challenging and blurring "long-established and traditionally-significant boundaries between distinct spheres" (Livingstone 2005, 163) between home and away, authentic and inauthentic, consumer and producer, mobility and fixity, individual and collective, local and global, public and private and stranger and friend. Rather than see fixity then as static and bounded or mobility as freedom and individualistic, these distinctions are increasingly blurred, each requiring the other to sustain individual activities and persistent identities.

In summary then, the decision to join Couchsurfing is closely connected to individual's expression of a subjective reality, with respondents describing how they were "imagined" Couchsurfers before the website existed, the medium offering a reality developing a subjective reality with and through others. Respondents described how they previously orientated towards travelers when at home, whether it be picking up hitchhikers or offering advice to tourists, highlighting how they sought immersion within local processes when travelling. Respondents also noted how this public production and consumption of and regulation of individuality had to be acknowledged and accepted by others such as friends, family, co-workers and house mates, sometimes leading to conflict. While self-interest is very varied, "different motives can be associated with the same action, and the same action may be explained by different motives" (Wang and Fesenmaier 2003, 43). Yus (2005) argues that if we were to look into the minds of both online or offline communities, one would find differing mental representations which, through steady and sustained interactions, end up intersecting one another, resembling one another, forming a stable but continuously re-negotiated set of communal representations. Couchsurfing as a participatory medium, where individuals talk through, creates a textual record of their interactions, building a sense of shared consciousness and collectivity (Turner 2006, 499), individual identity expressed through new "technologies of the self" requiring communication, interaction and exchange with others. Van Dijck (2007, 41) argues, that "[t]echnologies of the self are concomitantly technologies of sharing: they help form bonds... tapping into communal or collective culture that in turn reshapes... identity".

While the production and narration of self through blogging is primarily a solidarity activity of short duration with little reciprocity, the possibility of future reciprocation (expectancy) is a major motivation driving contribution in online communities, given members can obtain "benefits by making active contributions which, in turn, encourages them to continue participating themselves" (Wang and Fesenmaier 2003, 42). Rheingold (2000, 49) writes of a "gift economy" in which people do things for one another out of a spirit of building something between them, less a product of the social control and more a product of trust within ties (Plickert et al. 2007). Users in this gift economy participate because it enriches their lives, increasing "social capital" which Putnam (1995, 67) defines as "features of social organization such as networks, norms, and social trust that facilitate co-ordination and co-operation for mutual benefit". The reciprocity in Couchsurfing takes the form of hospitality and is built on the premise that those who contribute will, without "immediate" expectation, be rewarded themselves. Individuals who participate in this social network, although possessing different amounts of capital (social, economic, cultural, mobility, network) or access to capital can invest that capital into a social network without a guarantee of a particular return. Allowing "strangers" into one's home, although a risky venture given that "a member of the network may fail to perceive or act upon a mutual obligation" (Holt 2008, 232), augments the chance to transform social stock into symbolic capital and is heavily dependent upon an unspoken, intuitive agreement based on traditions, norms and accumulated trust and reputation. Even though unfilled obligations are commonplace, whereby an individual who may have previously received hospitality refuses to reciprocate as a host, the accumulated capital garnered by an individual through hosting is recognized and transferable within the wider social network, facilitating the acquisition of further capital at any point in the future.

Putnam (2001, 20) argues that social capital can thus be simultaneously a "private good" and a "public good" and even if guided by self-interest can only develop through interactions with others, lead to benefits for the broader community by facilitating collective action through network connections, the sense of reciprocal obligation even contributing to a sense of community or collective agency. It requires "a willingness to share resources when others request them, a commitment to put values in as well as take it out" (Rheingold 2000, 365). The person-to-person reciprocity is premised, "on the understanding of caring for a stranger in order to establish a relationship based on reciprocity and exchange" (Andrews 2000, 237). This is in direct contrast to commercial hospitality provision where the exchange of money absolves the guest of mutual obligation and

> [...] depends on a reciprocity based on money exchange and limits on giving pleasure to guests which ultimately impact on the on the nature of

behaviour and the experience of hospitality. Both host and guest enter the hospitality occasion with a reduced sense of reciprocity and mutual obligation (Lashley and Morrison 2000, 13).

Couchsurfers meanwhile prioritize immersion with the "Other" member and have an idealized picture of what constitutes a genuine, rewarding and "authentic" interaction in everyday local processes: primarily the absence of monetary exchange (Desforges 2001; Suvantola 2002). Zelizer (1994, 11) argues that once money invades the realm of personal relations, it "inevitably bends those relations in the direction of instrumental rationality". Rather than being entirely a person-to-person reciprocity, the whole community bears witness and benefits from non-monetary person-to-person hospitality, given that the motivation to participate is an anticipated reciprocity from the whole network implying trust and belief in the reciprocating nature of one's network.

3. Performing Mobility and Dwelling through Couchsurfing

Hannam (2006, 245) argues that "metaphors of performance and the development of the concept of performativity has been central to a more complex understanding of tourists' agency and their relationship with their hosts," identity creation and identification with others guided by performances and theatricality (Hetherington 1998, 150). A good performance requires one to learn how to be a good host or guest and at a most basic level, those joining and using the site, while doing so individually, must accept their actions and performance must be subservient to its common values and norms. This requires members to engage in "cultural interaction" without commercialization and payment, requiring cooperation, face-to-face engagement, intimacy, tolerance, respect, and reciprocity. Both the host and guest are judged and evaluated through references that pertain to these overriding values, with any notion that the host ignored the guest or the guest treated the host's home as a hotel or hotel seen as major transgressions. Reputation (the perceived commitment, values, integrity of an individual) is the result of identity being continually produced, the reputation and actions both online and in the physical realm having repercussions in and on each other. These reputations, can be seen as interpersonal surveillance producing a reflexive monitoring or surveillance of the self, that act as a tool for self-regulation, of one's own behavior, in order to take up preferred subject positions. Crouch et al. (2001, 257) argue that "[p]erformance may be something done for others as a display of identity, or for the self, in constituting and working identity".

One's reputation or performance isn't written by oneself then as in blogging or a diary but by those you host and those you surf with, and so taking care of one's reputation means managing the self and, in turn, to care for the self directly entails a care for those who write the references, and vice versa, entailing a sense of reciprocity that sustains the site and one's identity. Like commercial hospitality, guests are not merely passive observers of the staff's attempts to provide them with hospitality. They provide the conditions for that performance by colluding with the presentation. Unlike commercial hospitality however, the exchange takes place in the host's home, their private sphere (bedrooms, kitchens, and family rooms), where the guest has full access to its facilities (cooker, washing machine, fridge, shared meals) and the host's time. The hosts are obliged not simply to direct their surfer but engage with them, sharing their everyday lives, whether it's sharing meals or introducing the surfer to friends and family. Both the guest and host then perform, both having a vested interest in the performance being successful (Lashley and Morrison 2000), each interaction highlighting the importance of reputation as host and guest come to their own working consensus about what are appropriate and inappropriate enactions (cf. Edensor 2004). Individuals cannot simply rely on embodied habits and synchronized enactions to establish an emotional connection and so must become transparent, to make their lives as open as possible to be seen as competent, trustworthy, and cosmopolitan.

4. The Production of Locality

For many scholars, global processes such as mobility undermine sociality, locality and community. Tomlinson (1997, 14) proposes "that the paradigmatic experience of global modernity for most people is that of staying in one place", where they experience what global modernity brings to them, still relying and dependent on those neighbourhoods and people they have known for years. This seems to suggest that mobile practices help in undoing place and established identities, making geographic localization insignificant (Gustafson 2006); introducing "placelessness" (Relp 1976), frayed social ties; ultimately leading to the death of community (Putnam 2001). Yus (2005, 86) believes online communities, "produce(s) a reduction in the amount and quality of social encounters in physical environments, especially casual, non-profit-driven ones" removing the processes by which people meet people locally, the internet providing the means for mutual access to people scattered in geographically distant areas, and thereby favoring stay-at-homes. These readings of mobility characterize it as a freedom to live arid, individualistic, lonely lives "free of the many constraining attachments that make us grounded, well-adjusted human beings" (Benkler 2006, 356). This position, Kennedy and Roudometof (2001) argue, neglects how the nature of communities has changed in the era of reflexive modernity and globalization. They argue that community today is no longer actively generated according to fixed criteria ascribed by birth and social position, but through a voluntary and reflexivity process by members who choose to set up a community or seek membership in it. Given this, identity is no longer a matter of occupying an already given subject position (Diken and Laustsen 2001), with "individuals now seem to be more than ever prone to articulate complex affiliations, meaningful attachments and multiple allegiances to issues, people, places and traditions that lie beyond the boundaries of their resident nation-state" (Cohen 2006, 189). For Giddens, globalization points to the interlocking of the local and the global; that is, it "concerns the intersection of presence and absence, the interlacing of social events and social relations 'at a distance' with local contextualities" (1991, 21). He argues that "larger and larger numbers of people live in circumstances in which disembedded institutions, linking local practices with globalized social relations, organize major aspects of day-to-day life" (Giddens 1990, 79), the concepts of locality, belonging and dwelling being continually redefined as people's lives become increasingly global. Couchsurfing provides the means for individuals to reimagine the boundaries of their community, their home and identity through physical, virtual, communicative and imaginative mobilities, the highly interdependent "mobilities" which form and transform diverse networks, playing a "significant role in generating and maintaining complex connections in the networked society" (Urry 2002b, 2).

Greater connectivity, access to and penetration of local, national and global media, mean each individual can operate in multiple, partial communities; "the experience of locality being undercut by the penetration of global forces and networks" (Morley 2000: 14). Kennedy and Roudometof (2001) argue that we can no longer easily continue to inhabit entirely localized worlds even if we wish to do so as "the traditional notion of single, entirely separate and homogeneous cultures embedded in an ethnic or folk core is now completely unacceptable". As cultures increasingly overlap and interconnect with one another through "external networking" individuals will seek out a variety of appropriate people and resources for different situations.

The Couchsurfing project does not exist separately from locality, a global process creating placelessness and standardization, but through what can be considered "glocal" interaction, where globalization and localization are ultimately intertwined. Glocalization, "a global outlook adapted to local conditions" (Robertson 1995, 28), is a notion which helps one to grasp the many interconnections between the global and the local and a means whereby individuals can grasp and participate in new forms of global awareness by adapting global process to local realities, while maintaining and/or rediscovering local solidarities. Couchsurfing helps both hosts and guests re-approach the local for the first time in a different way, rather than through the guidebook, tour guide or serendipity. While it is impossible to accurately pinpoint the true status of "locals" and their true motivations to receive "others" into their homes, bedrooms and kitchens, individuals have noted their desire to learn specific languages, learn more about other cultures, meet like-minded others when they move to a new town, showing visitors their "true" selves as well as utilizing the site to create friendships, companionships and store up capital for future mobility. Members can also connect with like-minded others in the same geographic locality, leading to regular proximity, intimacy and interaction through scheduled and publicly announced events. Hospitality exchange and the obligations to perform in a certain way opens up parts of members surrounding locale to guests and even hosts as they perform locality by accompanying visitors around to places they might not have previously visited, such as tourist attractions. Members felt, given their decision to host others in their home, there was an obligation to share details about their locality and their lives, acting as an insider by spending time with their guests. Many altered their daily routines (work, family) around the surfer's needs, taking time out to cook or leaving work early, making this cosmopolitan part of their lives visible to others, their performance helping demonstrate and maintain a global belonging.

Couchsurfing's global scope is wide, its members neither local nor global, participants residing around the corner and around the globe, neither fully immobile nor mobile, very visible to its members but invisible within the wider continuum of mobility, transforming social, cultural and economic aspects of travel and everyday life. While to the outside observer, this may seem risky, boring, mundane, unspectacular in the organizing of experiences, often accompanied by lack of privacy and comfort; for the participants it concurs up a vital space for self-expression and representation that arises through discourses that are felt particularly intensively by many of the participants. Unlike the global penetration of tourism, participation in Couchsurfing is neither induced nor forced into an individual's home or lifestyle, but accepted as a tool to express aspects of individual identity; with individuals and their homes becoming part of a "larger temporal and lifestyle continuum" (Binkley 2003, 299) that no longer ends at the border of national cultures (Welsch 1999). While these social networks, unbounded by borders and boundaries might not correspond to traditional, authentic location-specific social networks (family, neighbors, workmates) or the "third places", (the local church, the pub), identified with "real" physical communities (Oldenburg, 1991); Harvey (1996, 314) argued that we can not go back over twenty years ago and "reject the world of sociability which has been achieved by the interlinking of all peoples and places into a global economy". He argues we must build upon it and transform it in socially constructive ways exemplifying "the ability of networks of affinity to leverage the internet and to translate virtual affinity into physical vicinity, and community action" (Castells 2007, 251). Therefore, as well as having the propensity of just reinforcing and boosting strong ties and existing relationships, technology can also by highlighting availability, help to create a sense of proximity and intimacy as well as contribute to "a sense of place" (Nyìrì et al. 2005) in a globalizing world. Even those members who are relatively immobile because of visa issues, family and job commitments, are key nodes in this glocal processes, as they "localize" a destination through a shared global belonging for their visitors through help advice, stories, translation, history (Salazar 2006) "to encapsulate the essence of place" (Pond 1993, vii, cited in Salazar 2006, 835). The exchange creates a window onto that place that refracts the visitor into national-territorial spaces, feeding into local processes. At the same time the host is refracted outwards onto the world.

   Hospitality exchange sites, adopted from globally circulating discourses generate via discursive interactions space where personal and global meanings are produced and negotiated by surfers and hosts; and at the same time the local is (re)produced in discourses of globalization. The spatial geographies of immersive travel once achieved by approaching locals while on the move have been blurred and fused in a global social network, which increasingly sets very specific form of conduct, when activated by users engaged in "self-directed networking" (Kellerman 2006).

Conclusion

   Beck (1997, 95) when referring to the individualization of the life course argues that "individuals must produce, stage and cobble together their biographies themselves... the individual is actor, designer, juggler and stage director of his own biography, identity, social networks, commitments and convictions". From new "technologies of the self" such as social networking sites, individuals in creating profiles, not only represent themselves, their cosmopolitan disposition and global (be)longing but also continually represent themselves in the context of their mobility and fixity (motility), highlighting that contemporary forms of mobility and dwelling are increasingly bound up with others. Even when temporary immobile individuals share their homes selectively to people with those they believe share common dispositions in the expectation of future reciprocation sometime in the future, the site requiring fixity and dwelling as well as mobility and movement to sustain it. The Couchsurfing site allows the individual to express personal identity through interaction, participation and exchange so that individuals can gain status, social capital and self-esteem by exercising agency, building a real and virtual representative reputation of autonomy, commitment and independence, which are developed and managed through reputation management.

While the site is sustained through the individualization of self-interest, it forms a collective sphere made of over a million individuals, who exchange information, resources, hospitality in a reciprocal manner, something that is extrinsically social and collective which cannot be explained away as simply a representation of aggregate of self interest — a notion which challenges our beliefs about the impact of social networking sites. I argue that, for individuals, the use of the sites tools has symbolic and practical resonance in creating real-world actions, which are neither anti-local nor anti-social but can form the basis for new cultural and social productions. The specific techniques constituted through the site result in real practices that shape people's lives, through which individuals assist themselves in becoming self-transformed, self-directed, self-managed by seeking out a variety of appropriate people and tools, who bear witness and help in that self-transformation.

With the activation of Couchsurfing, even the most immobile "local" or mobile subjects, can through the site seek out people, new affiliation, information and places beyond their local situation creating new forms of collective agency, that's neither local or global, creating a new sense of belonging as modern subjects as well as sociality, thick co-presence, intimacy and meetingness. The impulse that might make more time and capital resource rich individuals buy a package tour or travel abroad can be met while at home, much of the chagrin of the tourism industry who would prefer individuals to excise any curiosity about the world through an economic purchase rather than while at home.

For individuals who participate in the network who might live their whole life in one place or those with no home at all, Couchsurfing can give individuals the opportunity to develop a different sense of place both locally and globally, a sense of worth, identification and value resulting in openness to different cultures, peoples and genders. Respondents say they have become better informed, the site restructuring the search for the "local", while restoring a sense of identity and feelings of self-reliance and control, especially for those who felt undermined or underserved by an increasingly commodified, standardized and fabricated global tourism industry. Rather than passing through spaces on the way to somewhere else, somewhere better, the site offers encounters that challenge the very meanings we relate to tourism consumption and the distinctions we normally make between public and private, consumption and production, hosts and guests, home and away, with notions of leisure being bounded off in distinct spaces, times and even certain categorized activities becoming increasingly untenable. Veijola (2006) argues the obsession with the authentic is being replaced by an equal quest for the local as a basis for social life, identity and belonging. While sometimes hidden, "tourists" can now be found in inner city flats, suburban homes, sweeping the floor and cooking dinner challenging the host-guest paradigm, which assumes that "us" and "them" are clearly differentiated, physically and socially segregated from each other. The use of the private home is altered with project usage injecting dynamism into the home and the private sphere, entailing a reversal of existing spaces for other identities and practices, a commitment to an identity that runs very deeply within many of its users. This person-to-person connectivity means tourism as a form of leisure mobility is increasingly desynchronized; less collectively practiced and bounded to specific times, routes and paths, replaced by a more varied, flexible, personal and subjective pattern, as people live their lives in and through Couchsurfing, altering how they organize their lives.

While social networking has been criticized for the decline of social trust, social capital, privacy, autonomy and even community (Putnam 2001), leading to shallower and less intense social relationships, individuals working with one another via social networks are a growing force in our economy and society, as they create and manage ties once bounded and maintained by door-to-door and place-to-place relationships, transgressing what were considered sealed boundaries. For many the awards of travel such as meeting valued others with similar cosmopolitan dispositions had been transformed and unbundled from a process which required corporeal travel and serendipitous encounters to become a fluid part of their everyday lives through the medium of technology. Rather than destroying a "sense of place", the site creates a bridge to the hosts and guests' social networks and creates knowledge about locations, events, jobs, other people, and the world at large. Couchsurfing shows that these network ties governed by a framework for participants to conduct themselves by agreed norms, encountered in meaningful personal spatially intimate spaces; with a heightened sense of risk and trust can lead to intimate interaction and strong ties, even when individuals have never met before. Rather than technology causing reflexivity, the site appeared to help already reflexive individuals who had a strong sense of the role this technology could play to become more active, evaluative and reflexive in their home environment, reinforcing traits which they have established while on the road and during previous travels. These exchanges happen without the need for authority, expert voices or opinions, creating a cluster of like-minded producers and consumers that increasingly compete with conventional tourism. Couchsurfing should not be seen as some sort of utopian communal dream, but rather as a private "portfolio of sociability" (Castells 2001, 132), activation of the technology remains intermittent and place-dependent and while inextricably linked to power, the system tries to eliminate the possibility through the reputation system individuals might use and exploit "exciting", "authentic" insiders, for their holiday experience.

Members of the site "imagine themselves as those who influence the direction of their own moves" (Kesselring and Vogl 2004, 10), self-determining and self-monitoring their mobilities in a fashion that is very self-aware of the rhythm they wish to be a part of, gaining a foothold in a runaway world (Giddens, 1990). The site highlights how individual self-interest, activated and actioned through new technologies of the self have the power to affect personal mobility in contemporary life, whether at home or on the move, reinscribing the local through a global and user led participatory discourse. Even as leisure tourism becomes increasingly commercialized, individuals given the motivation can seek out and express identity from an increasing and wide ranging number of technologies that provide access to expressive and individual subject positions, enabling an individual to position themselves as in control of their self-image, providing the individual with desirable resources which may be experienced as personalized, authentic, capital intensive and identity-enhancing. They invest in an identity as a reflexive project with the aid of like minded others to transform themselves into the kinds of people they're supposed and want to be, resulting in new forms of individual production, consumption and forms of mobility that blurs the many dichotomies and metaphors we utilize to describe personal mobilities such as tourism which as a term is becoming obsolete as network based conceptualizations based on shared and specialized meanings and practices become increasingly attractive to individual self-fashioning.

Bibliography

Aas, K. (2007) "Analysing a World in Motion: Global Flows Meet Criminology of the Other". *Theoretical Criminology* 11 (2). 283-303.

Andrews, H. (2000) "Consuming hospitality on holiday". In C. Lashley, A. Morrison (eds.). *In Search of Hospitality: Theoretical Perspectives and Debates*. Oxford: Butterworth-Heinemann. 235-254.

Bauman, Z. (1998) *Globalization: the Human Consequences*. Cambridge: Polity Press.

Beck, U. (1998) *Democracy Without Enemies*. Cambridge: Polity Press.

Bechmann, J. (2004) "Ambivalent spaces of restlessness: ordering (im)mobilities at airports". In Bærenholdt, J. O. and Simonsen, K. (eds.). *Space Odysseys: Spatiality and Social Relations in the 21st Century*. Aldershot: Ashgate. 27-42.

Benkler, Y. (2006) *The Wealth of Networks: How Social Production Transforms Markets and Freedom*. New Heaven, CT: Yale University Press.

Binkley, S. (2007) *Getting Loose: Lifestyle Consumption in the 1970s*. Durham, N.C.; London: Duke University Press.

Boyd, D. (2007) "None of this is Real: Identity and Participation in Friendster". In Karaganis, J. (ed.). *Structures of Participation in Digital Culture*. New York: Social Science Research Council. 132-157

—. (2008) "Why Youth Social Network Sites: The Role of Networked Publics in Teenage Social Life". In Buckingham, D. (ed.). *Youth, Identity, and Digital Media*. The John D. and Catherine T. MacArthur Foundation Series on Digital Media and Learning. Cambridge, MA: The MIT Press, 119-142.

Castells, M. (1996) *The Rise of the Network Society*. Cambridge, MA: Blackwell.

—. (2001) Virtual communities or network society? In M. Castells, *The Internet Galaxy: Reflections on the Internet, Business, and Society*. Oxford: Oxford University Press. 116-136.

—. (2007) "Communication, power, and counter-power in the network society". *International Journal of Communication* 1: 238-266.

Clifford, J. (1997) *Routes: Travel and Translation in the Late Twentieth Century*. Cambridge, MA; London: Harvard University Press.

Cohen, R. (2006) *Migration and its enemies. Global capital, migrant labour and the nation-state.* Aldershot: Ashgate.

Conradson D. and Latham, A. (2005) "Friendship, networks and transnationality in a world city: antipodean transmigrants in London". *Journal of Ethnic and Migration Studies* 31 (2). 287-305.

Lashley, C. and Morrison, A. (eds.) (2000) *In Search of Hospitality: Theoretical Perspectives and Debates.* Oxford: Butterworth-Heinemann.

Cresswell, T. (2006) *On the Move.* New York; London: Routledge.

Crossley, N. (1999) "Fish, Field, Habitus and Madness: The First Wave Mental Health Users Movement in Great Britain". *The British Journal of Sociology* 50 (4). 647-670.

Crouch, D., Aronsson, L. and Wahlström L. (2001) "Tourist Encounters". *Tourist Studies* 1 (3). 253-270.

D'Andrea, A. (2006) *Global nomads: techno and New Age as transnational countercultures in Ibiza and Goa.* Oxon, UK: Routledge.

Diken, B. and Laustsen, C.B. (2001) "Enjoy Your Fight! — Fight Club as a Symptom of the Network Society". *Journal for Cultural Research* 6 (4). 349-367.

Du Gay, P., Hall, S., Janes, L., MacKay, H., and Negus K. (1997) *Doing Cultural Studies: The Story of the Sony Walkman.* London: Sage Publications.

Edensor, T. (2001) "Performing Tourism, Staging Tourism — (Re)producing Tourist Space and Practice". *Tourist Studies* 1 (1). 59-81.

Featherstone, M. (1991) *Consumer Culture and Postmodernism.* London: Sage.

Foucault, M. [Martin, L.H., Gutman H. and Hutton, P.H. (eds.)] (1988) *Technologies of the Self: A Seminar with Michel Foucault.* London: Tavistock.

Franklin, A. and Crang, M. (2001) "The Trouble with Tourism and Travel Theory". *Tourist Studies* 1 (1). 5-22.

Geertz, C. (1973) *Deep Play: Notes on the Balinese Cockfight. The Interpretation of Cultures.* New York: Basic Books.

Germann-Molz, J. (2004) "Destination World: technology, mobility and global belonging in round-the-world travel websites". PhD thesis, Department of Sociology, Lancaster University, UK.

—. (2006) "Watch Us Wander: Mobile Surveillance and the Surveillance of Mobility". *Environment and Planning A*, 38 (2). 377-393.

Giddens, A. (1990) *The Consequences of Modernity.* Cambridge: Polity Press.

—. (1991) *Modernity and Self-Identity*. Cambridge: Polity Press.

Gustafson, P. (2006) "Place attachment and mobility". In McIntyre, N., Williams, D.R. and McHugh, K. (eds.). *Multiple Dwelling and Tourism: Negotiating Place, Home and Identity*. Wallingford: CAB International. 17-31.

Hannam, K. (2006) "Tourism and development III: performances, performativities and mobilities". *Progress in Development Studies* 6 (3). 243-249.

Harvey, D. (1993) "From space to place and back again: Reflections on the conditions of modernity". In Bird, J., Curtis, B., Putnam, T., Roberston, G. and Tickner, L. (eds.). *Mapping the Futures: Local Cultures Global Change*. London: Routledge. 3-13.

Hermans, H. J. M. (2004) "Introduction: The dialogical self in a global and digital age". *Identity: An International Journal of Theory and Research* 4 (4). 297-320.

Hutnuk, J. (1996) *The Rumour of Calcutta: Tourism, Charity and the Poverty of Representation*. London: Zed.

Huxley, L. (2005) "Western backpackers and the global experience: an exploration of young people's interaction with local cultures". *Tourism, Culture and Communication* 5 (1). 37-44.

Hetherington, K. (1998) *Expressions of Identity: Space, Performance, Politics*. London; Thousand Oaks Ca.; New Delhi: Sage/Theory, Culture and Society.

Holt, L. (2008) "Embodied social capital and geographic perspectives: performing the habitus". *Progress in human geography* 32 (2). 227-246.

Kennedy, P. and Roudometof, V. (2001) "Communities across borders under globalising conditions: New immigrants and transnational cultures". Working Paper from *Transnational Communities* (WPTC-01-17).

Kellerman, A. (2006) *Personal mobilities*. New York, NY: Routledge

Lovin, G. (2007) "Blogging, the nihilist impulse" *Eurozine*. http://www.eurozine.com/articles/2007-01-02-lovink-en.html

Larsen, J. (2008) "De-exoticizing Tourist Travel: Everyday Life and Sociality on the Move". *Leisure Studies* 27 (1). 21-34.

Lash, S. and Urry, J. (1994) *Economies of Signs and Space (Theory, Culture & Society)*. London: Sage Publications.

Lashley, C. and Morrison, A. (2000) *In Search of Hospitality: Theoretical Perspectives and Debates*. Oxford: Butterworth-Heinemann.

Livingstone, S. (ed.) (2005) *Audiences and publics: when cultural engagement matters for the public sphere.* Changing media - changing Europe series, v. 2. Bristol, UK: Intellect Books. 163-185

MacCannell, D. (1999) *The Tourist: A New Theory of the Leisure Class.* (3rd Ed.). Berkeley: University of California Press.

Maoz, D. (2005) "The Mutual Gaze". *Annals of Tourism Research* 33 (1). 221-239.

Morgan, N. and Pritchard, A. (2005) "On Souvenirs and Metonymy — Narratives of Memory, Metaphor and Materiality". *Tourist Studies* 5 (1). 29-53.

Morley, D. (2000) *Home Territories: Media, Mobility and Identity.* London: Routledge.

Muecke, M.W. (2006) *Essays on Architecture and Other Topics.* Published by Lulu.com.

Nardi, B., Schiano, D., and Gumbrecht, M. (2004) "Blogging as social activity, or, would you let 900 million people read your diary?". In *Proceedings of Computer Supported Cooperative Work,* http://home.comcast.net/%7Ediane.schiano/CSCW04.Blog.pdf

Nielsen, L.D. (2005) "Reflexive mobility — a critical and action oriented perspective on transport research". In Thomsen, T.U., Nielsen, L.D. and Gundmundsson, H. (eds). *Social Perspectives on Mobility.* Aldershot: Ashgate. 47-66.

Nyíri, K. (ed.) (2005) *A Sense of Place: The Global and the Local in Mobile Communication.* Vienna: Passagen Verlag.

Oakes, T. (2006) "Tourism and the modern subject: Placing the encounter between tourist and other". In C. Cartier and Lew, A. (eds.). *Seductions of place: geographical perspectives on globalization and touristed landscapes.* London: Routledge. 36-55.

Oldenburg, R. (1989) *The Great Good Place: Cafes, Coffee Shops, Community Centers, Beauty Parlors, General Stores, Bars, Hangouts, and How They Get You Through the Day.* New York: Paragon House

O' Regan, M. (2008) "Hypermobility in Backpacker Lifestyles: the Emergence of the Internet Café". In Burns, P.M and Novelli, M. (eds.). *Tourism and Mobilities: Local-Global Connections.* Wallingford, UK: CABI Publishing. 109-132.

Pahl, R. (2000) *On Friendship.* Cambridge: PolityPress.

Plickert, G., Côté, R. R. and Wellman, B. (2007) "It's Not Who You Know, Its How You Know Them: Who Exchanges What With Whom?". *Social Networks* 29 (3). 405-429.

Putnam, R.D. (1995) "Bowling alone: America's Declining Social Capital". *Journal of Democracy* 6. 65-78.

—. (2001) *Bowling Alone: The Collapse and Revival of American Community*. New York: Simon & Schuster.

Rheingold, H. (2000) *The Virtual Community: Homesteading on the Electronic*. (2nd ed.). Cambridge, MA: MIT Press.

Robertson, R. (1995) "Glocalisation: time-space and homogeneity-heterogeneity". In Featherstone, M., Lash, S. and Robertson, R. (eds.) *Global Modernities*. London: Sage. 25-44.

Salazar, N.B., (2005) "Tourism and Glocalization 'Local' Tour Guiding". *Annals of Tourism Research* 32 (3). 628-646.

Scott, W.R. (1981) *Organizations*. Eaglewood Cliffs, NJ: Prentice Hall.

Simonsen, K. (2004) "Spatiality, Temporality and the Construction of the City" in Bærenholdt, J. O. and Simonsen, K. (eds.) *Space Odysseys: Spatiality and Social Relation in the 21st Century*. Aldershot: Ashgate. 43-61.

Southerton, D. and Tomlinson, M. (2005) "Pressed for time: The Differential Impacts of a 'time squeeze'". *The Sociological Review* 53 (2). 215-39

Sorensen, A. (2003) "Backpacker ethnography". *Annals of Tourism Research* 30 (4). 847-867.

Suvantola, K. (2002) *Tourist's Experience of Place*. Aldershot: Ashgate.

Tomlinson, J. (1997) *Globalisation and Culture*. Cambridge: Polity Press.

Yus, F. (2005) "The linguistic-cognitive essence of virtual community". *Ibérica* 9. 79-102.

Van Dijck, J. (2007) *Mediated memories in the digital age*. Stanford, CA: Stanford University Press.

Urry, J. (2000) "Mobile Sociology". *British Journal of Sociology* 51 (1). 185-203.

—. (2002a) "Mobility and Proximity". *Sociology* 36 (2). 255-274.

—. (2002b) "Mobilities, Networks and Communities". Paper for XV World Congress of Sociology, Brisbane, Australia.

—. (2003) "The Sociology of Tourism". In Chris, C. (ed.). *Classic Reviews in Tourism*. Clevedon: Channel View Publications.

—. (2007) *Mobilities*, Cambridge: Polity Press.

Vertovec, S. and Cohen, R. (eds.) (1999) Introduction. In Vertovec, S. and Cohen, R. (eds), *Migration, Diasporas and Transnationalism*. Cheltenham: Edward Elgar. viii- xxviii.

Veijola, S. (2006) "Heimat Tourism in the Countryside. Paradoxical Sojourns to Self and Place". In Minca, C. and Oakes, T. (eds.). *Travels in Paradox: Remapping Tourism*. Lanham: Rowman and Littlefield Publishers. 77-96.

Viégas, F. B. (2005) "Bloggers' expectations of privacy and accountability: An initial survey". *Journal of Computer-Mediated Communication* 10 (3). Article 12. http://jcmc.indiana.edu/vol10/issue3/viegas.html.

Welsch, W. (1999) "Transculturality: the puzzling form of cultures today" in Featherstone, M. and Lash, S. (eds). *Spaces of Culture: City-Nation-World*. London: Sage. 194-213.

Wang, Y., Yu, Q. and Fesenmaier, D. R. (2002) "Defining the virtual tourist community: Implications for tourism marketing". *Touring Management* 23 (4): 407-417.

Wang, Y. and Fesenmaier, D. R. (2003) "Understanding the Motivation to Contribute to Online Communities: An Empirical Study of an Online Travel Community". *Electronic Markets* 13 (1). 33-45.

Williams, D. R. and Kaltenborn, B. P. (1999) "Leisure places and modernity: The use and meaning of recreational cottages in Norway and the USA". In Crouch, D. (ed.). *Leisure/Tourism Geographies*. London: Routledge. 214-230.

Zelizer, V. A. (1994) *The social meaning of money*. New York: Basic Books.

LIST OF CONTRIBUTORS

Name	Affiliation
Yasmine Abbas	Harvard University, USA
Günseli Bayraktutan Sütcü	Baskent University, Turkey
Mutlu Binark	Baskent University, Turkey
Jed Brubaker	Georgetown University, USA
Fred Dervin	Universities of Turku and Joensuu, Finland
Katja de Vries	Vrije Universiteit Brussel, Belgium
Oliver Mauco	Paris Sorbonne University, France
Michael O'Regan	University of Brighton, UK
Tanja Riikonen	University of Turku, Finland
Cati Vaucelle	Massachusetts Institute of Technology, USA